In This Sign Conquer

A history of the Society of the Holy Cross
(Societas Sanctae Crucis)
1855–2005

In This Sign Conquer

A history of the Society of the Holy Cross
(Societas Sanctae Crucis)
1855–2005

Owen Higgs   David Houlding
Anthony Howe   Trevor Jones
Robert Mackley   Kenneth Macnab
Luke Miller   Geoffrey Rowell

Edited by
A Priest of the Society of the Holy Cross

continuum
LONDON • NEW YORK

Continuum UK
The Tower Building
11 York Road
London SE1 7NX

Continuum US
80 Maiden Lane
Suite 704
New York, NY 10038

www.continuumbooks.com

First published 2006

British Library Cataloguing-in-Publication Data
A catalogue record for this book is available from the British Library.

ISBN 0-8264-9186-3

Typeset by YHT Ltd, London
Printed and bound in England by
Antony Rowe Ltd, Chippenham, Wiltshire

Contents

Contributors

The Revd Owen Higgs SSC is Vicar of St Francis, Petts Wood.

The Revd Preb. David Houlding SSC is Vicar of All Hallows', Gospel Oak; and the International Master of the Society.

The Revd Anthony Howe SSC is Assistant Priest in the parishes of St Helen's, Athersley, and St Paul's, Monk Bretton, Barnsley.

The Revd Trevor Jones SSC is Vicar of St Peter, London Docks, and the archivist of the Society.

The Revd Robert Mackley SSC is Assistant Priest at Holy Redeemer, Clerkenwell.

Kenneth Macnab was until August 2005 a member of the Society and the Vicar of St Barnabas, Tunbridge Wells. He now teaches at The Oratory School, Berkshire.

The Revd Luke Miller SSC is Vicar of St Mary, Tottenham.

The Rt Revd Dr Geoffrey Rowell is the Bishop of Gibraltar in Europe, and the Visitor of the Society of the Holy Cross.

Acknowledgements

Most of the archives of the Society of the Holy Cross are maintained at Pusey House, Oxford. Thanks are owed to the Principal and Chapter for making them available to the authors of this history. Especial gratitude is owed by the editor to Fr Jonathan Baker SSC, the Principal of the House, and Fr Barry Orford, the archivist, for interest and assistance above and beyond the call of scholarly or archival duties.

Fr Trevor Jones SSC is the archivist of the Society and maintains a significant collection of material at St Peter's, London Docks. He is warmly thanked for his expertise and help.

Preface

David Houlding

In 1855 a group of priests who had come deeply under the influence of the Oxford Movement formed a new society under the leadership of Fr Charles Lowder, the vicar of the newly established mission parish of St Peter, Wapping, in the docks of London's East End. He established too a community of nuns under the dedication of the Holy Cross to work in the parish. He dedicated his life to working amongst the poorest of the poor for the mission of the Church. His new society was to give support and encouragement to priests working in these slum parishes to enable them to fulfil their mission. He recognized then, as we do now, that it all began with holiness of life.

Hence he formed a congregation of priests who would lead a disciplined way of life, uniting themselves under a common Rule, dedicated to the work of mission, and under the patronage of the Cross of Christ. At the altar, the priest is drawn wonderfully close to the saving act of Christ, and the Cross, therefore, must become a living reality in his life and work. There could be no better dedication for a Catholic priest. The Society grew astonishingly quickly, and under the mastership of Fr Alexander Heriot Mackonochie, the first vicar of St Alban's, Holborn, it flourished and exerted not undue influence in the Church, as its priests sought to promote the Catholic faith and practice within the Church of England.

The Society has had its ups and downs over the years, but it has consistently borne witness to Catholic truth and helped to further the practice of the faith. It has met with opposition and persecution, not least in its early days. In particular it helped to establish the practice of the sacrament of confession within the Church of England. It ran into more trouble over this issue in those early days than any other. Yet it stuck to its guns and prevailed: 'no desertion, no surrender', wrote Fr Mackonochie.

Despite setbacks, the Society has recovered its confidence and continues to be faithful to our inheritance and to look forward with hope and expectation for a new dawn for our Catholic movement within the Church of England. We have a roll now of over one thousand priests throughout the world, with 750 of them working in the United Kingdom. From the outset we have had a vision for unity with the Holy See and we continue to work for the reunion of Christendom: we need to move forward in faith, and in hope and in love. We have a positive agenda in front of us. We hold the faith once delivered to the saints; we work for the mission of the Church; we adhere to the gift of Holy Order in the Church, in accordance with the practice and discipline of the Universal Church, and we promote her unity.

In this book we are given a glimpse of the Church through the eyes of SSC priests. Inevitably it is not the whole truth. These essays, by young priests of the Society, are not intended to be a history of the Catholic movement within the Church of England since 1855, but rather, a bird's-eye view of the Church from the perspective of the Society of the Holy Cross.

We need now more than ever to remain united in our resolve and to stake our claim of rightful inheritance within the Church of England. Against the uncertain background of all that is going on in the Church, we need to stand together, to stand firm, to stand joyfully, and above all to stand up for Jesus.

1

The SSC in context[1]

Geoffrey Rowell

> Evangelical Vicar in want
> Desires a portable font,
> Will exchange the same
> For a portrait in frame
> Of the Bishop-elect of Vermont!

When, some twelve years ago, I gave a series of lectures to mark the 200th anniversary of the birth of John Keble, I began with this witty limerick of Ronald Knox. I do so again today because on this 150th anniversary of the founding of the Society of the Holy Cross, we need to remind ourselves of the society's roots in the Oxford Movement, ritualism, and the Catholic revival in the Church of England. If SSC is the portrait, then we need to place it in the frame of that wider movement of spiritual renewal of which it was a part, and which continues to nourish its spirituality.

As we all know, 1833 is the symbolic date for the beginning of the Oxford Movement – a date which became symbolic because of John Keble's Assize Sermon on 'National Apostasy' and because John Henry Newman, whose *Apologia pro vita sua*, giving his personal history of the development of his own religious opinions, imprinted that date on the history of the movement because it was so providential for him. In 1845 Newman converted to the Church of Rome, likewise providing another of those symbolic markers, particularly for Dean Church in his classic history of the Oxford Movement. As with the death of Pope John Paul II in 2005 (the close of an amazing and powerful papacy), we can surely understand the power of symbolic dates, and the marking out of time by personal lives. Yet recent scholarship has reminded us of the political context of the Oxford Movement, the questions posed for Anglican identity by the modifying of the old Anglican confessional state and the emergence of a more pluralist society by the removal of disabilities from Dissenters and Roman Catholics. Getting on for two centuries later the Church of England and Anglicans elsewhere (as indeed other Christian churches) are faced with the same questions of identity but this time in secular and multifaith contexts. The Oxford Movement question: 'On what ground do you stand, O presbyter of the Church of England?' is one that is still very much with us.

Recent scholarship has also pointed to a much more enduring vigour than had been supposed to be the case in the old high church tradition. The Oxford Movement in Oxford, and in the writing of the *Tracts for the Times*, was personal and focused. It would not have happened without the personal holiness and poetic gifts and pastoral and parochial example of John Keble. When Keble died members of the SSC, particularly Mackonochie and Lowder, were at his funeral. Richard Church, later to be Dean of St Paul's, wrote that there was

> a meeting of old currents and new. Besides the people I used to think of with Keble, there was a crowd of younger men, who no doubt have as much right in him as we have, in their way – Mackonochie, Lowder, and that sort. Excellent good fellows, but who, looked upon us as rather *dark* people, who don't grow beards, and do other proper things.

At the SSC May synod, five weeks later, Mackonochie paid tribute to Keble who had laid the foundation of the revival which had already grown through two generations.[2]

The Oxford Movement would not have happened without the genius of John Henry Newman. He was formed first by an evangelical conversion, and then, partly through the challenges in his own family from his atheist brother Charles, and his earnestly evangelical and then vaguely theist brother Frank, and partly by his encounter with the logical liberalism of Richard Whateley, leading on through the influence of John Keble in particular to his discovery of the Fathers and of the seventeenth-century Anglican tradition. Newman's genius fused all of this in a particularly personal and theological way. He said when he received his cardinal's hat in Rome towards the end of his life, in what we know as his *biglietto* speech, that he had spent all his life fighting against liberalism, by which he meant something quite particular – the heresy of resolving truth into an opinion. Newman stood for the objectivity of revelation, but a revelation that was also mystery. His theology was scripturally grounded, but that scriptural faith was mediated in multifarious ways in and through the worship and praying life of the Church and crystallized from time to time in creeds and conciliar definitions. The apostolic faith of the Church had always to seek understanding. He learned from John Keble Bishop Butler's aphorism that 'probability was the guide of life', and recognized that the assent of faith was never a simple *QED* matter but was grounded in the coming together of many cumulative possibilities. His engagement with the Fathers enabled him to see how doctrinal definition emerged from the worshipping life of the Church, and early doctrinal statements might not measure up to the more nuanced and detailed theological statements that emerged as the Church wrestled with an Arius or a Nestorius. Recognizing in his sharp and astute *Tamworth Reading Room Letters* that 'man is not a reasoning animal, but a seeing, feeling, contemplating acting animal', he saw in faith a principle of action: 'to act you must assume, and that assumption is faith'. His legacy to the Church of England, and his gift to the Church of Rome – not at the time a particularly welcome gift to either – was his 1845 *Essay on the Development of Christian Doctrine*. Believing in revelation, believing in incarnation, the faith once delivered to the saints was embedded in history, and the fullness of its meaning was only gradually appropriated. He was aware of the fragility of human language (including theological language): 'creeds and dogmas live only in the one idea they are intended to express' – and that idea was in the end the mystery of the creative, saving and sanctifying life of the One God in Trinity made known in Jesus Christ through the Spirit. If there was development of doctrine it was not change but explication, and the setting of that fundamental truth into the unfolding and changing scenes of human life and culture that was important. So he could say, 'It changes always in order to remain the same.'

If Newman was the theological genius of the Oxford Movement, Pusey's contribution was in a way no less, particularly following Newman's move to Rome. Again formed by the older high church tradition, learning of the Real Presence of Christ in the sacrament at his mother's knee, an early visit to Germany faced him with the challenge to traditional Christian orthodoxy posed by the rationalism of German Protestant theology. His Hebrew and Syriac learning made him acutely aware of the power of image and symbol in conveying theological truth. Pusey was profoundly convinced of the truth of the indwelling Christ – 'the secret is this, Christ in you, the hope of glory'. As he put it in the preface to his *Parochial Sermons*, the very heart of his preaching was 'the inculcation of the Great Mystery, expressed in the words to be "*in* Christ", to be "Members of Christ", "Temples of the Holy Ghost"; that Christ doth dwell really and truly in the hearts of the faithful'.[3] His sermons are almost ecstatic in character with his deep sense of the transforming grace of God. It was this which made him sympathetic to the pietist strain in the Lutheran tradition, with its emphasis on 'Christ in us', rather than the forensic theology so often associated with 'Christ for us'. As for Newman, the doctrine of deification – that our calling was no less than to become 'partakers of the Divine nature' – was central to his theology. It was this which undergirded his theology, and particularly his sacramental theology. His high theology of baptism, and his strong defence of baptismal regeneration, was because he saw this as the beginning of the transforming life of

grace. The sermon on the Eucharist, for which he was condemned by the Oxford authorities, was resonant with patristic
teaching, particularly that of St Cyril of Alexandria, who uses
the word μεταμορφωσισ – the word used for 'transfiguration'
for the eucharistic change; and also St Ephraim. Indeed, almost
all the quotations condemned by the Oxford Hebdomadal
Board were phrases from Ephraim and Cyril. This theology
undergirded Pusey's sense of the supernatural life of the
Church, its call to holiness, and the inseparability of that call
from its Catholic and apostolic identity. It was this which led
Pusey to be so major a player in the revival of the religious life
in the Church of England; to be a supporter of SSC; and to
place such a high value on the discipline of sacramental confession as that which enabled baptismal life to be sustained and
grow.

If the Oxford Movement did not start out by being concerned with ritual, liturgy and ceremony, the second generation
of those influenced by it became increasingly concerned with it.
The roots were many and various – the Romantic movement
with its change of sensibility in which emotion was seen as
revelatory of the human condition; the Gothic revival with a
conscious medievalism expressing both a continuity with the
past and a yearning for a more organic, even a sacramental
society, existing in tension with increasing technological
change and the urbanization consequent on the industrial
revolution. The ecclesiologists, with John Mason Neale and
Benjamin Webb as major protagonists, with their passion for
medieval churches and for their restoration were no less concerned with liturgy and hymnody. It should not be forgotten
that *Hymns Ancient and Modern* was an Oxford Movement
hymnbook, and that Neale's translations of hymns from ancient
Greek and Latin models were intended to make the richness of
Catholic devotion from both East and West part of Anglican
worship and spirituality. It is a heritage we need to defend
against the unbalanced subjectivity of many modern 'worship
songs' (there are 73 hymns or songs beginning with 'I' in
Mission Praise).

5

When Fr Mackonochie, vicar of this church, and Master of the Society of the Holy Cross, was challenged about the ritual and ceremonial practices of his church, he replied in a telling phrase that they were but 'the barest alphabet of reverence for so divine a mystery'. The defence of ritual was theological; aesthetic – there was an implicit theology of beauty; and also evangelistic. Catholic worship was seen as part-and-parcel of Catholic mission. The founding members of SSC were undoubted believers in a mission-shaped Church. In a church whose services had in so many instances become sadly wordy, dull, and sometimes slovenly, the ritualists showed that liturgy both taught and converted. It did of course go hand in hand with high ideals of pastoral care, and there were a number of observers who commented that it was because of the pastoral care that ritual innovations were tolerated. Part of the pro- gramme which was central to SSC was set out in the three volumes of essays (1866–8), *The Church and the World: Essays on Questions of the Day*, edited by an early member of the SSC, Orby Shipley, who in 1870 provided a liturgical guide drawing on Roman models, the *Ritual of the Altar*. For the Protestant *Record*, *The Church and the World* was 'a wretched compound of Sacerdotalism, Ritualism, and Jesuitry ... replete with insolence and presumption and [bearing] a thoroughly Roman face'. The strong strand of anti-Catholicism in Victorian England[4] played into a sometimes neuralgic hostility to all that was perceived as importing 'popery' into the established Church. The *Record*'s reference to 'Jesuitry' is symptomatic of this. Dr Peter L'Estrange, in his thesis on the English province of the Society of Jesus, notes alarmed reports of a phalanx of Jesuits disguised as Amazons invading the coast of Lincolnshire, and Jesuits mounted on dromedaries being seen on Hampstead Heath. Charles Le Geyt, another SSC priest, in the 1867 volume in an essay on 'The Symbolism of Ritual', wrote powerfully that the fundamental issue was between a sacramental and a non- sacramental religion. 'A Religion with a Sacramental system is of necessity a symbolical Religion', and it was the gradual decay of sacramental teaching in the Church of England that had led to the loss of ritual. Such symbolic and sacramental teaching was rooted in the Bible. 'To say we have outgrown teaching by symbolism, is to say we have outgrown the teaching of the Bible.'[5] In an essay in the first collection (1866) on 'The Missionary Aspect of Ritualism', R.F. Littledale (another SSC priest who was incumbent of St Mary the Virgin, Soho) pointed out that the gin-palaces of London attracted their customers with 'internal decoration, abundant polished metal, and vivid colour, with plenty of bright light', and secular organizations such as the Odd Fellows and the Foresters were much into processions, banners and music.[6] A set liturgy demanded ritual if it were to engage people. The Prayer Book without the ceremonial and drama that should express its meaning was like a musical score, which only the highly musically educated could hope to understand. Read the Passion narrative to an ignorant slum child – a street-Arab, in Littledale's words – or show that child a crucifix, and it will be the crucifix which will convey more vividly the meaning.[7]

Looking over the nineteenth century as a whole, a changing society inevitably produced a changing Church. Communications enabled the growth of central structures both nationally and in dioceses. Greater ease of travel meant new exposure to continental Catholicism, and there are many records of both clergy and laity finding that their caricature notions of Catholic worship were transformed by encounter with both popular piety and genuine devotion. Energetic bishops like Samuel Wilberforce could be far more present to parishes than their predecessors had been. As Anthony Russell noted in his book *The Clerical Profession*, the clergy in parallel with developments in other professions, became more professionalized. Training of clergy became more than just years of residence at Oxford and Cambridge, which themselves changed from being wholly Anglican institutions. Theological colleges such as Cuddesdon were concerned with formation, even though the word would not have been used. Patterns of daily prayer were inculcated and taken out into parishes. George Herring has shown how priests influenced by the Oxford Movement could, in places like Wantage, introduce daily sung services, so much so that, as Herring notes, 'By 1860 many rural Tractarian parishes were characterized by a full service sung to Gregorian chants by a surpliced choir twice daily, leading a regular congregation in relatively lengthy acts of worship, often including a sermon as well'.[8] Yet we must note Herring's careful statistical analysis that in the 30-year period from 1840 to 1870 there were probably only some thousand Tractarian clergy across the country, only some 5 per cent of the whole. Of these, Tractarians were most numerous in London, the home counties and the south-west, and just over half were in rural parishes of a thousand, and another 203 in market towns – and that is important to note in putting the undoubted achievements of Anglo-Catholic priests in urban parishes of social need in context.

If theological colleges and Tractarian influences contributed to the professionalization of the clergy, they did so in part by encouraging pastoral expertise and a willingness to grapple with some of the issues and defects of the parochial system. There was need for flexibility; for mission services of outreach; for the use of colour, music, and ceremonial to move the heart and teach the faith. There was also a need to gather those in the parish together into appropriate organizations. It was for this reason that church schools, and the founding of numerous guilds and societies characterized much of the pattern of the Victorian Church. The list of organizations connected with this parish of St Alban, Holborn, runs to over 35, amongst them, the schools, the Sunday schools, the Children's Penny Dinners, the Brotherhood of Jesus of Nazareth, the Confraternity of the Blessed Sacrament, the Church Burial Society, an association in support of Foreign Missions, the Guild of the Holy Family for Married Women; the Guild of St Mary the Virgin; the Guild of St Monica; a Bible class for women; a branch of the Girls' Friendly societies; sewing classes with Bible study; a Girls' night school; a Children's Guild; St John the Baptist; and the Dorcas Society. Fr Stanton held a Sunday afternoon tea with the aim of bridging the gulf fixed between the roughest of the lads and ourselves.

Any lad from fourteen to twenty-five can come if he belongs to the parish ... It doesn't matter what religion he is, Anglican, Roman, Jew, or nothing; we meet on the common ground of our common nature – which can enjoy a good tea and smoke, and sing the songs of the streets ... and tell the yarns of the week ... But the Religion of the thing remains in the fact that we meet together, sit down to a meal together, and are happy together. And that is something which helps to bridge over the yawning gulf fixed in society betwixt men and men.[9]

Fr Lowder at St Peter's, London Docks, listed the following achievements in an appeal for funds in 1880:

A Church built and consecrated; Schools for 600 children; A Hostel or Home for aged communicants; St Peter's Club and Dining Room provides meals for working men and their families at moderate cost; A Friend of Labour Society making loans to working men; a Penny Bank; St Agatha's Mission School and Infant School; St Agatha's Night School and Club; a Parochial Playground; together with a Convalescent Home, Benefit and Burial Clubs; three Mothers Meeting Clubs; Clothing and Boot Clubs ... String Drum and Fife Bands, Cricket Clubs and a Temperance Society. Four hundred and fifty communicants belong to the church; eight hundred children and lads are educated in the schools; between five hundred and six hundred members belong to the various Confraternities, Guilds and Clubs.[10]

It is all impressively energetic.

But still there was a concern for mission priests, powerfully stated in an essay in the 1868 *The Church and the World* collection by J.E. Vaux, who also had SSC links. Setting out the history of preaching orders in the Church he pressed the urgent need for a mission order.

For exceptional spiritual efforts, the agency to be employed must be exceptional, and what is more, exceptionally spiritual ... the more perfectly developed the spiritual ηθοσ of the operator (so to speak), the greater will be his power for good. The experience of the Church has ever uniformly pointed to the Religious Life as that by which this peculiar spirituality of mind is to be acquired – a life which, when not employed in actual ministrations, is spent, as far as possible, in communion with God, in contemplation, in prayer.[11]

Michael Hill, in his study of the revival of religious orders in the Church of England, shows how there was a continuous theme of colleges of unmarried priests as best fitted to provide for the mission needs of the burgeoning towns. Walter Hook in Leeds told Pusey that Robert Aitkin (the pioneer of parochial missions in the Church of England) had embarked on an experiment in Leeds in 1843.

> He has fitted up the school-room adjoining his church with cells, each containing a bed and a cross; he has some young men with him who have forsaken all; his rule is very strict; he has daily Communion; they fast till four every Wednesday, when he allows himself, and themselves, meat; on Friday, they fast till four, and then have fish. In the meantime he, having a family residing five miles away, sleeps in his cell four times a week ... his wife complains of his neglecting his six or more children.[12]

In 1866 the founding of the Society of St John the Evangelist under R.M. Benson became one of the most successful embodiments of this vision. At about the same time the SSC presented a memorial to Archbishop Longley of Canterbury, asking him to consider the establishment of 'Religious Orders of Men, living and working under Episcopal direction, in the Church of England'. In 1889 a debate in the Convocation of Canterbury, led by W.J. Butler, Dean of Lincoln, former vicar of Wantage and founder of the Wantage Sisterhood, pressed strongly for brotherhoods not only for mission, but for bridging the major class barriers of Victorian society and the Church.

The genesis of SSC has to be seen in the context of a concern for mission, a commitment to mutual support and spiritual discipline, and a Catholic conviction of the transforming reality of supernatural grace. SSC was anticipated as an association of clergy living under a common devotional rule by the

Brotherhood of the Holy Trinity in Oxford, which was founded in about 1845, counting among its members Henry Parry Liddon and R.M. Benson, and, importantly for SSC, the young Charles Lowder.[13]

The concern for retreats grew out of the same movement, and the first retreat in the Church of England was held at the instigation of SSC at Chislehurst rectory at the invitation of Francis Murray, the rector, though there was no silence but corporate reflection and prayer. Two years later Fr Benson conducted an Ignatian-style retreat for the Society, described by Benson in a letter to his mother as consisting of 'a nice little company, eleven and sometimes twelve. One or two of them were of such advanced holiness that it made one quite ashamed to sit as a teacher.' When Lowder spoke at the York Church Congress in 1866 he told the Congress that he himself had 'not had the privilege of belonging to a brotherhood, except in a modified form in a clergy house'. Donald Allchin notes Fr Benson's comments about the East End clergy, when Benson preached at the Jubilee of St Barnabas, Pimlico, in 1900.

> Although they were living in all the rigours of the Religious Life, they were not living under vows, but they were wholly dedicated – at any rate their great leader [Lowder] was wholly dedicated to God. They were not living under vows; but we must remember that vows do not constitute the religious life; [which is] the life of the Spirit within the heart of those who take the vows. The vows are the shelter of the Spirit ... And thus ... associated works tending more or less to what is called the Religious Life, have sprung up.[14]

Lowder's inspiration came in a significant way from what he read of St Vincent de Paul during the six weeks that Bishop Blomfield suspended him from his ministry at St Barnabas, Pimlico. He spoke of the 'deep impression' made on him by 'the sad condition of the French Church and nation in the sixteenth century', and the wonderful influence of the institutions found by St Vincent in reforming abuses and rekindling the zeal of the priesthood.

The deep wisdom [with which St Vincent] sought out the root of so much evil, in the unspiritual lives of the clergy, and provided means for its redress ... was well calculated to impress those who seriously reflected on the state of our own Church and people, and honestly sought for some remedy. The spiritual condition of the masses of our population, the appalling vices which prevail in our large towns, and especially the teeming districts of the metropolis, the increasing tendency of the people to mass together, multiplying and intensifying the evil, and the unsatisfactory character of the attempts hitherto made to meet it, were enough to make men gladly profit by the experience of those who had successfully struggled against similar difficulties.[15]

The objects which Lowder and his colleagues set before them were in principle identical with those of the Vincentian priests: 'the promotion of a stricter rule of life amongst the clergy, the establishment of home missions to preach the gospel to the poor, and the publication of tracts and pamphlets to defend and extend Catholic faith and practice'.[16] That was at the heart of it. In the commitment of SSC to this vision, in a church in which such a vision was strange, and, as John Shelton Reed has strongly argued, 'countercultural', there was bound to be conflict. And so, inevitably perhaps, SSC first came to public notice in the furore over *The Priest in Absolution* (denounced by Lord Redesdale in the House of Lords). This touched a raw nerve of Victorian propriety in providing a confessors' manual (a Romish book if ever there was one) which suggested that priests hearing confession should put indelicate questions to their penitents in relation to sexual sins. This particularly outraged those who in the Victorian patriarchal family believed this to be an inappropriate and unwarranted intrusion into family life. It kindled the kind of anti-Catholic hysteria which is evident in the anti-Catholic literature of the age, such as *The Awful Disclosures of Maria Monk* and Hogan on popish nunneries. The SSC was indeed concerned with the mission of the Church, with the deepening of priestly spirituality and holiness of life, and with what we would now call liturgical renewal. It

was circumstances which meant that it also became a brotherhood of mutual support in times of persecution and difficulty,
of which the Public Worship Regulation Act of 1874 was the
main symbol. Like all such organizations under pressure, this
doubtless increased its identity as what might be called a particular subsystem within the Church of England, and indeed
within the Catholic revival. But as we celebrate 150 years of
corporate life it is the central core value to which we need to
return and to see how such renewal can serve the mission of the
Church today.

Notes

1 This lecture was given to the Sacred Synod of the Society of the
Holy Crosss held on Tuesday, 5 April 2005 at St Alban's,
Holborn.

2 Michael Reynolds, *Martyr of Ritualism: Father Mackonochie of St
Alban's, Holborn* (London: Faber & Faber, 1965), pp. 112–13.

3 Quoted in Geoffrey Rowell, *The Vision Glorious: Themes and
Personalities of the Catholic Revival* (Oxford: Oxford University
Press, 1983), p. 80.

4 Cf. E.R. Norman, 'Anti-Catholicism in Victorian England', in
G.R. Elton (ed.), *Historical Problems: Studies and Documents*
(London: Allen & Unwin, 1968).

5 In O. Shipley, *The Church and the World* (London: Longman,
Green, Reader & Dyer, 1867), pp. 523–67.

6 Mary Heimann's study of Roman Catholic devotion in Victorian
England provides interesting contrasts and parallels with Anglo-
Catholic practice. See Mary Heimann, *Catholic Devotion in Vic-
torian England* (Oxford: Clarendon Press, 1995).

7 Shipley, *The Church and the World*, pp. 25–50.

8 George Herring, *What Was the Oxford Movement?* (London:
Continuum, 2002), p. 82.

9 G.W.E. Russell, *Saint Alban the Martyr, Holborn: A History of Fifty
Years* (London: George Allen, 1913), pp. 334–5.

10 L.E. Ellsworth, *Charles Lowder and the Ritualist Movement* (London:
Darton, Longman & Todd, 1982), pp. 162–3.

11 Shipley, *The Church and the World*, p. 182.
12 Quoted in Michael Hill, *The Religious Order: A Study of Virtuoso Religion and its Legitimation in the Nineteenth-century Church of England* (London: Heinemann Educational, 1973), pp. 304–5.
13 Jean M. Pailing, *Francis Murray of Chislehurst* (privately published, 2002), pp. 59–60.
14 A.M. Allchin, *The Silent Rebellion: Anglican Religious Communities 1845–1900* (London: SCM Press, 1958), pp. 186–7.
15 M. Trench, *Charles Lowder: A Biography* (London: Kegan Paul & Trench, 1882), pp. 64–5.
16 Ellsworth, *Charles Lowder*, p. 21.

2

The foundation of the SSC

Trevor Jones and Robert Mackley

In 1700 economic growth averaged 1 per cent per year and 13.4 per cent of people lived in large towns; by 1840 economic growth averaged 4 per cent and 28 per cent of people lived in large towns. This economic and demographic shift formed the social background to the foundation of the Society of the Holy Cross. Large-scale industrialization and rapid urbanization, combined with the forces within the Church of England unleashed by the Oxford Movement, led to a profound questioning of the catholicity and the effectiveness of the mission of the Church of England.

In 1845, following his study of the Arian controversy and the production of Tract XC, John Henry Newman despaired of the catholicity of the Church of England and repaired to Rome. He had inspired a generation of Oxford undergraduates with a renewed religious seriousness and an excitement concerning doctrine and belief which the old 'orthodoxism' of Oxford less easily produced. His way of walking, talking, even of kneeling in church, were aped and lauded by awestruck young men, and he opened their minds to the Church of the first centuries and to the reality of the sacraments of baptism, Holy Communion and ordination. When he studied the Church Fathers' debate with Arius, however, a small voice told him that the Church of England, if it had been around in Arius's day, would have been on Arius's side. Newman began to worry; the ultimate product of his concern was Tract XC, an attempt to demonstrate that the Church of England's Thirty-Nine Articles of Religion were at least patient, if not demonstrative, of a Catholic understanding of Christianity. When the bishops, whose authority he had exalted in his writing and teaching, disagreed with his tract, he felt he was finished. He retreated to Littlemore to ponder his future, and in 1845 he was received into the Roman Catholic Church. With him went a swathe of young men and his departure marked the end of the first phase of the Catholic revival in the Church of England.

In 1850 Henry Phillpotts, Bishop of Exeter, refused to induct the Revd George Gorham into the living of Bampford Speke on the grounds that he held heterodox views concerning baptismal regeneration. The Court of Arches upheld the Bishop's position when Gorham appealed, but when he appealed again, this time to the Judicial Committee of the Privy Council, Gorham succeeded. The Privy Council declared that the 'true and legal construction' of the Church of England's formularies permitted him to believe that regeneration did not automatically happen at baptism. Following this decision, major controversy enveloped the Church of England: Archdeacons Henry Manning and Robert Wilberforce, among others, argued that a secular body was being allowed to decide what was and what was not the doctrine of the Church of England. In total over 60 pamphlets and tracts were produced arguing the case back and forth. Manning declared that the Gorham judgment confirmed for him that the Church of England was completely Erastian in nature, simply an adjunct of the state, and not part of the Catholic Church able to pronounce on her own doctrines and teachings. Manning, Wilberforce and many other Tractarian priests seceded to Rome and for a while all sorts of apocalyptic responses were offered to the Privy Council's decision.

Was the Church of England Catholic? This was the question that faced Fr Lowder and his fellow-founders of SSC. Newman, Manning, Wilberforce and the others who left had decided that it was not; Pusey, Keble, Gladstone had decided that it was. The essentials were there, the sacraments, the scriptures, the creeds, the historic ministry of bishop, priest and deacon, but it needed missionary life injecting into it. As Newman wrote in the first *Tract for the Times*: 'I fear we have neglected the real ground on which our authority is built – our apostolical descent.' The first phase of arguing over rubrics in the Book of Common Prayer and establishing the patristic roots of Church of England teaching was over. What was needed now was a Catholicism to win not just professors but the proletariat.

It was not, however, simply a Church of England whose catholicity had been thrown into question and so needed declaring and robustly living out that was such a great spur for the foundation of the SSC; secondly, and just as importantly, it was the need for a priesthood to minister to a new England. Keble still lived the George Herbert dream of the *Country Parson*, of a rural nation with a rural heart and rural clergy. The pattern of the Church of England, however, no longer met the pattern of the nation. Tiny villages and hamlets had their own parish priest, but large cities and towns had one priest for thousands. Blomfield, the Bishop of London, supported by Pusey, among others, had set to work to remedy this with a huge programme of church-building in the capital city. The problem, however, was not merely lack of churches and clergy in the urban areas: what was being discovered was that rural methods of ministry could not simply be imported unthinkingly into the towns. Herbert had given the Church of England an inspirational model in his *Country Parson*, but a new model was needed for the nineteenth century, where over a quarter of all people now lived in towns and cities and where production was booming in coal, metals, cotton and shipping; by 1855 there were over 7,000 miles of railway track; the largest cities were no longer York, Norwich and Exeter but Manchester, Liverpool and Birmingham. It was into this fast-changing society that Lowder and his fellow priests stepped in the 1850s, and it was this great sweep of national economic, social and religious history interacting with Lowder's own personal journey that caused the birth of the Society of the Holy Cross.

Charles Fuge Lowder was born in June 1820 in Bath, the son of a banker. In 1840 he went up to Exeter College, Oxford. As an undergraduate he attended the University Church of St Mary the Virgin, where Newman's sermons guided him to the priesthood. Lowder took a second-class degree in 1843 and in the autumn of that year was made deacon to serve a title in the parish of Street-cum-Walton. On his ordination as a priest, by Bishop Denison of Salisbury, on 22 December 1844, he took up additional work as chaplain to the Axbridge workhouse.

As a deacon he had looked into the possibilities of mission work in New Zealand. The failure to achieve this ambition brought to the fore his other, parallel, and perhaps greater, ambition. He wanted to work in a parish with a more advanced Catholic pattern of worship, so he applied to become a curate at the leading ritualist centre of St Barnabas, Pimlico. This, the most Catholic building erected for worship in the Church of England since the Reformation, was from its foundation a centre of ritual controversy. W.J.E. Bennet, the first vicar, was long persecuted, and, unsupported by the Bishop of London, departed under pressure.

After the change of incumbent, Robert Liddel became vicar, but the problems continued. The assistant curates, Skinner and Lowder, carried out a vigorous, painstaking and committed parish ministry, but the proponents of the Protestant cause were not to be persuaded by energetic evangelistic and pastoral zeal.

The parish, then a maze of slum streets, had been created to serve the poor and had a claim to be the most Catholic parish in London, both in externals and in its teaching. In the atmosphere of a daily celebration of Holy Communion, with priest vested in cassock, surplice, black scarf and hood, daily Morning and Evening Prayer, a Sunday sung Eucharist and strict patterns of parochial visiting, Lowder regarded himself to be in the best possible situation for an Anglo-Catholic assistant curate.

Into Lowder's idyll dropped the case of *Westerton v. Liddel*, which was one of the great dramas of the early ritualist movement. Westerton, a parishioner of Protestant persuasion, challenged the legitimacy of a number of the furnishings that had given St Barnabas its Catholic atmosphere. These included the altar cross, candlesticks, credence table and rood-screen. The judgment, which went against Liddel, was challenged on appeal. During the course of these legal disputes, the atmosphere in the life of the parish was one of conflict and confrontation.

When the cases were concluded, Westerton sought election as churchwarden so that he could continue his persecution of Liddel and his opposition to the introduction of the Catholic faith and its ceremonial practices. To further his electoral cause he hired a man to walk around the parish carrying a sandwich-board proclaiming, 'Vote Westerton'. In what he later described as 'a moment of madness', Lowder gave some of the choirboys 6d with which to buy rotten eggs. These were then thrown (accurately) at the board-carrier. Lowder appeared before Westminster magistrates where he was fined £2. He later appeared before the Bishop of London on 6 May 1854, when he was suspended from duty for six weeks. Thus one of the heroes of the Catholic revival began his great work as a man with a criminal record and a diocesan black-mark.

Lowder spent his period of suspension out of the public eye in France at the seminary in Yvetot. While there, he read Louis Abelly's book *Vie de Saint Vincent de Paul*, and this meeting with the great French apostle of the poor marked the rest of Lowder's life. He concluded that England was in desperate need of priests committed to the service of the urban poor in the great cities, in the same way that St Vincent's Company of the Mission served the poor of rural France.

On his return to England, he completed his study of the life of the saint and meditated on the dual needs of a social order alienated from the message of the Gospel, and of his fellow priests who lacked the structure for carrying out missionary work exemplified by the Vicentians for mission. As a result of his study, Lowder called a meeting of handpicked, trustworthy and potentially sympathetic clergy. A group of six came together at the House of Charity, Soho, on 28 February 1855. They were Charles Maurice Davies, curate of St Matthew's,

City Road; David Nicols, curate of Christ Church, St Pancras; Alfred Poole and Joseph Smith, fellow curates with Lowder at St Barnabas and St Paul's; and Henry Augustus Rawes, warden of the House of Charity, Soho.[1] The six formed themselves into the Society of the Holy Cross (*Societas Sanctae Crucis*), and in this society and company they made promises binding on them until May that year. The promises were to maintain confidentiality in matters concerning the Society; to affirm the Nicene Creed; to give mutual help, both temporal and spiritual, to brothers of the Society. In this way they dedicated themselves to lives of self-disciplined service to the poor, and to the extension of the Catholic faith. Members were to undertake to be obedient to a rule of life in the period up until a second meeting in May when the future would be determined. Lowder, who appeared first on the roll of members, was elected the first Master, to serve for twelve months.

The first provisional Rule instructed:

1. Every Brother ... to pray daily for the Church and Society using either the Office or the Collects in the Office.
2. Every Brother ... to make on Sundays an offering to the Society to be used for the relief of the poor, the remainder given to the Society.
3. Every Brother ... to inform another Brother of any report he may hear either to his advantage or disadvantage.
4. When two Brothers meet, the elder is to salute the younger with the '*Pax tibi*'.
5. Every Brother ... to attend all the meetings ... and positively the Great Meeting on 3 May.
6. Every member ... to pay 20 shillings a year.

Unlike many other bodies founded during the second phase of the Catholic revival, the SSC was not intended to be a devotional society but one which provided a structure and support for mission priests. It was an original concept in the Church of England. It was different from a religious community; it was more than a group of friends with common interests; it was not a group of priests resident in an oratory. It was original and innovative because the founders had no models from which to work and because it was founded in response to unique social and economic conditions. The Society was a self-conscious expression of a Catholic priesthood dormant in the Church of England for too long.

In 1856 Lowder wrote that the Society had been 'ordered . . . by God's good providence . . . Its objects [being] to defend and strengthen the spiritual life of the clergy, to defend the faith of the Church, and to carry on and aid Mission work both at home and abroad.'

In that great endeavour the Society now set to work.

Note

1 Recent research by Fr Robert Farmer SSC indicates that the House of Charity was not the splendid Gothic Revival building now known by that name but a Georgian town house, then the diocesan House of Charity.

3

The Rules of the SSC and the Brotherhood Holy Trinity

Anthony Howe

A society is defined by its rules. The fundamental tenets of law have determined how people ought and ought not to behave for thousands of years. Western society is largely reliant upon legal codes which it inherited both from the Graeco-Roman systems, and from its undeniable Judaeo-Christian heritage: the Ten Commandments of Moses and of the teachings of Jesus. By governing the boundaries of what is acceptable, rules can shape, nurture and even encourage growth. Rules and their application, however, can also be vindictive, unjust and suffocating. A study of rules is necessarily more than merely a question of whether they are the prescriptive *thou shalt*, or the proscriptive *thou shalt not*. The two are complementary. What is more important is whether the rules aim to govern by encouragement or discouragement. Both might seek growth which in a religious context is spiritual, but whereas the former might succeed, the latter becomes a burden.

At the meeting in the House of Charity in Soho 1855, the six founding fathers of the Society of the Holy Cross decided that, like any society, this society should be bound by a Rule. At its heart would be simple instructions binding on all, aimed to encourage the ecclesial community that the SSC was to become. Practices such as prayer for one another, meeting together in chapter and synod and alms-giving were not new to the Catholic Church, but in this form they were new to the Church of England of the 1850s. That is what scandalized the Society's opponents from the start. Yet these simple instructions have been the mainstay of the SSC Rule, through its various revisions until the present time. In addition to this, the earliest members of the Society could also opt into one of three levels of a secondary Rule, according to degrees of circumstance and commitment. In the end, all of this amounted to one thing: mission. The SSC was to provide for the spiritual warfare its brethren were engaged in, by providing for the spiritual nourishment of those brethren. Yet the Rule that was eventually written, and indeed to some extent the SSC itself, was built on foundations that had been laid several years earlier, through a little-known guild, founded in Oxford, called the Brotherhood of the Holy Trinity.

In its foundation, development, and particularly in its set of rules, the Brotherhood of the Holy Trinity mirrors the Society of the Holy Cross to such a close extent that the study of the early history of the former sheds much light on that of the latter. The involvement of Dr Pusey in the construction of both sets of Rules, as well as the presence of the likes of Charles Lowder and many members of SSC on the roll of the Brotherhood, warrants a significant excursion into the history of this hitherto little-known organization, which could be said to have provided one of the foundations upon which the Society was built. The Brotherhood of the Holy Trinity is part of the forgotten history of Tractarianism. Founded in 1844 and only dissolved in 1932,[1] it numbered among its members Alexander Penrose Forbes, Henry Parry Liddon, Richard Meux Benson, Edward King, William John Butler, George Fredrick Bodley, John Stainer and Robert Bridges, as well as Lowder. Its origins lie at the heart of Tractarian controversies of the 1840s and 1850s, and also with the leaders of the Oxford Movement. A study of the early years of the Brotherhood of the Holy Trinity not only provides us with a further rationale behind what eventually became the Rule of the Society of the Holy Cross,

23

but also gives a fascinating and as yet undocumented insight into the mindset of those young men, many of whom were to go on to greater things in the Church.[2]

There is, however, a subtle difference of emphasis between the Rules of the SSC and the Brotherhood, which demonstrates precisely the significant difference between discouragement and encouragement. The Rules of the SSC have always aimed to encourage in its members spiritual growth. In this the Society has been largely successful. Those of the Brotherhood, on the other hand, became almost impossibly restrictive. Members were told what *not* to do. It is not suprising that this organization is no more.

The almost ubiquitous presence of Dr Pusey in many projects dating from what could be thought of as the second stage of the Oxford Movement provides the linchpin of this survey. His links to the origins of the Oxford Movement and the wide experience he had gained through the foundation of institutions and promulgation of doctrines which helped to shape the mid-Victorian Church had earned him the status of an elder statesman. Indeed, at the time of the foundation of the SSC, Pusey appeared to personify the whole movement, to such an extent that, to its critics at least, it even bore his name. When it came to the writing of its first Rule, the six founders of the SSC were left in no doubt as to whom they should turn for help.

In his advice behind the construction of a Rule, or more correctly a set of Rules for the SSC in 1855 and 1856, Pusey was not working from a blank sheet of paper. The seeds of what was to become the Rule of the Society were sown as far back as 1845, ten years before the foundation of the SSC, when Pusey was invited to draw up suggestions for a Rule for a small, newly reconstituted, devotional society of undergraduates at Oxford. That society was the Brotherhood of the Holy Trinity. It is with the Brotherhood that the history of the Rule of the SSC necessarily begins.

It is a story which is full of intrigue and complexity, not least because it started out its life as the Brotherhood, not of the Holy Trinity, but of Saint Mary. On 18 December 1844 a society called the Brotherhood of Saint Mary was founded in the rooms of Edward Freeman of Trinity College. The intention was to 'study ecclesiastical art upon true and Catholic principles'.[3] This was very much in accordance with a general renewal of interest in medieval art and architecture, which was occurring at the time. It is probable that the impetus lay in the foundation, five years earlier, of the Cambridge Camden Society by John Mason Neale and Benjamin Webb.[4] Like its counterpart, the Brotherhood of Saint Mary was interested in the use of churches; however, it differed from the Camden Society in that it was clearly grounded in the theology of art, rather than in the functional religious use of buildings. As such it was not an historical nor antiquarian society in the manner of other learned societies.[5] This meant that the appeal of the Brotherhood remained limited and its activities somewhat esoteric.

An early member of the Brotherhood was Frederick Meyrick of Trinity College, who later played an important part in its metamorphosis into the Brotherhood of the Holy Trinity. His memoirs include a brief but significant reference to this, dealing with the first years of the Brotherhood of the Holy Trinity.[6] Meyrick relates the aims of the Brotherhood of Saint Mary, stating that it was not to be confused with the Oxford Architectural Society, which was altogether more antiquarian and academic in outlook.

The Brotherhood's first minute-book covers the period 1844–56 and appears to date from no earlier than 1852. It indicates that, when founded in 1844, there had been four members of the Brotherhood. Besides Freeman these were James Laird Patterson of Trinity College, William Trevor Perkins of Merton and James Elwin Millard, headmaster of Magdalen School. Millard served as priest-master. The record shows eight further members in 1845 including James Henry Coleridge, Meyrick and J.W. Knott, later the vicar of St Saviour's, Leeds. Meyrick counts himself amongst the founders, and so it would appear that he joined the Brotherhood very early in 1845.

The young society remained small and, according to Meyrick, it soon began to flounder. This was a period of flux followed by reconstruction, when the name, aims and ethos of the Brotherhood were altered from those of an artistic theological society to a more devotional one. Again, Meyrick wrote:

> Having exhausted our subjects, or getting tired of them we determined to bring the society to a close; but it occurred to some of us that the nucleus thus formed might be useful to another purpose. Many young men came up to the University from pious homes and well taught at their schools, who found themselves solitary and lonely in their various colleges, and ran the risk of being absorbed into the idle or noisy set to be found in each college. It was thought that these men might be gathered up, and that they might find in a body of sympathizing elders a strength to resist the various temptations to which they were exposed. The members, therefore, of the society who were specially interested in architecture withdrew, and the others set out on their new quest.[7]

Although the change from an architectural to a devotional society must have been clearly defined, there is a degree of uncertainty as to the precise date when this was effected. The earliest minute-book records, before the minutes of a meeting in August 1852, that chapter meetings had been suspended for nearly two years prior to that date.[8] This suggests that the Brotherhood of Saint Mary continued to meet until 1850 in its original form, after which date it was disbanded. Since after 1850 little appears to have happened, it may be assumed that it was during these years that the idea of refoundation and redefinition occurred.

The minutes of this meeting do not refer to any refoundation. This would seem rather curious were it not for the existence of a loose sheet of paper in Liddon's hand which records a meeting in 1852, where it was decided to reconstitute the Brotherhood 'on its original basis'. If the Brotherhood was refounded in 1852, it would not be unreasonable to believe that the new dispensation, referred to by Meyrick, came into force that year. However, a closer examination of these minutes reveals a different story. No mention is made of a change in ethos, from an aesthetic to prayer society. If the Brotherhood of the Holy Trinity had come into existence at this meeting, the change, not least in name, would surely have been recorded. Likewise, the minutes refer to the Brotherhood of the Holy Trinity being 'revived on its original basis'. Yet, it is quite clear that the society was not being revived on its original basis. Furthermore, Liddon's undergraduate diaries make frequent mention of the Brotherhood of the Holy Trinity,[9] to which he was admitted on 23 November 1848, four years before the refoundation in 1852. Liddon's record of the reconstitution runs:

> At a meeting held in the Revd Frederic Meyrick's rooms present the Revd J.E. Millard, Meyrick, Jenkins, Liddon, Bramley (Lyson Birch), it was agreed;
> That the Brotherhood of the Holy Trinity should be revived on its original basis.
> That by its original basis be understood the first seven suggestions and that all old members being members of the English Church, and willing to abide by the suggestions should be invited to unite again upon that basis.
> That further necessary regulations be framed by brethren appointed for that purpose: and submitted to the chapter to be held on Ash Wednesday next, in P. Liddon's rooms in Christchurch.
> That the brethren be Millard, Meyrick, Liddon.

(The paper is signed 'H.P. Liddon', who added in pencil, 'Minute at meeting of reconstitution of the BHT in 1852'.)

The 'original basis' or the seven suggestions are listed at the beginning of the first minute-book.[10] As they clearly predate the lapse in meetings, it must be concluded that the Brotherhood went through not one but two periods of transition. The first involved a change in purpose and name; the second was more of a revival after a period of inactivity. It was also then that the Brotherhood sought to compose a set of more definite rules.

If this was indeed the case then it matches Meyrick's recollections. He describes how the original suggestions or resolutions came about as a manner of compromise from Pusey. Meyrick had been sent by the brethren, at the time of the first transition, to Pusey to seek his advice over the matter. The ensuing story reveals the difficulties involved:

> There was some difficulty in organising the new plan, and I was requested to ask Dr Pusey for his advice. Dr Pusey was at this time engaged in the institution and establishment of sisterhoods, and he grasped at this application, which he thought might be utilized for the institution of Brotherhoods also.[11]

If Pusey was, at the time, involved in the foundation of the Sisterhoods, the date must have been close to 1845, the date of the foundation of the Park Village Sisterhood. That would indicate that the Brotherhood of the Holy Trinity came into existence possibly as early as 1845. This date is highly significant. Not only is it possible to trace both the time at which Pusey first began thinking about what were to become the Rules of the Brotherhood and later, those of the SSC, but also the circumstances which surrounded his thinking.

By the mid 1840s, Pusey was evidently fired by the thought of a monastic revival and saw this as his chance. He had, however, misunderstood the brief, mistaking the Brotherhood to be pseudo-monastic. His initial suggestion, for example, that the brethren walk around with their eyes to the ground, thus avoiding temptation, was too strict. Meyrick, the voice of moderation, argued that such a practice was 'not natural for young men, nor good for them'.[12] Pusey went on to suggest that the brethren should wear a girdle of flannel or some other suitable material for self-restraint. This was hardly any better, if at all, than the first idea, and was not welcomed by Meyrick. On recounting the interview with Pusey to Basil Jones, the latter exclaimed, 'you will no doubt, call yourselves the Worshipful Society of Girdlers'.[13] Jones' light-hearted comment clearly illustrates the danger facing the Brotherhood. In a time when anything out of the ecclesiastical norm was regarded by the majority with suspicion, it would be foolish to draw attention to the fact by engaging in unusual public rituals. Nevertheless, it appears that, later on, some of the brethren and aspirant members did indeed take to wearing the girdle.[14]

Not all of Pusey's suggestions were, however, rejected:

> We did not accept either of Dr Pusey's proposals, but we accepted on his recommendation, the name of the Brotherhood of the Holy Trinity and some simple suggestions which might help us towards a good life, such as that we should rise early, use prayer, public and private, be moderate in food and drink, and avoid speaking evil of others.[15]

Pusey, who was responsible for the change of the Brotherhood's name to that of the Holy Trinity, also generated a simple Rule of Life for the Brotherhood. It is this which was referred to in the refoundation minutes and then copied into the front of the minute-book.[16] It is not difficult to detect similarities in these resolutions with parts of what later became the Rule of the SSC, particularly in the commemorations at morning and evening, study and mutual prayer.

The brethren were

1. To rise early.
2. To be moderate in food.
3. To devote some time in each day to serious reading.
4. To speak evil of no man.
5. To avoid dissipation.
6. To commemorate the Holy Trinity, by saying the *Gloria Patri* on first rising and the last thing at night.
7. To pray for (1) the unity of the church; (2) the conversion of sinners; (3) the advancement of the faithful; and (4) the members of the Brotherhood generally.[17]

These changes were, however, not universally welcomed by the brethren, for Meyrick tells us that those who maintained their architectural bent resigned, leaving the rest of the brethren free to undertake their reformation.[18]

No doubt these resignations must have gone some way to

disheartening those who remained with the Brotherhood. There were, however, enough remaining members to ensure that the reformation took place. The minute-book entry of August 1852 lists 47 members, including Alexander Penrose Forbes, Bishop of Brechin, Richard Meux Benson of Christ Church, Henry Parry Liddon and Edward King of Oriel and, of course, Millard, Meyrick and Knott. So a degree of continuity was maintained. There was still to be a priest-Master, who was assisted by the Almoner (in deacon's orders at least) and the amanuensis or secretary. The binding ethos of the society throughout this period was the seven resolutions.

In the light of this, it can be concluded that the Brotherhood underwent reformation before the gap of 1850–2, and that by 1845 this had in effect already taken place, ten years before the foundation of the SSC. As a result, all those who joined after 1845 joined the Brotherhood of the Holy Trinity and not the Brotherhood of Saint Mary. Furthermore, since after the lapse, the so-called 'original purposes' according to which the Brotherhood was to be revived were clearly those of the Brotherhood of the Holy Trinity and not of the Brotherhood of Saint Mary, and the latter must have been well and truly defunct long before 1850.

There are two questions which arise from this. Why did the transition of 1845 occur in the way that it did, and what caused the cessation of its meetings in 1850? At first, the answers to these seem obvious. Both mark a significant shift in the history of Tractarianism owing to two events which sent shock-waves to its very heart. The first was the conversion of Newman to Rome in 1845 and the second was the Gorham judgment on the efficacy of baptism in 1850. As both the conversion and the judgment caused considerable upset in the ranks of the movement, it is not unreasonable to believe that the ripple was felt in the Brotherhood of the Holy Trinity. People were shaken and as a result resigned, some submitting to the Roman obedience.

There was, however, another factor at work in 1850. By referring to an 'original basis', the 1852 minute implies that the

Brotherhood had moved away from such a basis in the first place. This would not be wholly unsurprising: it is not uncommon for a society to move away from its founding principles. But why did the meetings stop at all?

The answer is found in the form of a comment made by Benson during the course of an acrimonious debate on the reform of the Rule at the annual chapter meeting of the Brotherhood in 1865. Benson, who was then Master, resisted the attempts of Bright to push through reforms too hastily. Evidently emotions were high, and the threat of resignations even presented itself. In response Benson said:

> As for the succession of some brethren, with which we are threatened, unless we make some change, he would remind us that on the former occasion this recession was on the other side. We then lost some of the most valuable men, who were part now at work in the English Church. They felt that the Brotherhood was not considered by some of the brothers to pledge them to that fullness of aim, which they thought essential. Consequently the Brotherhood was for a time reduced to a very small number, though, thanks be to God, we are now a large body. But as the result of a change will not affect one side only, the master felt that he was acting for the interests of the Society, in saying that he could not consent to the subject being discussed before next General chapter.

Clearly the problem lay in the fact that for most of the brethren in 1850, the Brotherhood had lost its ground. They wanted a more formal structure and were not content with its rather loosely defined basis. This would not only explain why the meetings ceased but also why only Millard, Meyrick and Liddon are named at the meeting of reconstitution in 1852.[19] The revival was quick to take place, and by 1852, there were 47 members, including Benson.

This explains why the minutes mention the drawing up of a new and more detailed Rule. The 1844–56 minute-book refers to these as having been drawn up by 'an experienced clergyman as a standard to be aimed at, and as a guide to such as are willing to practise a stricter Rule, but not binding on the conscience of any'.[20] The clergyman in question was, once again, almost certainly Pusey. Meyrick recalls:

> Time passed, and some of the members were not contented with anything so vague; they wanted rules, not suggestions. If I recollect right, the chief mover in this direction was R.M. Benson later of Cowley, and he was supported by H.P. Liddon. I opposed, saying that principles were better guides to the conscience than rules.[21]

Benson and Liddon, who were both later members of the SSC, appear to having been arguing for a formally structured and constituted lay guild, founded upon a Rule of Life, which was binding to all. They laid the blame for the breakdown of the Brotherhood in 1850 upon the fact that it had been too loosely defined. It was for this reason, Benson later argued, that many of the members resigned.

Meyrick's opposition resulted in reference again being made to Pusey, who proposed a compromise. Instead of a Rule of Life, or indeed levels of Rules such as those written for the Society of the Holy Cross, there should be 'rules to be aimed at', which were not to be binding upon anybody except such brethren who wished to adopt them. Thus the situation of 1852 was resolved: Benson and Liddon had their Rule and Meyrick kept it optional.

What were these Rules? At the front of the 1844–56 minute-book, it is recorded that the Rule had been written by 'an experienced clergymen as a standard to be aimed at, and as a guide to such as are able to practice a stricter Rule, but is not binding on the conscience of any'. As the book appears to date from August 1852, it would follow that the additional Rule would date also from this time.

If Pusey was indeed once again involved in the drafting of Rules for the Brotherhood during this period, then this becomes crucial to our understanding of those written for the SSC, since we can positively identify the vein that runs through both. Proof of Pusey's hand is found in a copy of the manual of the Brotherhood printed in 1876, preserved in the

Brotherhood's archive which belonged to Darwell Stone, later Principal of Pusey House and the last Master of the Brotherhood. In it a manuscript gloss to the printed commentary on the Rule[22] in Stone's hand names Pusey as the author. Both Rule and commentary had been included in the Manual of the Brotherhood from the outset, although these remarks are dated to the feast of SS Philip and James, 1852 (1 May). This would, therefore, indicate that the new Rule was the result of the deliberations of the appointed brethren, as mentioned in the minutes of the meeting of reconstitution in 1852. That would concord with the scheme of refoundation suggested by Meyrick, as well as the date of suspension and reconvention recorded in the minute-book.[23]

It is no matter of coincidence that there are similarities between the 1845 resolutions and later the Rules of the Brotherhood of the Holy Trinity and the Rule written under Pusey's direction for the Society of the Holy Cross. We know from a comment made by Benson in 1867 that this was the Rule that was incorporated into the first manual of the Brotherhood, printed in 1852.[24] At the time, he claimed that this Rule had always been the basis of union upon which the Brotherhood existed.

A copy of the 1852 Manual survives amongst the Liddon papers at Keble College, Oxford. It is somewhat more elaborate than its successors and differs in format. It opens with a quotation from a letter concerning the Rule. This commentary found its way into the 1858 and subsequent editions, under the title of 'introductory remarks, by an experienced priest, are commended by the Brotherhood and the notice of its members as a useful interpretation of the preceding Resolutions'. In both the 1852 and later Manuals, these remarks are dated to the Feast of SS Philip and James 1852. The 1852 Rules were, with their many injunctions against even moderate excess, to say the least, ascetic.[25]

It might strike the modern reader as odd that an organization should go to the lengths of composing such a complex and harsh set of rules and then grant them optional status. After all, the very purpose of a Rule is to unite those who subscribe to it in a common way of life, as with, for example, the monastic Rule of St Benedict. Rules should, by their very nature, have a positive and distinct end. It is, therefore, hardly surprising that before long the question once again surfaced as to whether the Rule could and should be made obligatory for the brethren. The spectre of past failure still hung over the Brotherhood. It was to be one of the great weaknesses which was to dog the Brotherhood, but which the SSC managed to avoid. Whilst the SSC successfully catered both for various degrees of compliance and a unifying bond by instituting a general Rule binding on all and then three further standards of Rules to suit the personal circumstances of the priest, the Brotherhood initially had little more than a take it or leave it policy.

This eventually came to be regarded by some as unsatisfactory. Two years after the foundation of the SSC, the Brotherhood, forced to clarify matters, took an interesting lead from the SSC. On 20 January 1857 Brother John Greaves had advocated a stricter observance of the Rule and a more direct accountability to the Master. Accordingly, at the chapter held on 27 January 1857, the brethren sought to clarify by stating the objects of the Brotherhood:

> The objects of the Brotherhood of the Holy Trinity are Communion in prayer and works of charity, and mutual encouragement in regularity of life. To this end all Brethren, wherever residing, are supposed to adopt (so far as in their lives) the following Resolutions. Then shall follow the Seven resolutions as contained in pp 5 and 6 of the manual ... and ending thus '4 for each other as brethren'.[26]

As regards the *Rules to be Aimed at*, the brethren decided that it would be an appropriate optional extra, a tool for Lenten observance.

The fathers of the Society of the Holy Cross meeting in 1855 clearly learned from the machinations of their Oxford cousins and promptly avoided their mistakes. Whilst displaying some generic similarity with both sets of Brotherhood Rules, the Rule which came to be drawn up under Pusey's influence nevertheless managed to avoid from the outset the problems that had dogged the Brotherhood. This can be put down to two important differences. Whereas the 1852 Rule for the Brotherhood (as well as the later revision of it) was largely negative in ethos, those penned for the SSC were wholly intended to be positive by adding injunctions relating to the spiritual growth of the individual. In addition, almost from the outset, it was decided that there should be a greater degree of freedom concerning which set of rules a priest of the Society could subscribe to, whilst still retaining a sense of a binding common purpose. Whereas the Brotherhood had its original 1845 Resolutions and later a set of 'Rules to be aimed at', both of which were optional, the SSC from the outset in 1855 required its members to subscribe to one general Rule which became the Ordinary Rule, and then if they chose, to one of two further codes named after the colour of the cords worn with the SSC cross by the adherents: the White Rule (strictest and perhaps closest to the Brotherhood in nature), and the Red Rule. In 1856, when these were formally adopted, another Rule, the Green Rule, was also added.[27] Thus the Society avoided the problem of having no defining sense of purpose of a common Rule, but at the same time provided for varying degrees of choice as to how an individual could shape his life to that purpose.

The difference in ethos between the Rules of the two organizations is interesting. It is almost as if the purpose of one is a mirror image of the other, in that negative becomes positive, whilst retaining a clearly identifiable structure. Given the nature of its intended followers, the 1852 Brotherhood Rule is remarkably proscriptive. It is as if the brethren needed to retreat as much as possible from the world around them. It gives the impression of a sectarian, almost Johannine society which, although it existed in the world, wanted to have as little as possible to do with it. The monastic ideals which initially fired Pusey, even if somewhat tempered, are still evident. It is perhaps not difficult to see why – young undergraduates were (and still are) open to all manner of temptation. No doubt if Pusey could go some way to sparing the younger generation from all this, it was all the better.

Of course this sectarian attitude could not be further removed from the world of those six priests who met in the House of Charity in Soho on 28 February 1855. Unlike Pusey and most of the Brotherhood, they were parochial clergy, and as such they had very much been thrust into the world, and at its most worldly. London was then, as it is now, a huge and diverse city, in which dwelt both the super-rich and the extreme poor, and in which the Church often struggled to make itself heard. It is difficult for most living at the beginning of the twenty-first century to imagine just how bad conditions must have been for so many people in Victorian London. As we face today the problems of high-rise estates, so our forebears faced tenements and houses so overcrowded that in the parish of St George in the East End alone there were over 30,000 souls. Far from needing simply to retreat from the society in which they found themselves at work, these men had, following the example of St Vincent de Paul, the aspirations of reaching out into its darkest corners. And so from the very beginning the SSC was a missionary society, one which sought the transformation of the world through the Cross. The mission-fields were not only to be found abroad. People at home were in danger of forgetting God altogether.

It is no wonder that the Rule that was adopted needed also to be one of engagement. The Brothers of the SSC were secular priests through and through, and so it would have been utterly futile to have adopted a Rule which tried to protect its members from the world. Keeping one's eyes to the ground might be thought suitable for the Oxford Quad – it was certainly not always suitable for the East End.

Instead, this new Vicentian society needed to be one which provided active encouragement for its members in every aspect of their very practical priestly ministry. Lowder, writing in 1856 of the foundation of the Society, commented that its objects were 'to defend and strengthen the spiritual life of the clergy, to defend the faith of the Church, and to carry on and aid Mission work both at home and abroad'. As such, any Rule or set of Rules that it chose to adopt had to be one which both provided for the personal spiritual needs of individuals, and at the same time bound those individuals together as a community of prayer and support. To this effect a simple Rule, binding on all members, was drafted and remained provisional until the first SSC synod, on 3 May 1855, when it was formally accepted. This Rule, which was headed 'Rule until May 3rd' enjoined in six points the strongly fraternal nature of the Society:

1. Every Brother is to pray daily for the Church and Society, using either the Office or the Collects in the Office.
2. Every Brother is to make on Sundays an offering to the Society, out of which he is allowed to relieve the poor, the remainder being given at the next meeting to the Society.
3. Every Brother is to inform another Brother of any report he may hear either to his advantage or disadvantage.
4. When two Brethren meet, the elder is to salute the younger with the '*Pax tibi*', etc., but this need not be repeated again on the same day.
5. Every Brother is to attend all the Meetings of the Society he can; and positively the Great Meeting on May 3rd (Holy Cross Day), except by dispensation, which must be granted at the previous Meeting of the Society.
6. Every Member is to pay a subscription of twenty shillings a year by quarterly payments.

In its brevity, if not so much content, the first Rule of 1855 resembles the concept of the seven 1845 resolutions of the Brotherhood of the Holy Trinity. The nature of the Provisional Rule was highly practical in tone and so it is perhaps not surprising that it was felt that, like the Brotherhood, something more was required to deal with the spiritual side. Thus it was agreed at the May synod that two further Rules should be composed to which a member could subscribe, should he choose to do so, according both to personal circumstance and required spiritual sustenance.

The May Rule became the Ordinary Rule of the Society. In September that year the chapter agreed that a celibate order should be established within the Society, and to this effect Lowder, David Nicols and Henry Augustus Rawes set to work on what was to become the White Rule.[28] The following month it was resolved that a second voluntary Rule was also needed for married brethren and those single clergy who chose not to ally themselves to the celibate order. As such, the writing of a second optional Rule was also now required, the task being entrusted to F.H. Murray and G.C. White,[29] who were able to present their draft to the chapter on 8 December.

At the chapter meeting of 12 March 1856 the Society resolved that it should adopt the two voluntary Rules at its forthcoming May synod. Any full member of the Society, which was called the Higher Order could chose to adopt one of these Rules at his discretion. Those in the Lower Order, that is deacons, ordinands and priest-probationers who had yet to be admitted to the Higher Order, were to follow a separate simple Rule. On 3 May 1856, following an address by Dr Pusey 'on the Aim and Duties of the Priestly Life, and the cultivation of Personal Holiness', the Society in passing its first statutes, decreed in Item V 'that besides the Ordinary Rule of the Higher Order, there be two voluntary rules for the Brethren of greater strictness; one of which shall be restricted to celibates'.[30]

The Rules were then laid out in full. That for married and single men was named the Red Rule. (This was in effect the draft that had been presented in December 1855 and agreed on 12 March.) Like the Brotherhood Rule of 1852, the Red Rule consisted of twelve points. Through injunctions such as those to rise before 7 a.m., to keep the Church's fasts, to eat moderately and to make confession once a year, it is easy to discern the influence of the Brotherhood. Yet in addition, obligations of a more priestly nature were added, such as the daily recitation of Prime, Sext and Compline as well as Matins and Evensong, and daily spiritual, if not real, communion.

The Rule for the celibate brethren was a different affair altogether.[31] The draft penned in 1855 by Lowder, Rawes and Nicols and formally adopted at the May synod was austere, due in no small part to the fact that this was clearly based on Pusey's 1852 Brotherhood Rule, which it more or less wholly incorporates. The White Rule was divided into six sections under the headings of 'Daily Rule of Devotion, Food, Dress, Recreation, Study, and Society', with a list of injunctions under each heading. It is here that the now familiar SSC practice of making the daily commemoration first appeared. The celibate brethren were to begin the day by saying the *Gloria Patri* and making the sign of the Cross whilst saying *In nomine Patris, et Filio et Spiritui Sancto*, all of which was borrowed from the Brotherhood. Here we also see injunctions to early rising, modest eating and drinking, mental prayer and study, dress, conversation, avoidance of public theatres and other such spectacles, all familiar to the Oxford brethren. Occasionally, complete clauses appear to have been simply lifted out almost verbatim from the earlier version, such as that relating to the use of food 'to repair to the daily decays of nature, not for self indulgence',[32] or not quoting 'Scripture except for direct religious ends'.[33] However, the White Rule also added a great deal which would bring the priestly ministries of its adherents closer to Christ, through a series of rigorous daily exercises, such as commending the main courses of action in the day to God through ejaculatory prayer and seeking to promote the glory of God at every opportunity. And here is the subtle difference: the ethos of the White Rule aimed at building the priest up, by providing the spiritual tools necessary for his work. Lowder of all people would have known that this was not asceticism merely for asceticism's sake. Any mortification of the flesh was merely to help the furtherance of God's Church.

It was particularly to this end that the White Rule, like the Red, also contained numerous exhortations which genuinely aimed at enriching the life of the priest. Such matters as the daily reading of Scripture and reception of Communion, suitable preparations for so doing, self-examination, recollection and mental prayer, as well as the saying of the offices at nine, twelve and three, in addition to Matins, Evensong and Compline, were all intended to bring this about, by promoting a standard of priestly life that had hitherto been unknown.

In all, the original White Rule adopted in May 1856 contained a total of 34 injunctions, appertaining to almost every detail of the ideal celibate priestly life. Although it was later to be revised, it was to some extent the standard by which the Society could set its mark. That was evidently what the Society itself thought, since barely more than four months after it had been put down in the statutes, the Red Rule was again revised, bringing it far more into line with the White Rule.[34]

This revised Rule of September 1856 followed the structure of the White Rule with headed subsections. It is introduced in the minute-book as being 'an amended copy of the Red Rule', which is misleading, since it is completely rewritten. Whilst the new Red Rule was still rather more liberal than its White counterpart, this is relative, and much of it, including the complete sections on 'Dress, Recreation, Study and Society', were identical, so that the minute-book simply refers the reader back to the White Rule rather than copying out these sections once again.

With the demise of the original twelve-point Red Rule, it was clear that there needed to be something in its place. Thoughts of revision must already have been in the minds of the brethren even when they met in May 1856, for at the chapter meeting on 5 August W.H. Lyall presented his suggestions for a new Green Rule. In September, after the new Red Rule had been accepted, it was resolved that a Green Rule should also be drawn up. For this task, Lyall was joined in a subcommittee by Frs Goulder, Poole and Bryan King. When the committee reported back to the chapter on 11 November 1856, it presented a Rule, which once again followed the structure and some of the injunctions of the White Rule, but which was closer in ethos to the original and now rejected version of the Red Rule.[35] Thus by the time the SSC met for its third synod in May 1857, the Red and Green Rules were ready to be accepted for general use.[36]

Whilst the original all-or-nothing policy of the Brotherhood was doomed from the start, the degrees of commitment which came to be adopted over time by the SSC managed to prevent a similar crisis from occurring. It was an ingenious, if not rather Anglican, solution. In a church in which clergy were permitted to marry, there was necessarily going to be a mixed bag of priests who were drawn to the ideals of the SSC. Lowder, in his celibate state, adopted and kept the White Rule until his death. But others who might have been attracted to the missionary ideal of the Society would have been excluded from membership due to their marital status. What might have been appropriate for young single curates or austere Oxford dons could not be forced on all of the ritualist clergy. Pusey, a widower by this time, would have been well aware of this. At least one other optional rule was not merely desirable but required.

It might be tempting to think that in his part in the construction of this trinity of rules for the SSC, Pusey was guided by more than the Rule he had previously written for the Brotherhood of the Holy Trinity. Pusey did have a clear devotion to the Trinity – both the Brotherhood and his Sisterhood came so to be dedicated. The existence of three rules for one society could well be seen to be an expression of Trinitarian theology: equal, yet different, just as the persons of the Trinity are equal but different. But this is at best mere conjecture. What is certain is that the existence from 1856 of one general, and three progressively demanding Rules, marked the type of practicality which was a distinguishing mark of the SSC. So whilst the White Rule, adopted in December 1855 by Lowder and in 1856 by Pusey, was highly ascetic and closest to that of the Brotherhood, the SSC Rule, as it came to be, clearly refuted the pseudomonasticism of some rather overzealous if well-meaning undergraduates.

This practicality which governed the decision not only to adopt variable degrees of Rules, but which also lay behind the positive outlook of the original Provisional Rule, was one which was grounded in the type of incarnational theology

which inspired the founders of the Society and which naturally
lent itself to the protection of the Holy Cross. The ideals set out
between 1855 and 1857 were no pie-in-the-sky, impossible-to-
achieve wonderlands. They were instead ideals of engagement
and mission, sustenance and growth, firstly of the priest-
Brethren, and then through them, of the people of God. Just as
the Cross was not a matter of mere romanticism, neither was
the work of Christ's Church undertaken by the priests of the
Society. At times, their work was joyful, at others painful. But
in good times and bad, the Rule which was generated from
those early days of 1855 and 1856 formed and, more importantly, resourced a Society which has held together now,
sometimes against the odds, for 150 years.

We could very well leave the Brotherhood of the Holy
Trinity in 1855, since from that date it and the SSC had
notionally little more in common than a degree of mutual
membership. It is, all the same, an interesting case in point (and
one which ultimately vindicates the wisdom of the Fathers of
the Society) that the subject of the Rule continued to prove
something of a bone of contention for the Brotherhood.
Whereas the SSC flourished with its three sets of rules which
could be adopted by individual members at their choice, and
which were largely positive in the encouragement of a dee-
pened spiritual life, the Brotherhood battled with the whole
question of having a single Rule of Life, which was merely
optional. It had, of course, been a point of debate from the
earliest days, but it was only during the 1860s that it was driven
close to a point of schism. After much heated debate, and not a
little acrimony, the Brotherhood came to a consensus. From
1870 there was one set of obligatory rules, some of which
applied to undergraduate brethren and others to nonresidents.
These rules remained unchanged until the final demise of the
Brotherhood in 1932.

The Brotherhood had by 1870 come of age, and began to
settle down. After 1870 the excitement that had not only
fuelled its controversies, but also its prayers, became more
restrained. Youthful zeal tends to moderate over the years, and

in any case there were soon to be other battles to fight. The Brotherhood had grown and the Church of England had changed beyond the expectations of those first members of 1844 and 1845. The original Oxford Movement, from which the Brotherhood and later the SSC emanated, was little more than a recollection, in the minds of the young undergraduate Brothers and the ritualist slum-priests who inspired them. There were different problems facing the English Church, and whereas both the Brotherhood and the Society continued to exist alongside each other, it was eventually only the Society that was able to stand up and face them. It cannot be a mere coincidence that, in the end, it was the positive Rule of engagement chosen by the SSC rather than the simply negative Rule of abstinence of the Brotherhood which won the day, since it is largely the engagement with humanity that lies at the heart of the Incarnation. Even so, without the Brotherhood, one might wonder whether the Society we have inherited might have been what it has been, or even if it might have ever been at all.

APPENDIX

Brotherhood *Rules to be Aimed at*, 1852[37]

1. To rise an hour before the time of Morning Chapel, with a view to devoting the interval to private prayers. When in the country to rise at six in the summer and at seven in the winter for like purpose.

2. Daily
    (a) To commemorate the HOLY TRINITY by saying the *Gloria Patri*, at least the first thing on rising in the morning and the last before going to bed.
    (b) To use the accustomed prayers (i) For unity; (ii) For the conversion of sinners; (iii) For mutual perseverance and advancement;[38] also the form of intercession 'Remember O Lord', as at pp. 15, 16 and 17.[39]

    During Lent
    (c) To say together, as may be conveniently arranged, the Gradual Psalms (pss. 120-134 inclusive) on Wednesdays, and the Penitential on Fridays.

3. To devote an hour in every day to Theological reading, of which Holy Scripture shall always form a part; or when this is absolutely impossible, half an hour to reading, in this case, of a strictly devotional character; unless the daily service be said or heard, and then at least a quarter of an hour.

4. To aim continually at increased self-collectedness, and at offering up to God every thought, word and action.

5. To shun all unedifying and frivolous conversation, especially when in female company.

6. To repeat evil, or speak disparagingly to no one, unless duty, or love to some other require it: and to improve every other opportunity of promoting peace and goodwill.

7. Never to quote Holy Scripture except for a religious end.

8. With the intent of taking food as a repair of the daily decays of nature, and not for self indulgence:
    (a) To observe the fasts of the Church as health shall permit.

   (b) When at home, or alone,
      (i) to take the *plainest* things at table
     (ii) not to eat meat twice in the day, unless health require it
    (iii) not to drink wine or beer,
    (iv) not to eat between meals
   (c) When in society,
      (i) not to eat above three kinds of food, besides soup or fish.
     (ii) not to drink *in all* above three glasses of wine.

9. To observe becoming simplicity in dress,
    (i) if in Holy Orders, to wear nothing unclerical.
   (ii) if laymen, to avoid extravagance in dress, with an especial view to the exercise of charity.

10. To set apart one tenth of the income for God's service, unless the claims of any near and dependent relation, or the smallness of the income itself, prevent it.

11. To avoid attendance at the theatre and opera, as well as all places and practices in any way connected with the promotion of known deliberate sin.

12. To keep careful guard over the eye, when in the streets or elsewhere, so as not to look at anything hurtful unless it is a duty.

Suggestions[40]

1. To practise confession to a priest.
2. To receive the Blessed Sacrament, if possible, every week, and on the Greater Festivals.

SSC White Rule 3 May 1855

Daily Rule of Devotion

Rise at 6 a.m. in Summer, and before 7 a.m. in the winter.
Commend the Day to God at first waking by saying *Gloria Patri et Filio et Spiritui sancto*, or some other form – and at rising

sign yourself with the sign of the Cross saying *In nomine Patri et Filio et Spiritui Sancti.*

Employ at least half an hour daily in mental prayer.

Communicate daily, if possible: and if not make a solemn act of spiritual communion. In both cases fasting, except by medical, or other authority.

Say Matins and Evensong daily and secure previously ½ an hour for private morning prayer and preparation for Holy Communion.

If you have received Holy Communion use some ejaculation frequently with respect to it – as 'Abide with me Lord'. If you have only made Spiritual Communion, renew it by other higher acts.

Pray daily at least ¼ of an hour for the conversion of sinners, and always at Holy Communion.

Use thanksgiving for ¼ of an hour after Holy Communion.

Choose daily an ejaculatory prayer to be used every hour, supplying it afterwards if omitted – one grace to be cultivated – one temptation to be resisted.

Examine yourself twice daily, including in one at least a special examination on any leading fault.

Read daily at least 10 verses of Holy Scripture on your knees, as God's voice to you.

This may be blended with mental prayer or with study.

Read a Spiritual Book for a quarter of an hour daily.

Say an Office for each of the hours 9, 12, 3 and Compline.

Say grace before and after every meal, and mentally at times during it.

Commend to God by ejaculatory prayer the main courses of action in the day.

Food

Use all food to repair the daily decays of nature, not for self-indulgence.

Do not take food out of meals, unless ordered by a Physician, or faint and exhausted.

Take at home the plainest food at table.

Abstain from flesh meat, wine, and luxuries on all Fridays, and fasts out of Lent – and in Lent at least on fours days of the week unless a physician order otherwise.

If you dine out do not take above three varieties of food, or three glasses of wine.

Dress

Avoid all ornament and everything unclerical – and use simplicity of dress.

Recreation

Avoid theatres, balls, cards, and any public amusement except music, in which there is nothing immoral.

Study

Avoid all frivolous, or objectless reading.

Do not read about sin (as in trials or newspapers) except as a duty.

Gain if possible an hour daily for study of Holy Scripture, or theological reading.

Begin to prepare each sermon whether written or oral on your knees.

Restrain curiosity.

Society

Never repeat evil or speak disparagingly of any one; except as a distinct duty – but rather endeavour to make an excuse for anyone who may be evil spoken of or speak some good of them – or if you know of none, be silent or turn the conversation.

Do some act of penitence for every instance of evil speaking and ask God for special forgiveness for it.

Do not interrupt others in conversation, but allow yourself to be interrupted, and often keep silence as a mode of self-discipline and collectedness.

Avoid frivolous and unedifying conversation, especially in female society.

Seek, if you are in Society, in whatever way you can to promote the glory of God.

Never quote Holy Scripture, except for direct religious ends.

Keep a careful watch over the eyes when in the street, and elsewhere; and do not needlessly look at the faces of women.

SSC Red Rule, 16 September 1856

Daily Rule of Devotion

Rise not later than 7.

Commend the Day to God at first waking, by saying *Gloria Patri et Filio et Spiritui Sancto*, or some other form; and at rising sign yourself with the sign of the Cross saying *In nomine Patri et Filio et Spiritui Sancti*.

Use mental prayer daily.

Communicate if possible on all Sundays and Festivals, and that fasting, except by medical, or other authority. If hindered from Sacramental Communion make an act of Spiritual Communion as early in the day as possible.

Observe strictly the Rule of the Church to say Matins and Evensong daily either publicly or privately.

If you have received Holy Communion use some ejaculation with respect to it, as 'abide with me LORD' - If you have only made Spiritual Communion, renew it by other higher acts.

Pray daily at least ¼ of an hour for the conversion of sinners, and always at Holy Communion.

Use preparation before and thanksgiving after Holy Communion.

Choose daily an ejaculatory prayer, one grace to be cultivated, one temptation to be resisted.

Examine yourself twice daily, including in one at least a special examination of some leading fault.

Read daily a portion of Holy Scripture on your knees, as GOD's voice to you. This may be blended with mental prayer or with study.

Read a Spiritual Book for ¼ of an hour daily.

Say daily Prime and Compline, or an Office of those times which may be Family Devotion – also an intermediate office which may be Sext, Nones, or the Office of the Society.

Commend to God by ejaculatory prayer the main actions in the day.

Food

As the White Rule except art 4.

4. Abstain from flesh-meat, wine and luxuries on all Fridays and Fasts out of Lent; and in Lent at least 3 days of the week; unless on the authority of your director or medical man.

The rest as the White Rule.

SSC Green Rule, 11 November 1856

Rise not later than 7.30 a.m.

Commend the day to GOD at first waking (and at night at going to bed) by saying *Gloria Patri*, etc., or some other form; and at rising (and lying down) sign yourself with the sign of the Cross saying *In nomine Patri*, etc.

Communicate on all Sundays, and Festivals, if possible fasting. If hindered from Sacramental Communion, make an act of Spiritual Communion.

Endeavour to observe the Rule of the Church to say Matins and Evensong daily, either publicly or privately.

Use preparation before and thanksgiving after Holy Communion.

Examine yourself daily.

Read daily a portion of Holy Scripture on your knees, as

GOD's voice to you – this may be blended with mental prayer or with study.

Say daily a midday office of those times, which may be the Office of the Society, and Compline which may be family devotion.

Say grace (at least privately) before and after every meal.

Food

Use all food to repair the daily decays of nature, not for self-indulgence.

Observe the days of fasting and abstinence approved by the Church.

Dress

Avoid unclerical attire.

Recreation

Avoid all theatres, balls, cards, and such other amusements as might prove an occasion of scandal.

Study

Give if possible at least half an hour daily for study of Holy Scripture, or theological reading.

Begin to prepare each sermon, whether written or oral, on your knees.

Society

Do not speak evil or disparagingly of anyone, except as a distinct duty.

Avoid frivolous and unedifying conversation, especially in female society.

Never quote Holy Scripture, except for some religious or useful purpose.

Notes

1 A number of letters addressed to Darwell Stone as Master of the Brotherhood survive in its archive at Pusey House. They indicate that the Brotherhood had outlived its usefulness and that the overwhelming majority of the correspondents advocated its dissolution.

2 Little or nothing has been written about the Brotherhood. Where it is mentioned in printed works, it is either brief and incidental, or consigned to a footnote. Biographers of Gerard Manley Hopkins, who considered joining his friends in the Brotherhood, have shown interest, but no serious study has been made of the records. The minutes are now deposited at Pusey House, Oxford.

3 W.R.W. Stephens, *The Life and Letters of Edward A. Freeman* (London: Macmillan, 1895), p. 58.

4 May 1839. In 1846, when it moved to London, it changed its name to the Ecclesiological Society, the name it still bears.

5 It is difficult to gain a clear picture of the precise activities of the Brotherhood of Saint Mary. There are, for instance, no extant minutes of any of the meetings. All that we know is that which is contained in the prefaces to the first minute-book of the Brotherhood of the Holy Trinity, and of the earlier manuals. Even then, we are only informed of the date, purpose and founder members of the Brotherhood of Saint Mary.

6 Frederick Meyrick, *Memories of Life at Oxford and Experiences in Italy, Greece, Turkey, Germany, Spain and Elsewhere* (London: John Murray, 1905), pp. 173ff.

7 Ibid., p. 173.

8 Pusey House Library (PHL): Brotherhood of the Holy Trinity minute-book, Vol. 1 1844–56, MSS. To be referred to as BHT minute-books.

9 PHL: Liddon papers, Box 12. Liddon records chapter meetings of the BHT and not the BSM on 25 April, 15 June, 19 November and 17 December.

10 See p.29.

11 Meyrick, *Memories of Life at Oxford*, p. 174.

12 Ibid., p. 174.

13 Ibid., p. 174.

14 Including Gerard Manley Hopkins, although he never became a full member.

15 Meyrick, *Memories of Life at Oxford*, p. 174.

16 Ibid., p. 174.

17 PHL: BHT minute-book, Vol. 1, pp. 4–5.

18 Meyrick, *Memories of Life at Oxford*, p. 174. Edward Freeman resigned for this reason.

19 See above.

20 PHL: BHT minute-book, Vol. 1, p. 5.

21 Meyrick, *Memories of Life at Oxford*, p. 175.

22 'Remarks by an experienced priest, are commended to the Brotherhood to the notice of its members.'

23 It appears that the Rule was not immediately adopted by the Brotherhood. We read in the minutes of the chapter meeting held on 1 March 1856 that the new optional Rule was formally adopted at that time, for it informs us that the amanuensis was instructed to send out a revised copy of the Rules to the absent brethren.

24 It is interesting to note that while these optional Rules were printed in the 1852 manual, the seven resolutions which formed a foundation of the society were not. However, the Rule was only formally adopted in 1856.

25 See Appendix.

26 PHL: BHT minute-book, Vol. 2, pp. 23–4.

27 PHL: SSC minute-book, Vol. 1, pp. 164, 172, 185ff.

28 Ibid., 14 September, p. 34.

29 Ibid., 13 October, pp. 38, 42.

30 Ibid., 3 May 1856 pp. 98ff.

31 Ibid., 3 May 1856 pp. 129–34.

32 White Rule, Food, no. 2; BHT, Rule 8.

33 White Rule, Society, 6; BHT, 7.

34 PHL: SSC, Vol. 1, 16 September, pp. 168–71.

35 Ibid., 11 November 1856, pp. 185–8.

36 Ibid., 5 May 1857.

37 Keble College, Oxford: from Liddon's own copy of the manual 1852. Signed 'H.P.L. June 22nd 1852'.

38 From the 1852 manual: Daily Devotions. Third Hour. For the peace and unity of the Church. Sixth Hour. For the conversion of Sinners and the awaking of the listless. Ninth Hour. For the advancement and the perseverance of the faithful.

39 The Intercession to be used daily: 'Remember O Lord, according to their several necessities, our brethren, whose names Thou knowest; and grant that we may each of us this day do which is well pleasing in Thy sight, think upon us, O Lord, for good, and spare us, according to the greatness of Thy mercy, through JESUS CHRIST our Lord. Amen'.

40 By 1858, these two suggestions had been replaced by three extra rules: To practise self examination daily. If the conscience be troubled, to open one's grief to a priest. To receive Holy Communion if possible, every week, and on the greater festivals.

4

Dr Pusey and the SSC

Robert Mackley

> It seems beginning at the wrong end for the ministers to deck
> their own persons: our plain dresses are more in keeping with
> the state of our church, which is one of humiliation: it does
> not seem in character to revive gorgeous or even in any
> degree handsome dresses in a day of reproach and rebuke and
> blasphemy: these are not holyday times ... the garment of
> mourning were fitter for us than one of gladness.[1]

So wrote Edward Bouverie Pusey, Doctor of Divinity, Canon
of Christ Church, Regius Professor of Hebrew and (after
Newman's conversion to Rome) the leader of the Oxford
Movement. He was writing to a friend concerning observance
of the Ornaments' Rubric of the Book of Common Prayer and
responding in particular to a report that a pious young man had
decided to deck his rooms in black velvet for Lent.

In that one paragraph can be seen both the reason for Pusey's
initial enthusiasm for the Society of the Holy Cross and the
reason for his eventual resignation from it. Pusey longed for
holiness; he had an exceptionally keen sense of sin and he
wanted the priests of the Church of England to eschew establishment luxury and indulgence and seek holy living as a matter
of urgency. The SSC with precisely this aim at its outset, could
not but commend itself to Pusey. Equally, however, as an
academic and as a spiritual contemplative, the revival of a

religion of the senses that the ritualist movement heralded would never be of great interest to him. The SSC shortly after its inception was to come to the forefront of ritualist and Catholic advance and Pusey was never an enthusiast for 'ultra-ritualism'.

On 17 January 1856 Pusey met with the initial membership of the SSC at the House of Charity in Soho to discuss the Society, its objects and its work; he wanted especially to know more about the promise of obedience, the promise of secrecy, the coloured badges and 'the expediency of act II of the Red Rule on confession'.[2] Already, however, on 10 January he had been conditionally elected should 'he express a wish to join the society'[3] and a dispensation granted to him to pass through both the lower and the higher orders on the same day, in the event of his admission. They were keen to have Pusey, who would give to them what Newman believed Pusey had given to the Tractarians – 'a position and a name'.[4] At the next meeting, when the venue changed from the House of Charity to Titchfield Street, the Secretary of the Society was instructed to write to Pusey informing him of the change, even though he was not yet a member: his importance was considerable and he was to be deferred to. Pusey, though, was keen to join; any organization whose aims were stated as being 'to promote a stricter rule of life amongst the clergy' was bound to win his approval.[5] So it was that on 26 April he gave notice that he wished to join, and on that same day was received into both the higher and lower orders. On 3 May Pusey was listed among the brethren for the first time and was received into the White Rule, a Rule which, significantly for later disputes, made no mention of compulsory or regularized sacramental confession. Any question as to the precise motivation of Pusey's joining would have been answered by the title of the talk he gave to the chapter on that third day of May: the 'aims and duties of the priestly life and the cultivation of personal holiness'.[6] That was Pusey precisely. At the same meeting he was elected a senior vicar of the Society and appointed to a committee of three to organize a retreat for brethren in July. The retreat was to be in

Oxford, at Pusey's house, and at the 5 June meeting Pusey was appointed to preside over the spiritual conferences at the retreat, covering the themes of mental prayer, conversion, confession, direction and the work of the Society itself. In the end, the Thursday, Friday and Saturday of the retreat were given over mostly to the subject of confession.[7]

At an early stage Pusey was already considerably involved, not only in the spiritual growth of the brethren but in the wider life of the Society: he was both a senior vicar and was called upon to arbitrate in a dispute between Charles Lowder and Bryan King (rector of St George in the East, London) concerning 'the standing of the [SSC] Missionary Body with reference to the Rector'.[8]

At the annual general meeting of 1857, Pusey was re-elected a senior vicar of the Society, but by the same time the following year, he had ceased to be a vicar and was not even present at the 1858 AGM.[9] Already there were signs of Pusey's enthusiasm waning as the Society became more committed to supporting King's ritualism at St George's and the explicit encouragement of sacramental confession. Nonetheless, this decline was far from rapid, and at the July retreat of 1858 held at Cuddesdon, Pusey's sermons were read at mealtimes, along with Thomas à Kempis, St Gregory on Job, St Augustine on St John and the Lord's Prayer. This was praise indeed.

The Society, however, was set on a collision course with more moderate and diplomatic Tractarians. At the meeting on 14 September 1858, it was reported that one of the brethren, Fr Poole, had been deprived for hearing confessions. Fr Lowder, the Society's Master, demanded that something be done to vindicate the doctrine of confession and absolution which had been impugned by the deprivation of Poole. It was further reported that another Brother had been forced to remove an altar cross from his church in Sydenham.[10] There is no indication that anything was done about either issue, but it was clear that the temperature of the brethren was high and Lowder and G.C. White (now Master) were in no mood for compromise. In October, White showed the draft of an address to

Convocation on the subject of confession to the chapter and in January, R.F. Littledale (now also a member) suggested that the Society address the question of a good manual for confessors: a suggestion with which the Master agreed. Significantly, Pusey was not present at any of these meetings.

On Rogation Monday 1859, Pusey was present at a meeting of the Oxford chapter. He suggested the establishment of an association to promote intercessory prayer on behalf of the unconverted. 'It would be an encouragement to individuals in prayer', said Pusey, 'to know that there is an association by which perpetual intercession on behalf of the unconverted and those in danger of falling into sin is carried on night and day so that at whatever hour anyone may be praying for this object he may be sure that at least one other is uniting with him in the prayer'.[11] It was agreed that this would be 'most advantageously formed' without reference to the Society or the Oxford brethren, although many of the associates would doubtless be drawn from brethren of the SSC. At the meeting on Holy Cross Day the terms of association were changed from a requirement for fifteen minutes of prayer for the unconverted each day to five minutes. This was at the suggestion of Fr Chamberlain and provoked 'considerable discussion'. There is no record of Pusey's views on the subject, but he was not known for ever supporting less prayer. Although there is no explicit mention of Pusey and his brethren disagreeing on this, the indication of 'considerable discussion' by the secretary suggests that the change was not achieved amicably. At the AGM on Holy Cross Day 1860, at which a relic of the true cross was exposed for veneration, another sign of growing extremism, it is Benson who is described as taking the lead in the association, producing a manual of prayers, organizing meetings of associates and receiving Chamberlain's suggestions of local wards of associates and the devising of a proper form of admission. Pusey is not mentioned once; nor indeed was he present at the meeting.[12]

In October 1861 a list of brethren was produced: it did not contain Pusey's name.[13] There is no explanation for this, for

Pusey was still a member; moreover, it seems unlikely that the secretary would forget someone so important as Dr Pusey. It is suggestive, therefore, of a loosening of ties between Pusey and the Society and of a cooling in the relationship between the two. Intriguingly, when Littledale suggested again that the Society produce a manual for confessors, and it was agreed that various people be written to for advice, Dr Pusey was referred to as 'Dr' and not 'Br', despite other brethren from whom advice would be sought (such as Benson) being called 'Br' by the secretary.[14] In May, Baird, the secretary, reported that he had received a response from Pusey, but the contents of his letter were not indicated.

The Catholic temperature of the Society continued to rise, and by June 1863 even its membership was starting to complain, Fr Gilbertson objecting to the 'extremism' of members' practices, especially in elevating the Host. Even the former Master, Fr White (Vicar of St Barnabas, Pimlico), was concerned, worrying that several secessions to Roman Catholicism among the brethren meant that it was even more important that members should 'know the exact ground upon which the Church of England stands'.[15] By August, Holy Communion was being called 'the Holy Eucharist' in the Society's minutes.[16]

At the half-yearly meeting in September 1863, 'Br Smith stated that Br Pusey had resigned'.[17] Pusey's membership of the Society had lasted only seven years. It had begun with considerable enthusiasm on both sides: Pusey hosting and leading retreats, giving talks, attending meetings and suggesting extra-societal activities such as the Association for Promoting Intercessionary Prayer; for their part the Society had fast-tracked him through the orders, appointing him a senior vicar and (as we have seen) reading his sermons in the company of those of Thomas à Kempis, St Gregory and St Augustine. Pusey's enthusiasm, however, had been for personal holiness and the increase of clerical discipline and devotion. As the Society became embroiled in controversy about ritual, and as the membership profile became younger, so its reputation for extremism grew. Young Turks had no time to wait for their forefathers such as Pusey, Carter, Bright and Liddon; they wanted a Church of England inwardly and outwardly Catholic. The Church should be obviously Catholic from first glance and not need it proved by debating the minutiae of the Ornaments' Rubric in the Book of Common Prayer.

This was not to be the end of Pusey's relationship with the Society, however. In 1873 the Society petitioned Convocation for provision of a Catholic liturgy that would remedy the 'incompleteness' of the Prayer Book. The bishops in Convocation ignored most of the petition except for the request for the 'licensing of duly qualified confessors'. The Society had only meant by this to refer to unbeneficed or unlicensed priests, but was misunderstood to mean that the bishops should arrange for confessors to be trained. There was uproar; Pusey described the petition as 'ill-advised' and sought to calm the situation while at the same time defending the right of priests to hear confessions: 'if something is good for the soul', he argued, 'it ought not to be put off to a possible death-bed'.[18] Together with 28 other clergy (none of them 'advanced ritualists', apart from Fr Mackonochie) Pusey published a declaration drawn from the Prayer Book, the canons and the homilies. A committee of the brethren of the SSC, which had been considering a response to the episcopal disapproval of their original petition, decided that Pusey's declaration was 'likely to do its own work, and that absolute silence is the best course to recommend to the SSC'.[19] This was a rare moment of SSC discretion.

When John Chambers, a member of the Society, published his manual for confessors, *The Priest in Absolution*, in 1870, little impact was made. The Society had requested the book but had not overseen its writing. Nonetheless, it had acquired the copyright upon Chambers' death in 1874 and was seen to be closely associated with the text. When in 1877 Lord Redesdale denounced it in the House of Lords, however, a new storm occurred. Pusey, although not directly concerned with the controversy which surrounded Redesdale's parliamentary speech, saw that in attacking a book whose conception he regarded as 'unwise' and whose language he thought insufficiently 'guarded', many would use the opportunity to impugn the practice of sacramental confession itself.[20] His response was to bring forward his edition of the Abbé Gaume's *Manual for Confessors*. He had worried about, and consequently delayed, work on his adaptation for years, for fear of its impact on people. However, as he wrote to Henry Parry Liddon in August 1877: 'If I had published Gaume in those former years, *The Priest in Absolution* never would have been compiled. Chambers asked me to put out Gaume, and it was only on my continual delay that he published.'[21] Pusey blamed himself in part for the row that had erupted around the heads of the brethren of his former Society, and it should be remembered that while the hotheadedness of the young priests now influencing the SSC in the late 1870s annoyed him, he still retained much sympathy with his Catholic colleagues. In his later years he did 'advance' his vesture, but like Keble he would have been perfectly happy to celebrate Holy Communion in tippet and hood until his dying day. His sympathy for those who wanted something more visually robust remained, however, for their 'loyal self-sacrifice in winning souls had endeared them to him'.[22] This warm letter to a former Master of the Society, Mackonochie, in 1874 demonstrates this: 'Your strength is and will be in the hearts of your people. These you have won wonderfully. Courts cannot really move you while you have them ... If the younger clergy will but win their people first as you have ... It was a grand Roman boast, "*Volentes per populos dat jura*".'[23] Certainly Pusey himself made and heard confessions, but as a member of the first generation of Anglo-Catholics, and as not only their leader but a wider religious leader in Oxford and in the Church of England generally, he did not and could not seek the advance of the practice, indeed of Catholic ritual generally, in the same way as did his brethren in the SSC. He felt that their disregard of the law, even the consequences of the Purchas judgment of 1871, which had not only the authority of the Privy Council but also of the archbishops and bishops, put them (and as a result the whole high church movement) in an impossible situation. How could he explain this to 'Englishmen [who] love what is legal'?[24] It was frustration at the actions of ritualist and SSC clergy which threatened the movement as a whole which caused him to write angrily to William Bright: 'I have a thorough distrust of the Ultra-Ritualist body. I committed myself some years ago to Ritualism, because it was unjustly persecuted, but I do fear that the Ritualists and the old Tractarians differ both in principle and object'.[25] Pusey's relationship with the SSC, therefore, was a varied one. He loved and supported enthusiastically their call for greater clerical holiness, but as the Society became more of a campaigning body for ritualism, and a campaigning body which lacked diplomacy and discretion, he had to part company with it. He remained a good friend of Mackonochie, however, and both Mackonochie and White (another former Master) signed Pusey's declaration on confession in 1873. He remained a leading light in the Church Union and a supporter of Catholic faith and discipline all his life. As the *Doctor Mysticus* of the Catholic movement, a man of deep prayer and penitence, Edward Bouverie Pusey could declare with all the brethren of the Society of the Holy Cross, '*In hoc Signo Vinces!*'

Notes

1 H.P. Liddon, *Life of Edward Bouverie Pusey*, 4 vols (Oxford: Longmans, Green & Co., 1893), Vol. 2, pp. 142–3.

2 PHL: SSC minute-book (1855–60), p. 138.

3 Ibid., p. 140.

4 William Oddie (ed.), *J.H. Newman, Apologia pro vita sua* (London: 1993), p. 132.

5 PHL: SSC minute-book (1855–60), p. 154.

6 Ibid., p. 158.

7 Ibid., p. 160.

8 Ibid., p. 163. The Society had established a mission house in the parish, with King's consent, but precisely who was in charge of the mission was not agreed.

9 Ibid., p. 216.

10 Ibid., p. 260.

11 Ibid., p. 308.
12 Ibid., p. 31.
13 Ibid., p. 35.
14 Ibid., p. 47.
15 Ibid., p. 107.
16 Ibid., p. 118.
17 Ibid., p. 129.
18 L.E. Ellsworth, *Charles Lowder and the Ritualist Movement* (London: Darton, Longman & Todd, 1982), p. 120.
19 Quoted in Ellsworth, *Charles Lowder*, p. 121.
20 Liddon, *Pusey*, Vol. 4, p. 304.
21 Ibid., p. 306.
22 Ibid., p. 272.
23 Ibid., p. 277.
24 Ibid., p. 272.
25 Ibid., p. 271.

5

The First Decade: 1855–65

Kenneth Macnab

One might be forgiven for assuming that the story of a small group of friends who could meet around one table with a singularity of purpose over a relatively short period of time would not be too complicated, particularly when the manuscript sources are hardly vast. Two manuscript minute-books cover the ten years which separate the initial meeting of six priests in February 1855 and the May synod of 1865. A further manuscript-book lists the members of the Society with their dates of proposal, election and admission to the two orders, together with their proposers, seconders and addresses. Such an assumption, however, flatters to deceive when applied to the first ten years of the Society's history. None of the three volumes reveal their secrets as easily as one might imagine. In places the minute-taking is clearly less than accurate, to judge from internal evidence. From 1861 various meetings go unrecorded, witnessed by blank pages in the second minute-book. The list of members appears to have been compiled retrospectively in 1865,[1] initially by the then secretary, Edgar Hoskins, and close examination shows that Hoskins faced the same confusions, contradictions and lacunae in 1865 as modern readers of the minute-books do 140 years later. Perhaps it is significant that Embry passed over this period relatively quickly in his history of 1931.[2]

Yet these difficulties should not surprise us. The infant SSC was an organization with fairly loose initial aims. Its priorities shifted as the need arose and as it had to react to external events and pressures. For a year or so one particular item, such as mission work, dominated the Society's thinking only to be replaced relatively quickly by another all-consuming interest such as retreat provision. During these years the Society was evolving quickly and, to an extent, was thinking on its feet. One clear example of this is the need for constant revision of the statutes and the Rules of Life. They were an organic creation, in need of refinement as the brethren lived them rather than treated them as a sacrosanct pattern set in stone. It is only with the passing of time, the growth of numbers and organization and the election of Fr Mackonochie, a Master with a clear administrative ability, vision and the support of very capable officers, that the SSC settled down into the pattern of life which it has known ever since.[3]

However, this is not to imply that the first decade of the SSC's history is entirely chaotic. Various themes recur. One is the development of various Rules of Life.[4] Another is the numerical expansion of the Society. A third is the provision and publication of devotional, liturgical and catechetical material. Another is the importance of retreats and the recovery of an ascetical tradition, and a final theme is the essential part that missions played in the Society's work and self-understanding.

There is something of an irony that the May 1855 meeting[5] of the Society describes itself as 'The Great Annual Meeting' when it had an attendance of four.[6] Of the initial six members of the Society who made their promise on 28 February, C.M. Davies never came to another meeting. Alfred Poole sent his apologies in May. J.S. Boucher had been admitted as the seventh member of the Society on 31 March but, like Poole, had to send his apologies.[7] Recruitment was crucial. Almost every meeting records invitations issued to likeminded priests who might be interested in being proposed. Permission was asked of the other brethren to mention the Society to friends. If they responded positively they were proposed, elected to the Society and subsequently admitted first to the Lower Order and then to the Higher.[8] Relatively few people who were approached seem to have turned down the invitation, although the minutes are singularly discreet about recording anything which might be construed as rejection.[9]

Although the list of members does not contain all those elected and admitted before 1865 it is possible to reconstruct such a list for the years 1855 to 1861 from the minute-books (see Appendix, p. 72–4). During these six years 51 brethren were admitted to the Society, of whom nine left for one reason or another. This lapse rate of nearly 20 per cent is surprisingly high. Hence 42 admitted members are found on the printed roll for October 1861 (the first such roll to have survived) together with the names of nine brethren who were elected but not yet admitted. The puzzling 52nd entry is the name of J.M. Neale.[10] A further 30 priests had also been elected to the Society during these years but were not yet admitted,[11] making a total of 81 names in the reconstructed register. In addition, 25 priests had been contacted with a view to joining the Society but had not allowed their names to go forward. Lowder served as Master for the first three years (elected in 1855, 1856 and 1857) followed by George Cosby White (1858–61) and J.C. Chambers (elected for one term in 1862) before A.H. Mackonochie was elected for the first time in 1863.

It is also possible to reconstruct a register of attendance at synods and chapter meetings. What is clear is that the Society relied on a small number of priests, mostly in central London, for its day-to-day and month-to-month business. Some members, such as Lowder, Newton Smith, Nicols and Cosby White seldom missed a meeting. Others, particularly those who were later known as 'country members', rarely appeared between one synod and the next. These figures show the importance of a batch of admissions in 1859. In R.F. Littledale, J.A. Foote and A.H. Mackonochie the Society admitted three young priests (Littledale was 26, Foote 29 and Mackonochie 34) who were not only highly talented in different ways but were committed to the round of chapters and committees. Within a short time they were indispensable to the Society, not least by turning up to almost every meeting, volunteering for all sorts of tasks and proving voluble contributors to debates. Over the next three decades the Society put Littledale's considerable learning to good use.[12]

The question of recruitment highlighted two problems for the Society. One was the notion of 'secrecy' which, as Embry comments, was an unhappy word. If a Society is a secret one, how does it advertise its existence when it is specifically looking to recruit others? To meet this objection, brethren frequently requested and occasionally received a 'Digest of the aims and work of the Society'.[13] However, such openness occasionally had to be balanced by a plea for confidentiality. The May synod in 1858, for example, reminded brethren, 'That no member be allowed to divulge the proceedings of the chapter, except so far as the publication is authorised by the Society, or to mention the names of the brethren except for the purpose of inducing men to join the Society, and that every such communication be regarded as strictly confidential.'[14]

The other problem was the increasingly nation-wide location of the membership. Priests in rural parishes or in the industrial Midlands and North could not be expected to travel to London every month. Bryan King investigated the possibility of setting up a branch of the Society in Cambridge in 1858,[15] but it was Oxford which established the first provincial branch of the Society the following spring, with R.M. Benson as its provincial vicar[16] and Dr Pusey the most prominent member, at least at its first meeting. As the membership grew, Mackonochie was convinced that further branches would be required. At the September synod of 1864 he envisaged similar branches being established in Manchester and Liverpool 'before long'[17] and planned a trip as Master later that autumn. These two new branches were formally sanctioned in December, had Rules drafted for them in January, and were included as separate entities on the printed paper for the 1865 May synod, the first to be spread over two days.[18]

If the Society was, from the first, a confidential one, it also had a clear impetus to look beyond its own boundaries. From the earliest years publications were an essential part of its vision. The May synod of 1856 appointed a committee to take on the task of providing a *Manual for the Poor* to be published in twelve parts at a penny a part.[19] The Bishop of Brechin was happy for SSC to use some of his work as the framework and provided considerable encouragement, but the scheme ran out of steam. As Lowder commented in his Master's Address in May 1857, the mission work at St George's-in-the-East had engrossed the Society's whole attention.[20] Small booklets were produced for the clergy, including the Society's liturgical books in Latin. The need for tracts on moral theology and the hearing of confessions was an early preoccupation. In later years this would lead to J.C. Chambers' *The Priest in Absolution* and the crisis of the 1870s.[21] In the 1860s the Society's tract committee was into its stride and produced a large number of publications from the presses of G.J. Palmer. Publications, and their finances, increasingly dominated the Society's business meetings. Larger books such as Lowder's *Five Years at St George's Mission* were supplemented by smaller pamphlets on liturgical and devotional themes. A news-cutting of an advertisement from the *Church Times* of 16 July 1864, pasted into the SSC minute-book, demonstrates the range. There are tracts at a halfpenny each for Advent, Christmas, Lent, Passiontide, Easter, Ascension Day and Whitsuntide; penny pamphlets on Self-Examination, the Four Last Things, Devotions for Non-Communicating Attendance at the Eucharist, Catechism on the Holy Communion and Eucharistic Hymns; two pence could buy *Plain Words about Self-Examination* or *Meditations on the Passion*; *Pardon through the Precious Blood* cost four pence and *The Altar Manual* was available in a variety of bindings costing up to 1s 6d per copy.[22] A book-hawker had been engaged in August 1862, but he proved a shortlived luxury. Within twelve months both the salesman and Palmer the printer were owed money by an embarrassed Society.

These publications were largely aimed at catechetical work in mission districts. When A.R. Venables set sail for the diocese of Nassau in February 1864, with the SSC's farewell service for him ringing in his ears, he went with nearly 2,000 SSC tracts in his luggage. By this date SSC brethren were active in missions in the modern sense of the word: preaching and teaching weeks with preparation and follow-up. Very often these took place in Advent or Lent, and Mackonochie made several pleas for brethren to coordinate their efforts.[23] However, in the first five years of the Society's history the word 'mission' had a rather different connotation and involved it in the difficult and confusing world of the evangelization of the East End of London.

The first year or so of SSC's history is relatively silent on 'mission'. However in February 1856 Bryan King, the rector of St George's-in-the-East and a brother-elect of the Society asked for help in mission work in his poor, populous and dilapidated parish. At once SSC came to his aid and arranged for Fr White to preach on three evenings a week and set about looking for another brother to conduct mission services. The initial impression, set down in March 1856, makes for emotional reading a century and a half later. 'In this most destitute place much opposition was made, the mob resorting to the throwing of missiles and mud at the clergy, in addition to blasphemy and violent language'.[24] The minute-book records that rather than backing down the SSC decided that 'To do any lasting good, there must be a resident Priest on the spot' and 'It was agreed that a Mission House and Room for Prayer should be taken by the Society'.[25] This was the start of the Society's involvement with Wapping and what became Lowder's life's work at St Peter's, London Docks. The infant Society threw all its energies into the East End. Wellclose Square and Calvert Street had mission houses and chapels bought or built, sometimes with liturgical blessings performed with some style by the assembled brethren.[26] A refuge was established with members of a Sisterhood looking after the women. Schools were planned and teachers engaged. There were to be protests and riots concerning the supposedly advanced ritual and an equally firm reply from SSC that colour and liturgy had its place as an evangelistic tool and witness to theological truth.

The story of the St George's Mission is a complicated one.[27]

It is tempting to ask what a young society such as SSC was doing involving itself to quite such a dramatic extent. St George's Mission dominated the Society's thinking for most of 1857 and 1858, even to the extent of passing the accounts through the Society's minutes, the sum of £961 3s0d, and running up a bill of £21 0s 4d on legal opinions. There also appears to have been confusion generated by the overlapping responsibilities of the SSC, Bryan King as rector of the parish, the Bishop of London and the diocese's own missionary body. From 1860 or so the greatest fuss had died down and the mission continued as an agenda item for SSC more on the grounds of report than formulating new policy. When an outbreak of rioting disturbed King's parish once again in March 1860, the SSC's resolution to 'express its sympathy with Br. King, and to offer its co-operation in any feasible way'[28] reveals that the relationship between the parish and the Society had changed subtly. However, Lowder and several other members of the Society had moved to Wapping and its surrounding neighbourhood where they were to do famous work for many years and where SSC was to find a spiritual, if unofficial, home at St Peter's.

One thing which this episode and others like it revealed to Mackonochie was that many SSC priests were in an anomalous position regarding the parish system. He preferred the idea of a missionary order. To this end Mackonochie stressed the need for good theological formation of ordinands and he was keen on an idea, which had Benson and Chamberlain's support, of a college in Oxford for poor students bound for ordination.[29] The foundation of Keble College, half a generation later, stemmed from a similar concern.

Allied to this concern was the development of retreats for clergy. Lowder first proposed a Society retreat in January 1856[30] and F.H. Murray of Chislehurst organized and hosted one the following month. Following a silent retreat which addressed mental prayer, spiritual reading, theological study and confession, it was agreed to hold a similar retreat every July. The next two retreats were held in Oxford: at Dr Pusey's house in July

1856 and Canon Chamberlain's vicarage at St Thomas's in 1857, when St John Chrysostom's *De Sacerdotis* provided strong meat for meditation. The following year Fr Benson arranged to use the new theological college at Cuddesdon during a vacation. Bishop Wilberforce sent his friendly greetings to the twelve retreatants, of whom only eight were members of the Society. In 1859 the Society returned to Chislehurst, having been let down at Harlow, and in 1860 there were two retreats: the first at Chislehurst and the second at Cuddesdon, which the Bishop (remarkably) and the Warden of All Souls attended alongside more obvious high church retreatants.[31] The Bishop and the Dean of Westminster returned for the 1861 retreat, led by Carter of Clewer. These were certainly not events restricted to the ranks of SSC, but they were firmly organized by the Society and some of its senior members. During the 1860s retreats were held further afield: at St Aidan's Birkenhead and St Augustine's, Canterbury, and from 1862 monthly day-retreats were held in London, usually at one of the great Anglo-Catholic churches such as St Alban's, Holborn, or All Saints, Margaret Street. Increasingly this met a need, and Mackonochie pleaded for priests who felt they had the expertise and gifts to lead such days. By 1864 very nearly every SSC chapter meeting had an agenda item which referred to retreats which had taken place or were about to do so.

If the Society's work popularizing retreats was adopted in part by the Anglican Establishment, the SSC retained during these years a cutting edge which could be fiercely anti-Establishment when it came to defending the Catholic faith. From time to time bishops and courts moved against individual members, and the Society rallied to their aid. The first of these was the case of Alfred Poole of St Barnabas, Pimlico. Poole's licence was suspended in 1858, principally for the offence of having heard a woman's confession. The Archbishop of Canterbury sided with the Bishop of London and refused to give Poole a hearing – a right which the secular courts upheld. At root was not only the place of sacramental confession but the security of the incumbent and his relationship with his bishop.

In the end John Keble came to Poole's rescue and offered him a post in his country parish at Hursley, but not before SSC had printed thousands of pamphlets and subscribed to the 'Poole Defence Fund'.[32] Evening Communion was another target of SSC's ire involving, as was inevitable, the rejection of the eucharistic fast. On this occasion SSC developed a more subtle approach, invoking the help of senior clergy in the diocese of London to criticize the growing practice. Another *cause célèbre* was the publication of *Essays and Reviews*.[33] 'Br Benson spoke of a volume of *Essays and Reviews* of an infidel tendency lately put forth by six priests of the Church of England and desired that some means might be adopted for its contradiction', recorded the minutes of September 1860.[34] In February 1864 the book was still causing members of SSC much excitement and outrage.[35]

In the ten years of its 'manuscript period' the Society had grown many times over. The six brethren of 1855, of whom only three had remained longer than two years, had grown to 105 by the synod of May 1866. The Society had developed and refined its Rules of Life to sanctify and form the lives and ministries of many priests. They had taken the Gospel out with missionary fervour. It had built a professional organization and was establishing itself across the country. It had stood up to the bullying tactics of bishops and Protestant opposition. In Mackonochie, a dynamic young Master, things seemed set fair for years of sustained growth and influence. Embry's verdict is hard to resist. '[Mackonochie] was not one of the Founders, but he so truly interpreted their design and ideals, to which was added his own wisdom, fervour, fearlessness and sanctity, that he became the real Master Builder of SSC.'[36]

APPENDIX 1 ADMISSIONS TO THE SOCIETY 1855–61 AND ATTENDANCE AT SYNOD AND CHAPTER

	Date admitted	Oct 1861 roll number (52)	May 1865 roll number (82)	May synod 1855	Meetings 1855–56 (13)	May synod 1856	Meetings 1856–57 (12)	May synod 1857	Meetings 1857–58 (12)	May synod 1858	Meetings 1858–59 (10)	May synod 1859	Meetings 1859–60 (10)	May synod 1860	Meetings 1860–61 (11)	May synod 1861
1 Lowder, C.F.	28.2.55	1	1	√M	11	√M	9	√M	10	√	9	√	6	√	3	√
2 Poole, A.	28.2.55	2	2	A	6	√	5	√	5	√	1		1			
3 Davies, C.M.	28.2.55				9											
4 Rawes, H.A.	28.2.55			√				A								
5 Smith, J. Newton	28.2.55	3	3	√	12	√	8									
6 Nicols, D.	28.2.55		4	√	11	√	10	√	4							
7 Boucher, J.S.	6.4.55	4	5	A												
8 Lyall, W.H.	14.9.55	5	6		6	√	10	√	8	√	9	√	6	√	7	√
9 Goulden, C.J.	13.10.55	6	7		1	√	1	√	1	√	1	√	1	√	2	√
10 Murray, F.H.	13.10.55	7	8		6	√	4		8	√	2	√M	3	√M	9	√M
11 White, G. Cosby	13.10.55	8	9		8	√	7	√	9	√M	8	√	7			
12 Caffin, C.S.	17.01.56	9	10		1	√	1	√		√	1	√	1			
13 Mossman, T.W.	4.4.56	10			1			√								
14 Pusey, E.B.	26.4.56				3	√		A								
15 King, B.	3.5.56	11	11				5	√	2	√	2	√	1			

No.	Name	Date													
16	Brownlow, W.R.	2.7.56	12	12	2		1		1						
17	Collins, R.	2.7.56	13	13	2	✓									
18	Chamberlain, T.	7.7.56	14	14	1	✓	1								
19	Huntingford, G.W.	7.7.56	15	15		✓	2	✓		✓		✓		✓	
20	Marshall, J.W.	7.7.56			8	✓	4								
21	Harrison, C.	14.9.56	16	16	1	✓	2	✓	1	✓	1	✓	1		
22	Benson, R.M.	11.11.56	17	17	2	✓	3	✓	3		3	✓	2	✓	
23	Neville, W.F.	10.2.57	18	19	1	✓				✓				✓	
24	Eagleton, J.	10.2.57	19	17	4		4	✓	3	✓	1	✓			
25	Binney, J.E.	10.2.57	30	18	1				3		2	✓		✓	
26	Lyford, C.	2.4.57	20	20	1										
27	Lee, F.G.	2.4.57	21		1	✓	3	✓				✓			
28	Davies, E.H.	5.5.57	21	21		✓	1					✓			
29	Martin, H.	5.5.57	31			✓	2								
30	De Burgh, H.	5.5.57				✓	5								
31	Oxenham, H.N.	5.5.57				✓	3								
32	Chambers, J.C.	10.11.57?	24	22	2		3	✓	5	✓	2	✓	2	✓	
33	Littledale, R.F.	4.5.58	25	25				✓	9	✓	9	✓	8	✓	
34	Fish, J.L.	4.5.58	22	23			1	✓							
35	Cleaver, E.D.	4.5.58	23	24				✓	1	✓	2				
36	Gilbertson, L.	14.9.58	32	28					1	✓					
37	Venables, R.A.	14.9.58	29	26					1		1	✓			
38	Edwards, J.	14.9.58	26	27					5	✓	3	✓	1	✓	

		Date admitted	Oct 1861 roll number (52)	May 1865 roll number (82)	May synod 1855	Meetings 1855-56 (13)	May synod 1856	Meetings 1856-57 (12)	May synod 1857	Meetings 1857-58 (12)	May synod 1858	Meetings 1858-59 (10)	May synod 1859	Meetings 1859-60 (10)	May synod 1860	Meetings 1860-61 (11)	May synod 1861
39	Foote, J.A.	8.2.59	27	29								2	✓	8	✓	9	✓
40	Bradley, R.H.A.	8.2.59	33	30								1	✓	3	✓		
41	Mackonochie, A.H.	8.3.59	28	31								2	✓	8	✓	9	✓
42	Cooper, J.H.	3.5.59	34	67									✓	1			
43	Wornwall, S.P.	3.5.59											✓				
44	Liberty, N.	9.8.59	35	33										2	✓		✓
45	Carter, T.T.	14.9.59	36	34										1		1	
46	Lamphier, W.H.	13.12.59	37	35										1	✓	1	✓
47	Baird, J.W.	13.12.59	38	36										3	✓	8	✓
48	Winter, R.R.	13.12.59	39	37										1			
49	Poole, H.J.	14.2.60	40	38										2	✓	8	✓
50	Lyne, J.L.	14.9.60	42	68												1	
51	Reece, W.S.	11.12.60	41	39												1	

Key: ✓ indicates attendance at synod
✓ M indicates election as Master at synod

74

Notes

1 See this volume p. 112, n.5.

2 J. Embry, *The Catholic Movement and the Society of the Holy Cross* (London: Faith Press, 1931), Chapter 1.

3 One small example of this is the fact that Mackonochie introduced printed agendas in his first year as Master (1863). There is a perceptible change in the 'professionalism' of the SSC at this time.

4 See Chapters 3 and 4 of this volume.

5 The words 'meeting', 'chapter' and 'synod' were not used with their present precision until the 1860s. In this chapter we generally use the slightly later convention of talking of the May and September meetings as 'synods' and the monthly meetings between the synods as 'chapter meetings'.

6 PHL: SSC papers, Ch 71/A1, p. 21.

7 Boucher soon moved from St Paul's Grammar School in Knightsbridge to Birkenhead and then to the Training College in Carnarvon. Boucher's name remained in a senior position on the roll for many years without obviously attending a meeting of any kind.

8 As the distinction between a Lower and Higher Order developed in the late 1850s, the first members were deemed to have been elected and admitted to both at the same time.

9 For example, Fr Gutch and Fr Beckett both replied that they had too many commitments to join another society. The recording of the fact that H.A. Rawes became a Roman Catholic in 1856 was the exception rather than the rule. Of the initial six members, Embry claimed that Hawes, Nicols and Davies all became Roman Catholics. However, Davies and Nicols are both included in the 1865 edition of *Crockford's* though without current Anglican appointments. Nicols, in particular, attended SSC meetings as regularly as anyone and was elected secretary in May 1857, before he suddenly disappears from the minutes later that year. The resignation from the Society of its most prominent member, Dr Pusey, went unmentioned for a couple of years and that of Henry Nutcombe Oxenham was ignored completely.

10 This is a puzzle. Neale's name appears nowhere in the minutes

and a pencil note next to his name, presumably in the hand of the secretary, says 'Can't find, ask Bown'.

11 PHL: SSC papers, Ch 71/A2, p. 192. In September 1864 many of the Brethren-elect who fell into this category were erased from the roll if they had been elected before May 1861 but not subsequently admitted.

12 For Littledale see new *Oxford Dictionary of National Biography* (Oxford: Oxford University Press, 2004). Littledale is best remembered now as the translator of the hymn 'Come down, O Love divine', but he was a scholar of considerable achievement and a man of prodigious energies. Despite his book *Plain Reasons against Joining the Church of Rome* (London: SPCK, 1880), the sisters of St Katherine's Convent, Queen Square, where he was chaplain before his death in 1890, did precisely that in 1908.

13 PHL: SSC papers, Ch 71/A1, pp. 181ff. The first request for this came as early as the meeting of October 1856. It is not clear whether anything came of this request.

14 Ibid., pp. 257f.

15 Ibid., p. 285.

16 Ibid., p. 301.

17 Ibid., A2, p. 192.

18 Ibid., p. 239.

19 Ibid., A1, p. 30.

20 Ibid., p. 218.

21 Throughout 1859 it was proposed to hold monthly lectures on moral theology and the skills required in hearing confessions using St Barnabas' College and Archbishop Tenison's Library as venues. These appear to have been poorly attended and shortlived. The idea surfaced again under Mackonochie's mastership when practice in hearing confessions was built into local chapter meetings.

22 PHL: SSC papers, Ch 71/A2, p. 182.

23 See, for example, ibid., p. 103.

24 Ibid., A1, pp. 91f.

25 Ibid.

26 Ibid., pp. 215ff.

27 See particularly L.E. Ellsworth, *Charles Lowder and the Ritualist Movement* (London: Darton, Longman & Todd, 1982), pp. 21ff.

28 PHL: SSC papers, Ch 71/A1, p. 320.
29 See, for example, ibid., A2, pp. 63ff.
30 Ibid., A1, p. 79.
31 Ibid., A2, pp. 257ff.
32 Ibid., A1, p. 299.
33 *Essays and Reviews* was edited by Benjamin Jowett. It was essentially a broad church work which attempted to reconcile Christian doctrine with the recent scientific theory on evolution and also with biblical criticism. It attracted a great deal of opposition from traditionalists and two contributors were unsuccessfully prosecuted.
34 Ibid., A2, p. 2.
35 Ibid., p. 170.
36 Embry, *The Catholic Movement and the Society of the Holy Cross.*

6

Mackonochie and the controversies over confession and ritual

Kenneth Macnab

If the giant figure of the first ten years of the Society's history was Charles Lowder, the towering presence of the next 20 years was Alexander Heriot Mackonochie of St Alban's, Holborn. In 1880, after a gap of four years, Mackonochie found himself once again addressing the brethren of SSC as their Master. Thinking back to his last Master's Address, he commented:

> The future which then [1876] seemed to be opening before the Society was not, in God's Providence, to be realized. He willed us to sustain a shock which should threaten even our existence as a Society; and yet the same Goodness and Wisdom which then threatened to overwhelm us, had continued our life, in order, as it would seem, that the victory might be won by the few and the weak, trusting more in the supernatural force with which He fills us.[1]

The history of SSC in the years following 1865 falls into two distinct phases. There were twelve years of rapid growth, during which the Society successfully implemented a deliberate policy of recruitment and expansion of its activities. For a supposedly 'secret society' it worked surprisingly hard at maintaining a high profile. However, even as the SSC seemed to be flourishing in a way the founders could hardly have imagined, the shadows were lengthening. From 1870 the clouds grew darker until fierce storms broke over the Society between 1874 and 1877. When they subsided, the Society had not disappeared, as had seemed likely to some of the brethren and as had been hoped by some of the bishops. However, even with Mackonochie back at the helm, the Society had lost almost half of its brethren and, arguably, much of its influence. The years from 1880 to the First World War were, more often than not, quiet ones.

Embry commented on the appropriateness of Mackonochie's tribute on the death of John Keble being one of the first pieces of printed material the Society produced.[2] The Master's Address of May 1866 was distributed from the presses of W. Knott of Holborn, a name to be synonymous with Anglo-Catholic printing for the next century. Although recent research has warned against driving too great a wedge between the Oxford men of the period 1833–45 and a later 'ritualist' generation,[3] the men of the 1860s and 1870s still seem to belong to another era from that of the Professor of Poetry and Fellow of Oriel who had spent long years as a country parson. The protagonists of the next phase of the Catholic Revival's history are men who were photographed in cassocks rather than painted by Richmond in breeches: the granite-like, single-minded Mackonochie; the gentler and much-loved Lowder, more ready to see both sides of a problem; E.G. Wood, the Cambridge canon lawyer and the hot-headed young men like Orby Shipley who were the *enfants terribles* of early Anglican papalism.

Mackonochie was elected Master in 1863 and was to be re-elected to the position every year until an amendment of the statutes precluded his re-election in May 1876. In these thirteen years the membership of the Society rose from 54 to 377.[4] What sort of society did Fr Mackonochie preside over? What sort of men were his brethren and where did their ministry take them?

Nigel Yates made extensive use of the SSC's list of members, compiled by various hands between 1865 and 1884.[5] Tracing 462 of the names of those who joined the Society during these four decades and who were ordained between 1841 and 1874, Yates reached some striking conclusions. Members of the Society tended to be offered livings sooner than the average Anglican priest. Nearly 60 per cent of them were appointed to livings held by private patrons and only 15 per cent to livings to which bishops appointed. Some 75 per cent of the membership of the Society had attended Oxford or Cambridge colleges compared with 67.5 per cent of the clergy generally. Only 29 had attended one of the new theological colleges. A surprisingly high 10 per cent were appointed to canons' stalls. Yates concludes: 'Emerging from this clutch of statistics one is left with a clear impression that the ranks of the ritualist clergy were drawn predominantly from those of a good family, well educated and owing their preferment to clerical and landed interests with which they frequently had close personal connections'.[6]

Similar analysis of the 1866 roll yields further conclusions. Three years into Mackonochie's tenure of the mastership the roll listed 105 brethren. The Society had almost doubled its membership in three years. It is tempting to suppose that the majority conformed to the Anglo-Catholic priest of folklore: young, not long down from Oxford, celibate, working in a slum parish, probably in London. A careful analysis of the roll, however, tells a different story. The third edition of *Crockford's Clerical Directory* had been published the previous year and, though it lacks some of the accuracy of later editions, it is possible to trace 83 out of 105 members of SSC in its pages. Later editions of *Crockford's* increase the number whose careers can be found to 91.

Although Victorian editions of *Crockford's* do not include the year of birth in an entry, as recent editions have done, it is possible to make an educated guess at the ages of SSC priests from the date of their first degree and subsequent ordination to the diaconate. Many, perhaps most, would have been ordained at the canonical minimum age of 23. Very often this ties in with having taken their first degree at what one might suppose to be the age of 21 or 22.[7] In 1866, 21 per cent of brethren (where details are known) were in their twenties, 46 per cent in their thirties, 25 per cent in their forties and only 8 per cent in their fifties. The oldest member of the Society, Thomas Chamberlain of St Thomas the Martyr, Oxford, was 56. Some 40 per cent of the Society were under the age of 35 and 82 per cent under the age of 45. Lowder turned 46 in June 1866 and Mackonochie was 41 in August, having been elected Master at the age of 37. Hence the Society of 1866 was principally, but by no means exclusively, a society of relatively young men. The only Tractarian 'grand old men' in the roll were Chamberlain, Carter of Clewer and Prynne of St Peter's, Plymouth. Priests whose names were to become famous in later years, such as Benson of Cowley, were still in their thirties and early forties. One name was to become mildly notorious: Br Lyne (better known as Fr Ignatius of Llanthony). The earlier curious anomaly whereby men such as Pusey and Liddon had been elected without applying, however much they supported the general trend of the Society, had already been ironed out.[8]

Of the 91 members of the Society in 1866 who can be traced, 80 were engaged in parish ministry, five worked in universities and schools and a further five were chaplains. Two of these were in the forces and the other three worked in a hospital, a convent and as a domestic chaplain. Lyne was living the Benedictine life in Norfolk.[9] Of the parish clergy, 30 were in London and sixteen in provincial cities. The roll drew attention to four of the recently formed local branches: Liverpool, Manchester, Plymouth and one for Leeds and Wakefield. Given the prevailing 'Lancashire Low' churchmanship and the fiercely Protestant tradition of the diocese of Liverpool, it is perhaps surprising to find that eleven of the brethren lived and worked in industrial Lancashire. Seventeen members of the Society worked in suburbs or country towns and fourteen, nearly a sixth of those of those whose details are known, held rural livings. Certainly famous Anglo-Catholic parishes were well-represented on the roll: St Barnabas, Pimlico; St Peter's, London Docks (as it became); St Alban's, Holborn. These were balanced, however, by parishes, rural and urban, which were far from purpose-built Anglo-Catholic shrines.

Similarly, the roll shows a breadth of background, education and priestly formation. References to the new theological colleges are sketchy in the early editions of *Crockford's*. Only one priest on the roll of 1866 is credited with having attended Cuddesdon, although it is clear from other evidence that he was not alone.[10] Educational details are known for a further 69 brethren. Thirty-seven were members of Oxford University, of whom seven came from Christ Church (Pusey and Liddon's college) and six, including Lowder, from Exeter College. Cambridge supplied 22 priests, five of whom had been undergraduates at Trinity College. Six priests had been to King's College, London, and five attended the staunchly Protestant Trinity College, Dublin.[11] It is impossible to say what proportion of the Society was married and what proportion lived a celibate vocation. Mackonochie, who believed the celibate calling to be a 'higher life'[12] knew that several of the brethren had taken vows of celibacy in one form or another even if the number who did so formally through the Society remained very small. The question of celibacy became more of an issue in the twentieth century. Certainly, the Society elected J.C. Chambers, a married priest, as its Master in 1862 and in later years discussed setting up a sustentation fund to support the wives and children of priests who might be ejected from their livings in ritual prosecutions.[13] This would not seem to be the action of a Society which tolerated married clergy on sufferance.

By the time the Society next printed the roll five years later the Society had once again more than doubled in size. However, despite this rapid growth, its expansion had been consistent. The 1871 roll contained 262 names plus the additional names of nine ordinands. Of these, the ministries of 204 have been traced. The general composition of the Society had not changed. Some 21 per cent of those whose details are known were in their twenties, 39 per cent in their thirties, 28 per cent in their forties, 9 per cent in their fifties and 2 per cent in their sixties. Roughly 42 per cent of the Society was under 35 years of age and 77 per cent under 45. If anything, the membership of the Society was getting slightly older. A few older men had joined SSC in the intervening five years, of whom W.J.E. Bennett of Frome was the most prominent.[14]

Neither had the geographical spread of the brethren changed between 1866 and 1871. Some 28 per cent lived and worked in London and 10 per cent in industrial Lancashire and Yorkshire. For the first time, the 1871 roll gave details of the province to which each brother belonged: 7 per cent were to be found in Scotland (the northern province), 14 per cent in the eastern province, 18 per cent in the western province (which included Wales); and 59 per cent in the southern province. This last province, however, was enormous, stretching from the diocese of Canterbury to the diocese of Exeter (before the creation of Truro) and from the English Channel to the northern border of the diocese of Oxford.[15] There were ten local branches: three in Scotland; one in Wales; three in the north of England; Plymouth, Brighton and Oxford in the south. There were 6 per cent of the brethren living in the city and university of Oxford, but this included several Cowley fathers who were soon to leave SSC when Fr Benson came to the opinion that living under two Rules was unsustainable.[16] An analysis of the parishes where the brethren worked indicates a similar range with many more country brethren than we might have assumed. Once again, the names of some parishes, whether urban (such as St Augustine's, Kilburn) or rural (Bovey Tracey, for example), are found time and time again. Some incumbents seem to have had a policy of making sure that their curates joined SSC or, perhaps, of offering titles to ordinands who would be keen to join.

So it is clear that SSC was, from its first decade, a broader organization than the caricature picture of 'London, Brighton and South Coast' Anglo-Catholicism lampooned in a later generation. It was predominantly a young man's society, but not exclusively so. Many of its members worked in slum parishes, but many did not. It recruited its membership from the four corners of the British Isles and had a handful of members abroad. By 1871 three of these, to the Society's intense pride, were colonial bishops: Venables of Nassau, Jenner of Dunedin and Staley of Honolulu. To the common charge that SSC was a 'secret society' the easiest answer was to say that it was particularly successful at recruiting new members and making its work better known. A simple graph shows the dramatic expansion of the Society. It shows too the equally dramatic numerical effect of the events of 1877–8.[17]

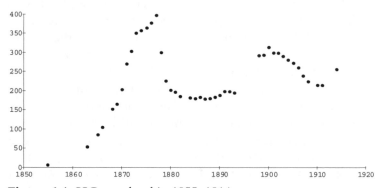

Figure 6.1 SSC membership 1855–1914

How was this growth achieved? In part it must have had much to do with the individual examples of its existing members. In part there must have been an element of success breeding success. In part it presented a vision of priesthood and sanctification of the clergy which was radically different from that which was current at the time. It is perhaps no coincidence that SSC flourished at the same time as new theological colleges were beginning to prepare men for ordination in a more 'professional' way than the older model of 'reading for holy orders' under a tutor. Following one of the SSC Rules of Life gave a structure and a sanctification to priestly ministry which Anglicans had seldom met before. Perhaps there was an element of Victorian 'clubability' forged in public schools and universities which appealed to some. Perhaps men in poor, demanding or unresponsive parishes, then as now, valued the company of likeminded priests, particularly if marooned in unsympathetic dioceses and deaneries. Perhaps the SSC appealed to the same instincts which led other men to join

Freemasonry.[18] These are all conjecture.[19] What is certain is that expansion was a deliberate policy of the Master and his council.

Near the end of his Master's Address for May 1866, Mackonochie described himself as being dissatisfied with membership merely passing a hundred.

> I conceive that the work of the Society is by no means commensurate with the work which God has been pleased to effect by it, and that, conversely, the blessing which we obtain is stinted by our own want of earnestness in pressing the Society on others. It is quite true that we must be careful to admit none but those who are thoroughly Catholic, in the very best and highest sense of the word ... I believe that if we would all bestir ourselves, there are enough of such men among our own acquaintances to double the number of the brethren of the Society in this one year.[20]

Eighteen months later the SSC took the initiative and organized a conference of priests to coincide with the Church Congress meeting in Wolverhampton. Despite the fact that preparations were rushed and the notice given was very short, it was a great success. Two booklets were rushed through the presses: one explicitly describing the 'Nature and Objects' of the Society and the other a more wide-ranging 'Address to Catholics' over the signatures of Mackonochie and the four vicars. This was only part of the busy work of the Society's tract committee which attempted, sometimes unsuccessfully, to meet twice a month. Mackonochie acknowledged that such a blatant exercise in what we might call recruitment and retention involved a deliberate change of policy. He had reminded the brethren in 1866 that 'secrecy' referred not to the existence or the name of the society but to the roll and proceedings. Increasingly he felt that the word only served to excite the curiosity of SSC's opponents.[21]

In the Master's Address of May 1868 (which that year had a particularly bitter edge)[22] Mackonochie asked the question,

> Are we to be contented only with what we have done, or, like the hundred and twenty going forth from the Upper Chamber, to

limit our field of action only by the boundaries of the world? If the latter, we must strive for an increase in our Society, for more intercommunion, for better organisation ... we must increase – not rashly, and in haste, but by pressing wherever we can the acceptance of a portion with us as a great means of glorifying our Lord.[23]

A conference similar to the one organized in Wolverhampton was attempted again in 1869 when the Church Congress met in Liverpool. Numbers attending were down on the earlier conference but more priests joined the Society. However, Mackonochie was still not satisfied and was particularly critical of the poor attendance at chapter (the meeting held monthly in London) and the twice-yearly synod. Throughout this period only a fraction of the Society ever appeared at chapter; the attendance was usually under 20, sometimes in single figures; and synod, which was of obligation, always had dozens of defaulters. It may well have contributed to the chaos of 1877–8, when many members had not kept themselves abreast of fast-moving events until they were upon them. Even then, barely a third of the Society came to London for an emergency meeting when the future existence of the Society was at stake. As he drew his 1870 Master's Address to a close, Mackonochie returned to the question of recruitment. Many in his audience must have thought that he had said enough on the subject by the middle of page 3, but he returned to it on what was to be page 8 of the printed record. He posed a very simple sum:

The section of the Church of England represented by the Islington Clergy have told us recently that of her 18,000 clergy they can claim but 5,000. Surely the remaining 13,000 should yield to this Society more than 200? In the face of approaching Disestablishment[24] these are not the days to sit still. If there be anything to be done to gain to ourselves a larger spiritual power than we possess already it must be done. What the English Church Union is to Churchmen at large, that – and much more than that – we ought to be to the Catholic priesthood.[25]

Mackonochie's dreams were large ones. 'If every Brother in his own neighbourhood would try to seek out some four or five Priests like-minded with himself, get them proposed, elected, admitted, form them into a Branch ... we should soon find ourselves reaching out towards 1,000 brethren, instead of just passing 200'.[26]

Anglo-Catholics frequently claim 'not to play the numbers game'. Mackonochie in 1870 certainly did. However, the next three years were to be bruising ones, reflected in the brooding atmosphere we can still sense in the printed pages of the *Acta* and Proceedings. Internationally, the First Vatican Council (1869–70) horrified Mackonochie. At home the Purchas judgment and the persecution of Archdeacon Denison and W.J.E. Bennett had gone as badly as they could have done. In 1873 he reflected, 'Our own Society ... has developed from secrecy to the most open publicity, so far as its existence and objects are concerned ... Truly we must be careful how we boast of so wide an extension. It is of the nature of religious bodies, as they grow in extent, to become weak in the limbs and joints – in energy and coherence: nor is it to be supposed that we shall have altogether escaped this evil'.[27] Seventeen members of SSC had resigned that year. Mackonochie did not go into details but some brethren had opposed the petition to Convocation which had been drawn up that winter on the grounds that it was needlessly provocative. The 1872 revisions of the Society's formal documents did not please everyone. They contained more definite Catholic phraseology than before which, to some, would prove a red rag to an episcopal bull. Perhaps Mackonochie was beginning to sense cracks in the Society. However, the persecution of Anglo-Catholics which was unleashed by the Public Worship Regulation Act of 1874 may well have acted as a final recruiting sergeant for the Society and had the effect of binding the brethren together. Although numbers of new admissions slowed over the next four years, Francis Bagshawe reported a roll of 397 in May 1877. It was not to be as high a number again for many decades. Over the next two years this figure was to fall by nearly a half. Episcopal disapproval, when turned directly on the Society rather than towards individual brethren, very nearly divided and ruled.

The crisis of 1877–8, which is seen so graphically in the fall in membership of the Society, hinged, in the first instance, on the way in which SSC went about its uncompromising promotion of sacramental confession. Given that three of the Society's principal objects were personal sanctification of the members, mutual encouragement in priestly work and pastoral ministry and the promotion of the Catholic faith, its insistence on the importance of confession may not seem surprising or unduly controversial after the passing of 130 years. However, we can also see that there was an inevitability about some of the battles which erupted in the very different world of the 1860s and 1870s. Despite the place which 'ghostly counsel' retained in the rubrics of the Book of Common Prayer, and despite the examples of post-Reformation use of confession in the Church of England,[28] nothing in the Catholic revival raised the hackles of English opinion, both within and without the Church of England, as sacramental confession. In a notorious phrase, the evangelical Dean of Ripon, Hugh McNeile, gave vent to his feeling that, were it left up to him, hearing confessions would be a capital offence in English Law.[29] In two separate, if overlapping, crises in the 1870s the subject was to set SSC firmly against the episcopal establishment. The first of these, the 1873 petition to the bishops in Convocation, was a very deliberate move on the part of the Society to raise the subject. The second, the far more damaging case of the book *The Priest in Absolution*, seemingly came upon the Society out of the blue in the summer of 1877. Forced into a position where the Society had to decide how best to respond, all sorts of other questions about SSC's identity and policy came to the fore.[30]

The May synod of 1866 heard a report of chapter discussions during the previous year which had frequently returned to the desirability of confirmation at a young age and thus hearing the confessions of children. 'Several of the brethren were able to testify from experience to the amount of sin and sorrow which have been saved, especially to boys, by this means under the grace of God ... It was felt that, while much is done for women, scarcely a hand is raised to help men to repent.' Proposals to leave tracts on confession at casino doors may seem faintly ludicrous. Far more sensible, and common practice in later years, was the suggestion that times for confession should be advertised so that men (in particular) could walk into a church anonymously and know that there would be a priest there 'who would ask no questions as to who he was, but faithfully discharge his duty for the healing of his soul'.[31]

How were the clergy to be equipped for this specialized ministry? Church of England clergy lacked the thorough seminary training of contemporary Roman Catholic priests. It was to be several years before training for hearing confessions became part of theological college life, and then only in a small number of institutions. Moral theology did not hold a particularly prominent place in Anglican universities and the great tomes of seventeenth-century moral theology such as Jeremy Taylor's *Ductor Dubitantium* went only so far in equipping a curate for the sins of nineteenth-century urban life. There were contemporary manuals on hearing confessions published on the continent but, as yet, no equivalent Anglican versions.[32] The very word 'Priestcraft' was anathema to many Anglicans.

Mackonochie, himself a confessor much in demand, was keen to meet the need. His immediate practical suggestion was to ask local branch meetings and chapters to discuss, as a standing item on each agenda, a theoretical case for the confessional. Sensibly, he suggested that the junior member of the Society present should be the first to express an opinion, having heard the sample case. Perhaps it would be difficult for a curate to contradict his incumbent if the older man had given an opinion first. Do we see a faint prefiguring of Fr Couratin's famous 'box tutorials' at St Stephen's House a century later? How widely followed this advice was, and how long it remained part of branch meetings is unclear. What is certain, however, is that it was taken up with alacrity but also with some misgiving. Mackonochie had to give further sensible advice a year later. Where several priests at a meeting might work in the same, or neighbouring, parishes, it would sometimes be easy to identify parishioners if examples were taken 'from life' and the seal might be in jeopardy. The Master suggested that cases of conscience might be pooled from branches across the country to guarantee the anonymity of penitents.[33]

The first reference we find to *The Priest in Absolution* is in the summer of 1866 when Mackonochie reports that 'the [Tract] Committee have placed the Manual for Confessors in the hands of Br. Chambers, who undertakes to bring it out in parts on his own responsibility. The title will be "The Priest in Absolution". Part I is nearly ready'.[34] This sentence was to be important eleven years later when the furore over the book erupted in public. Chambers was dead by then and SSC made the point that it had bought the copyright and the remaining copies of the book in part as an act of charity to Mrs Chambers. Therefore we may assume Chambers paid for its publication and printing himself. To that extent SSC could claim that *The Priest in Absolution* was not an official publication of the Society in the way that other tracts were. At the same time, the motivation for the book lay firmly and squarely with the Society. Chambers, one of its senior members and a former Master, had proceeded with his work at the Society's request and with its knowledge and blessing, but without its editorial oversight or control.

The first part was soon finished and Chambers set to work on the more substantial second part. This was finished by 1870, though Chambers could not find a publisher. Rivington and Masters, publishers well known to Anglo-Catholics, both declined to publish it. Chambers admitted to being relieved. He was concerned that the book should find its way into the hands and studies of *bona fide* confessors rather than public bookshops. Chambers' hunch was to be proved right by subsequent events. The May synod of 1870 not only thanked Chambers for his labours but passed a resolution 'that [this synod] relieve him of all responsibility with regard to it; that it acquire the possession of the copyright, and sell it at 5s a copy to members of the SSC'.[35] Why this was not acted upon is a mystery. Chambers still owned the copyright and the copies at his death in 1874.

The advertisements for the book which appeared in the Society's literature in 1870 urged brethren to purchase Part II directly from Chambers at St Mary's, Crown Street, though Part I was on sale at Masters & Co in New Bond Street. On Chambers' death a special notice was circulated to brethren asking for loans or gifts of £5 to buy the copyright and remaining copies for the Society.

Part I is a slim volume of barely 90 pages, which deals in a general way with moral theology and the place of sacramental confession within that context. It was likely to be less inflammatory than Part II which gave 300 pages of details and examples of various sorts of sin. Some brethren suggested that the book be published in Latin. This, however, would have defeated Chambers' intention of providing a practical manual for working parish clergy whose Latin might not have been as good as it had been at school. Of these 300 pages, precisely three went into some degree of detail about sexual sins. They had no more capacity for titillation than the medical textbooks which could be found on any Victorian bookseller's shelves. Yet they were doubly controversial when combined with Chambers' acknowledgement that at times a confessor needs to question a penitent to help self-examination or for the sake of clarity. Chambers' book is discreet and responsible, if rather dull. Later generations had other and better books such as Pusey's translation of the Abbé Gaume,[36] or Belton's *Manual for Confessors*[37] on their study shelves. *The Priest in Absolution* retains its place in the bibliography of books on penance and absolution for historical rather than practical reasons. However, if it ever entered general circulation it would offer the coarsest opponents of SSC the opportunity to ask John Bull how he felt about his wife and daughters being grilled about their sex lives by prying clergy. It would also give John Bull an opportunity to ask the bishops what they were going to do about it.

With the exception of buying the copies, *The Priest in Absolution* disappears from the records of the Society between 1870 and 1877 when it re-entered SSC's life in the most dramatic way possible.

As the 1860s gave way to the 1870s the persecution of Anglo-Catholic priests and causes intensified. At the end of Mackonochie's first trial for ritual practices at St Alban's, Holborn, Sir Robert Phillimore's judgment given in March 1868 decided many points in the priest's favour. On appeal, however, the Privy Council overturned much of this. Matters intensified at St Alban's throughout 1869 as Mackonochie refused to compromise, and in November 1870 he was suspended for three months for continued disobedience.[38] At the same time the evangelical Church Association moved against the relatively soft target which was John Purchas's advanced, if eccentric, worship at the proprietary chapel of St James, in Brighton. Once again, Phillimore decided some points in Purchas's favour. Anglo-Catholic satisfaction was shortlived. Once again, the Judicial Committee of the Privy Council overturned Phillimore's judgment. The Church Association seemed triumphant.

If moderate and cautious high churchmen were outraged, Mackonochie's next address to SSC was a battle-cry. 'The war is now openly declared against the very life of the Church. We must sacrifice that, or fight for it to the end.'[39] He rejected a suggestion of compromise which had been made, improperly he felt, through a member of the laity by the Bishop of London.

While we could enter into such a negotiation if the Catholic principles of Doctrine, Ritual and Practice were granted, it would be impossible to do so without such a foundation; and although the bishop's letter contained some most generous expressions of willingness to make any sacrifice in order to avoid a schism, which he deemed must inevitably issue from the present divisions, it gave no hint as to the nature of the sacrifices which he contemplated. The synod [of September 1870] thought that unless a basis were offered by the bishop, it would be impossible for the clergy to suggest one ... Now, my brethren, I have only in conclusion to bid you, in God's name, put on the whole armour of God for the coming struggle.[40]

Part of the coming struggle was a petition to Convocation which a committee of SSC started to draw up during the winter of 1871–2. It argued for the official provision of a more Catholic liturgy than that of 1662, urging that the Prayer Book of 1549 should be the model for future Anglican liturgical reform. Other liturgical requests to provide for the times and situations for which the 1662 book makes no provision included eucharistic propers for feast-days and at funerals, reservation of the Blessed Sacrament, consecration and use of holy oils, harvest festivals, non-communicating attendance at Mass and 'the advisability of providing for the education, selection, and licensing of duly qualified confessors'.[41] In draft form the petition was presented to the chapter meeting of March 1873 by Lowder in the presence of 36 brethren. Opinion was divided with the local vicar of the Oxford branch reporting his branch's unanimous opposition. Some wanted a more moderate document which men like Pusey and Liddon would be happy to sign. After a long debate the petition was accepted by an unknown majority. Two months later 480 priests had signed it, both members of the Society and like-minded nonmembers, as it was not to be presented in the Society's name. However, the Master's Address reveals seventeen resignations. Mackonochie's tone is bullish: 'when the Society has come to a conclusion, it would seem that only one course remains for any whose heart is in the welfare of the Society, and that is, to use every endeavour that the vigour of the Society and its work may not suffer through that which he himself may think a mistake'.[42]

The bishops, not surprisingly, ignored the calls for collects, funeral services and harvest festivals and concentrated on the single clause on confession. In good Anglican style they set up a committee. Far from training and licensing confessors as the petition requested, its task was to curb the practice. For some evangelicals, the fact that the subject was being discussed by bishops at all was a step too far and pressure from the Church Association was redoubled. Members of SSC who spoke in the debates at the June and July chapters seem genuinely and naively surprised at the furore. It was proposed to send a memorial to the bishops signed by priests who both heard and made their own confessions, and an amendment added that it should be a document which could be signed by Anglo-Catholicism's elder statesmen: Pusey, Liddon, King and Carter. Mackonochie and Lowder, not for the first or the last time, took different lines. For Lowder, 'the primary object of the Society is to deepen the Spiritual life, not become pugnacious; we must be careful not to increase differences in the Society. [I] would rather wait, than compromise the whole Catholic body'.[43] Mackonochie, in an ambiguous phrase, commented, 'We must not look to great names for success',[44] and the outspoken Orby Shipley 'objected to giving the power of ruling the SSC into the hands of Priests who are external to the Society'.[45]

The bishops' committee's report emerged at the end of July and was predictably condemnatory of confession in any circumstances beyond the special provisions in the Prayer Book rubrics. Pusey, Liddon, Carter and Bright produced a response on their own initiative which was published by *The Times* in December. Only 29 names were added to it, including Mackonochie's. This was in stark contrast to the 480 names on the original petition which had started its life with the SSC. Pusey deliberately avoided sending it to 'those of the advanced school ... It is the rallying of the old school for whom the young ones have been speaking and whom they profess to represent'.[46] After all its hard work and nervous energy expended over the previous two years, the 'young ones' of the Society's convocation committee reported to the January 1874 chapter: 'absolute silence is the best course to recommend to the SSC'.[47]

For most of the following three years the controversy over confession took its place within the wider debates of the Society over the persecution of the Public Worship Regulation Act which passed into law on 5 August 1874. This was the most draconian legislation yet attempted to bring ritualistic clergy to heel, and in the course of the next decade four priests, members of SSC at one time or another, ran the full gamut of the legislation until they were gaoled for 'Ritual Offences'. Many others had their parish work interfered with. There was widespread opposition to the Bill. Churchmen of various shades of opinion were horrified by the use of the secular courts and judges without any ecclesiastical authority whatsoever. Even the old Court of Arches, hamstrung though it may have been by the right of appeal to the Judicial Committee of the Privy Council, was still an ecclesiastical court with a certain ecclesiastical authority. Questions of authority, jurisdiction and obedience were raised for priests of all traditions. For the ritualists there was the issue of the extent to which liturgical and ritual externals enshrined non-negotiable religious truth.[48]

In what was becoming an annual call to arms, Mackonochie warned his brethren in May 1874, 'Remember, WE MUST FIGHT – let us fight bravely and wisely'.[49] It is to the credit of the Society that in the course of the next few years when the battles of ecclesiastical politics could have easily swamped all other considerations, the *Acta* of the chapters and the proceedings of the synods demonstrate that a range of activities and topics continued. Mission work with children and the provision of church schools was a subject to which SSC returned time and again; new branches were set up in the west country, the relationship between Christians and Freemasonry was debated. However, the bulk of the Society's business fell into two categories: what we might loosely call 'ecclesiastical politics' and 'ritual details'.

In the first category, there were several debates on disestablishment, a subject on which the Society seems to have divided evenly. Many brethren, including Mackonochie, hated establishment with every fibre of their being and wanted the bishops removed from the House of Lords. Even establishment's supporters assumed that disestablishment of the Church of England was an inevitability. The example of the Church of Ireland, disestablished in 1869, was before their eyes. Many SSC priests saw this as a golden opportunity to set God's Church free from the Erastian shackles which were part of the

Reformation's legacy.[50] Surprisingly few put forward the opposing Anglo-Catholic argument that establishment, in itself highly regrettable, is a historical fact which provides a privileged boat from which to catch the souls of English men and women for the Catholic faith.

As the PWR Act (as it was universally known) bit, and as SSC priests were increasingly targeted, the Society had a change of leadership. In May 1876 Mackonochie finally was allowed to step down as Master. The brethren's first choice was to ask Lowder to take up the post once again. He politely refused. Within minutes of the hasty election of the Vicar of St Barnabas, Pimlico, Francis Bagshawe, the brethren were involved in a heated debate. Some wanted to defuse the situation by toning down the language of the Society's official documents. They felt that giving up words like 'Mass' would be a concession worth making. Fr Stanton made a powerful rejoinder. 'There were some who would stake all upon the Mass. The term is most dear to us – it is a shibboleth of the Catholic Church - no word expresses what we mean like the word "Mass". We want Mass for the living, and we want Mass for the dead'.[51] Later the synod debated a motion which proposed active resistance urging brethren to consider the PWR Act court null and void, remain in their parishes if inhibited or deprived and continue to minister to their people until prevented. The debate produced many amendments. Lowder introduced the question of the ordination oath, and pointed out the difference between a bishop's supposed authority under the state's PWR Act and his real authority if he comes as a father in God. Mackonochie, who spoke from experience, argued that 'The priest has nothing to do with the PWR Act – his jurisdiction is from God, and it is his duty to remain in his parish. When turned out of his Church, his duty is still the same ... God gives the charge of souls and only God can take it away'.[52]

The second category of debates, 'ritual details' makes for weary reading 130 years later. Liturgy was something on which each one of nearly 400 brethren had a view. The Society had been committed to supplementing and adapting Anglican liturgical provision from 'Western' or 'Roman' sources since the 1860s. This approach held that as the Church of England was part of the continuing life of the Catholic Church therefore her liturgical points of reference must be contemporary continental Catholicism. At first this provoked almost no comment. As the Society grew, however, there were calls to permit greater flexibility. In particular, some brethren wanted ceremonial to be based on the Sarum use of the pre-Reformation Church. 'The second year of King Edward VI' was their touchstone, drawn from the preface to the Prayer Book. They emphasized Catholic continuity not so much with contemporary Roman Catholicism as medieval English Christianity. Both approaches had their passionate advocates and eloquent proponents. In many respects it was a pointless argument which generated more heat than light and divided men who believed the same things about the Eucharist. Rather against expectation, a committee made up largely of 'Western rite' enthusiasts proposed a degree of liturgical flexibility for the brethren, permitting Sarum interpolations. Presumably it made little practical difference in most parishes.[53] It is tempting to see the Anglo-Catholicism of cruel myth in some of these debates: arguing about the cut of maniples while the Catholic understanding of the Eucharist was being attacked wholesale. It is also interesting to see a terse note appear in the formal papers reminding brethren not to boo or cheer during debates and circulate position papers privately. It would be unfair to be too harsh on the brethren, but they needed to remember F.H. Murray's warning in September 1874: 'In a few months the question for all of us to consider will be, not whether we should follow the Roman or Sarum Use, but what we can save of any ritual at all'.[54]

Ellsworth, in her vivid account of the events of the 1870s, comments that

> none of these [ritual] disputes appears to have damaged the Society ... They do, however, reflect the divergence of opinion inherent in any large society, and they show that some brethren were not

always entirely in sympathy with the Society's tenor and actions. The tendency in the 'seventies of two-thirds of the membership to be absent from the synods meant that some were not even aware of them. The implications of this revealed themselves in 1877.[55]

In his thirteen years as Master, Mackonochie had from time to time reminded the brethren that they were a private society if not a secret one. In his Master's Address for May 1875 he had urged greater caution than usual with the Society's papers, suggesting that brethren, if needs be, destroy them. The wisdom of this dramatic sounding proposal became only too clear when a copy of Part II of *The Priest in Absolution* came to Lord Redesdale through the hands of a Protestant agitator, Robert Fleming. Having warned the Archbishop of Canterbury first, Redesdale denounced the book in a speech to the House of Lords on 14 June. With only two days' warning, Bagshawe wrote in the first instance to his own bishop, Jackson of London, explaining some of the background. He made clear that the Society had requested such a book in the first place as a practical guide for priests; it had left the contents in Chambers' hands and had only later purchased the copyright from his widow. For some of the brethren it was a book gathering dust on their shelves, while others did not know of its existence at all. Jackson's reply was blunt. 'In my judgment, a system of confession which makes such a book necessary or even useful to the Confessor carries with it its own Condemnation.'[56] To this Bagshawe replied in terms which hint at one possible way forward for the Society: 'I cannot help feeling, after listening to a debate such as that on Thursday night, that our practice with regard to confession is very widely misapprehended. One of my objections to *The Priest in Absolution* is that its language is not calculated to remove that misapprehension'.[57]

A.C. Tait, the Archbishop of Canterbury, contacted F.H. Murray of Chislehurst, whom he suspected, correctly, of being a longstanding and respected member of the Society. Following an initial meeting between the two men, Murray reported to the Master's council, who sent a delegation to Lambeth on

28 June. Lowder was present, but not Mackonochie, who argued that to take any part would be tantamount to saying that the book demanded an apology. That same afternoon Bagshawe delivered specimen copies of the book, the statutes and Office book to Jackson for examination. The bishops were horrified at what they read. Jackson then sent the documents on to Tait, who gave the SSC a deadline of 5 July to repudiate *The Priest in Absolution*. Meanwhile, the bishops in Convocation continued to discuss confession in general and the book in particular, wisely debating the principle rather than the personalities.

A special chapter of SSC was summoned for 5 July, attended by a mere 75 brethren. A statement as to how the book came to be written, drafted by Lowder, T.W. Perry and the lawyer Walter Phillimore, was agreed for circulation to the bishops. Not for the last time, Lowder, the founder, and Mackonochie, the longest-serving Master, found themselves painfully at odds with each other. Mackonochie thundered against doing anything which might permit an interpretation of backing down. Lowder eventually secured a compromise whereby SSC assured the bishops that it would not supply further copies of the book in deference to the wishes of the Archbishop. Far from being mollified Tait was furious that the books had not been burned. In the meantime the bishops had issued a resolution expressing 'strong condemnation' of any doctrine or practice of confession which would make a book such as *The Priest in Absolution* necessary. It seemed that SSC was to be formally censured. Lowder, perhaps unwilling to see 22 years' work disappear, proposed to chapter the following week that the Master in council take 'any steps necessary' to defend the Society. Once again, Mackonochie and Lowder had to disagree. Mackonochie called on the brethren to suffer and bear the brunt of any attack. 'The leading mind among the Bishops was simply hatred to the Society ... *The Priest in Absolution* was a mere catspaw to work the ruin of the Society.'[58] A further compromise resolution passed which permitted Bagshawe to appear before the bishops, but only if they summoned him to do so.

At the same chapter, Newton Smith proposed a motion which indicates the way in which some brethren were reacting. Smith's proposal was for the Master to refuse to accept any resignations until May 1878. This motion, although defeated, clearly shows that the council was worried about, and presumably had received, threats of resignation. In the course of this one chapter meeting three possible ways forward for each individual brother had been displayed: outright defiance, submission to a greater or lesser extent and the option of walking away. Brethren were to choose all three paths of action in the course of the next eighteen months.

During the summer of 1877 there were relatively few developments, although interest in the press was acute. It seems likely that the bishops imagined, and perhaps hoped, that SSC would implode without further episcopal intervention. Bagshawe, who appears from the papers as a gentle and indecisive man rather out of his depth, must have dreaded the prospect of the September synod as much as another archepiscopal carpeting. The two-day synod started, as usual, at St Peter's, London Docks, at 9 a.m. on 13 September. Surprisingly, still only 133 brethren bothered to attend. After the Office, elections, admissions and Mass came formal items of business. These included reading out a long list of resignations and correspondence from local branches and individuals. The thrust of most of these was to argue that the Society must not disband. A letter from the Bishop of London was read, 'condemning many of the terms used in the Statutes, and the whole tone of the Society', and another from Dr Pusey 'deprecating the use of the term "Mass" in the Statutes and urging moderation generally'.[59]

The atmosphere must have been electric as Bagshawe then suspended standing orders and asked for discussion of a proposal to disband the Society with effect from 15 September, made by E.G. Wood and seconded by R.R. Bristow. Bagshawe made it clear that he supported the motion.[60] Member after member, including Mackonochie and Archdeacon Denison, rose to protest that they had only had 24 hours' notice of this resolution. Bagshawe backed down and reinstated standing orders, bringing the proposal to disband as an amendment to the first item on the printed agenda which proposed a committee to modify the statutes. Moving the amendment, Wood argued that the SSC was over-emphasizing its own importance. It was, after all, a voluntary society. If it was formally censured by the bishops, by implication the Catholic faith and everything it stood for would be seen to be officially censured too. Tinkering with the wording of the statutes would be useless. In Wood's eyes, much of the present trouble could be laid at SSC's door. The memorial of 1873 had thoroughly frightened the bishops and the PWR Act was a direct outcome. Wood drew an analogy with the suppression of the Jesuits by Clement XIV for the sake of the peace of the Church.[61]

The two most powerful speeches against disbanding came, unsurprisingly, from Lowder, speaking emotionally in his own church about how his whole ministry had been bound up with SSC and 'feeling the weight of the Cross', and from Mackonochie. Still grumbling that the brethren had only had 24 hours' notice, he resorted to legal tactics. Only a majority of the whole Society, not a majority of those present, could vote to dissolve the Society. In addition, Mackonochie had been assured by his lawyers that disbanding would leave the brethren individually and corporately liable to actions in Chancery. In a final act of defiance, he threatened what might be called a 'Continuing SSC', pledging that he 'would hold on, with any who chose to join him, as the SSC, in spite of any vote for disbanding'.[62] The motion was lost by 67 votes to 9. On the following day the brethren debated whether they should revise their statutes and publish them. After a long debate it was agreed to set up a committee to revise the Statutes, Lowder once again being asked to serve. A final little motion on the second day, moved by Mackonochie, concerned resignations from the Society. Mackonochie must have known that he was rubbing salt into Bagshawe's wounds. He later apologized for seeming to tell the Master what to do. The motion fell, but the incident rankled sufficiently for Bagshawe to include it as a detail in his letter to the brethren dated 15 October and posted from Eastbourne, where he had been sent on doctor's orders. Bagshawe had intended to resign immediately, but it had been put to him that he could still help with the revision of the statutes. In doing so, Bagshawe concluded that if revision proved unsuccessful, 'I shall feel that I have done all that I can for the Society, and ask you to elect another Master who can carry out the policy of resistance'.[63] He did not attend a chapter or synod in person again.[64]

The committee worked through the winter of 1877–8 and submitted its proposed amended statutes to the Archbishops of Canterbury and York and the Bishop of London. Tait thought that the bishops would still be unhappy with them, but was pleased to see 'Eucharist' and 'guidance of souls' replacing 'Mass' and 'Confession'. Thomson of York thought it sensible to keep the bishops as far distant as possible from SSC. He had apparently been tipped off that the revised statutes were likely to fall at the May 1878 synod. Thomson's informant was right. Of the Society's elder statesmen, Lowder and Carter were unworried about the proposed changes, but Mackonochie was implacable. Before the debate started he had already insisted that the minutes of the April chapter be altered to record his words accurately: 'he [Mackonochie] would as readily give up the Nicene Creed as adopt them [the revisions]'.[65] The motion for revision was defeated by 58 votes to 51. The hardline confrontational party in the Society, with Mackonochie its chief proponent, had triumphed. The brethren braced themselves for the expected episcopal censure to come, but it never materialized. Perhaps the bishops thought that they had divided and ruled. After all, in the previous twelve months, 122 brethren had resigned and five more had died (though 24 had been admitted). The next twelve months were to see 72 further resignations including the Master, secretary, treasurer and other officers. One member died and only four were admitted. Perhaps subtler forms of pressure could be used on parish clergy who remained in the Society.

Bagshawe sent the May 1878 Master's Address, read out before the decisive vote, from his convalescent bed. He was able to find charitable and generous words for Mackonochie. 'Although he has not agreed with me in judgment upon all points, he has never failed to give me his generous counsel and support.'[66] But if the bishops thought that it was only a matter of time before the SSC folded completely they were wrong. Wisely, Carter of Clewer was asked to fill the breach left by Bagshawe's resignation for the year 1878–9. His Master's Address for the following year is the work of an experienced priest. He admits that he would not have been unhappy had the revisionists prevailed, acknowledges that division persists within the Society and he makes an impassioned appeal 'above all things still to be one in heart and in mutual charity, that the bonds of past associations and of a common faith, which still knit together the Brethren who have left with those of us who still remain in our sacred fellowship, may be felt to be precious'.[67] At the synod which followed Carter's Address, Mackonochie was elected by the brethren to serve again as Master.

What conclusions can be drawn from this detailed story of conflict within and without the Society? John Sheldon Reed argues that 'it is difficult to say whether the activities of the Society of the Holy Cross generally helped Anglo-Catholicism or hurt it. There is no question, however, that the SSC shaped both the movement and the public perception of it'.[68] Did the SSC also shape the way in which the wider Catholic revival was persecuted? E.G. Wood's claim that the petition to Convocation had contributed materially to the PWR Act and its implementation has an element of the chicken-and-egg argument. To what extent did the victory of the hardline party in 1877 and 1878 divide the SSC from other more moderate high churchmen who were slowly being appointed to positions of responsibility in the Anglican establishment? By the 1880s R.W. Church, the semi-official historian of the Oxford Movement, was Dean of St Paul's; Butler of Wantage, founder of a religious order, was Dean of Lincoln; and even Liddon was thought to have been offered the Bishopric of St Alban's. Did the hardliners' victory guarantee that SSC would only ever attract those on the topmost pinnacles of the Church of England? At the same time, perhaps the continued existence of the SSC made men like Church and Liddon more reasonable in the eyes of Downing Street.

Reed draws a parallel between *The Priest in Absolution* and the Tractarian's publication of Froude's *Remains* and Newman's *Tract XC* nearly 40 years before. 'If Newman and his friends published ... with apparent indifference to likely reactions, their successors often seemed not so much indifferent as flatly uncomprehending.'[69] This comment rather misses the point. It would have had little meaning or significance for men like Mackonochie or Stanton. To them trimming God's truth for the sake of political expediency would have verged on blasphemy. Reading the papers of the SSC and the bishops one often thinks of the Gospel saying about how the children of this world are wiser than the children of light. Yet perhaps it was only Mackonochie's toughness and singleness of vision which allowed the SSC to survive at all. Had the Society remained in the hands of the unimpressive Bagshawe it is hard to see it withstanding further onslaught from Protestant bishops. It is hard to envisage the saintly Lowder, who had endured much bitter persecution in Wapping but still agonized over his ordination vow of obedience, regarding bishops and brethren alike with a steely glint in the eye. However, another of Reed's pithy judgements is hard to resist. 'The society served the larger movement by providing it with what amounted to shock troops: in the legal cases that followed in the wake of the PWR Act, it is fair to say that the English Church Union provided the defence, but the SSC supplied the defendants.'[70]

For a society which was criticized for being a secret one (highly reminiscent of the ignorant jibes against Opus Dei in modern times), the SSC had seldom been out of the headlines for many years. Its influence was out of all proportion to the size of its membership, even at its height when it boasted a mere 400 members out of a total of 18,000 Anglican clergy.[71] It is not easy to make a case for SSC as an astute political body, but equally it is easy to forget that its chief mission was to promote the consecration and sanctification of priests' lives. That work continued morning by morning in busy and faithful parishes. Had the SSC been a society of dilettantes looking for a clerical version of the gentleman's club or Freemason's lodge it would have joined any other number of Victorian brotherhoods remembered only in learned footnotes. The romantic picture of the SSC slum-priest living, working and dying amongst the poorest of society may owe something to Anglo-Catholic hagiography, but neither is it a work of fiction. That mission work, still recognizable in the parishes of the twenty-first century, 'eventually won for the entire Anglo-Catholic movement a measure of tolerance and even admiration from those who otherwise had little use for it'.[72]

During the next 35 years the life of the Society was never to scale the dramatic heights it knew in the 1870s. Life settled down for the brethren who remained, and the annual round of synods and chapters proceeded with comparatively little incident. Even with his somewhat hagiographical view, Embry described Mackonochie's second period as Master (1879–82) as 'uneventful and fallow years'.[73] However, that is not to say the Society was not busy. Missions and retreats continued. A torrent of learned papers emerged from individual brethren and the committees on a variety of liturgical, legal, theological and practical subjects. SSC made an impassioned call for the anointing of the sick to be restored to the life of the Anglican parish.[74] Priestly celibacy was an issue much debated in the years after 1878.

Controversial questions continued to demand the brethren's attention. One of these was the long process whereby SSC tried to come to a mind over the Order for Corporate Reunion.[75] This organization, with an innocuous-sounding name, belongs to one of the more curious byways of Anglo-Catholic history. In much the same way as it is hard now to see how men like Pusey, Liddon and Lord Halifax were taken in by Fr Ignatius, so it is hard to see how some members of SSC took the OCR (as it was generally known) seriously. The project proposed healing Christian division by consecrating three Anglicans to the episcopate on a ship on the high seas, thus avoiding questions of jurisdiction. The consecrators were to be bishops whose episcopal orders Rome would recognize as valid, using a valid form to administer the sacrament. Who these shadowy consecrators were to be was a closely guarded secret. It was rumoured that at least one was an Orthodox bishop, thus helping to heal an older schism. From a later vantage point it seems to be a story from the memoirs of *episcopi vagantes*.

The OCR impinged on SSC in two ways. First, prayer for reunion, which had been part of the aims of the Society from the very beginning, had suffered several setbacks in Anglo-Catholic eyes. The definition of Papal Infallibility at Vatican I seemed to have dented the prospects of reunion with Rome. Even diehard Western rite Anglo-Catholics such as Mackonochie saw nothing strange about espousing 'Catholicism without the Pope'. A more sympathetic and nuanced approach to papal authority was to come in the twentieth century. So the OCR to some seemed to be doing something rather than nothing. At the same time, official Anglican discussions with Old Catholics and Nordic Lutheran churches renewed controversy over the Jerusalem bishopric and rumours of Anglican and Free Church collusion in the mission-field led many to fear that the ecumenical drift of the times was leading in a Protestant direction. Closer to home, SSC and OCR overlapped in the person of one of the three future 'bishops', T.W. Mossman, who had been a member of the SSC for several years. Mossman tried to enlist the SSC's support. Opinion was mixed. Many of the senior members of the Society, led by Carter, felt that he should be kept at arm's length, and Mossman was, eventually, expelled from the Society.[76]

There is little evidence in the Society *Acta* and proceedings of the trials and persecutions Mackonochie was enduring at St Alban's, Holborn. Successive suspensions and threats to deprive him elicited friendly motions of support, but he did not wear his suffering on his sleeve. In 1880 Mackonochie led the Society's mourning for its saintly founder, Charles Lowder, who died on holiday at Zell-am-See on 9 September. Lowder's whole ministry had been bound up with the SSC, and vice versa. Although there had been no formal connection between the SSC and St Peter's, London Docks, it remained the Society's spiritual home under R.A.J. Suckling (who later exchanged livings with Mackonochie) and L.S. Wainwright.

Mackonochie's second spell as Master saw one further outbreak of resignations in 1881 when some brethren took exception to Stewart Headlam, the prominent Christian socialist, who addressed the September synod.[77] The heartland of the Society may have been poor urban parishes, but the brethren's high doctrine of the incarnation and pastoral calling did not mean that the majority embraced Headlam's politics. Mackonochie's defence the following May is fascinating:

> The name Socialism has a bad mark upon it; but so much the more, if men, and even our Brethren, who have examined this 'Christian Socialism', find in it only those precepts which our Lord and His immediate followers adopted to the letter, ought we to be glad to have an opportunity thoroughly, from the lips of Christian men, to hear what claim it may, or may not, have on our attention. These are days of active thought, so that we cannot afford to shut ourselves up in our own nutshell.[78]

Mackonochie's second period as Master came to an end at that synod and he was succeeded by H.D. Nihill of St Michael's, Shoreditch. Nihill had been a vigorous member of the Society for many years and was an expert on its statutes. His term of office, however, ended on a sour note over how the Master should treat resignations, especially those being used as threats in debates. His position had clearly become unbearable. 'My object today has been to try to bring to the surface certain elements of discontent that are floating about among us ... I know that there are some among us who think that the time is come when SSC has done its work and had better be laid to rest ... But I, for one, am not convinced of it yet.'[79] That final sentence is a strange one for a man who was about to resign from the Mastership and the Society after 21 years as a member.

Mackonochie was elected Master for one last time in 1885,

but his health was already failing and he rarely managed to attend chapters and synods. Consequently he made way after only one year for E.G. Wood. One of Wood's early duties was to pay tribute to Mackonochie who died visiting his old friend (and a former member of SSC) the Bishop of Argyll and the Isles on 15 December 1887. As priest, politician and pastor, what Embry calls the 'Governor', Mackonochie had served the Society for nearly 30 years. Even in the most difficult days, he never lost his confidence in what SSC was and his high vision of what it might be. Wood, whom Mackonochie had opposed with all his might in 1878, presented the Society with a cross in Mackonochie's memory for the Masters to wear. In a light-hearted comment, the sentiment of which was deadly serious, Wood regretted that the rubrics do not provide for the *Te Deum* at a Requiem.[80]

With the deaths of Lowder and Mackonochie, the SSC moved away from the first generation of brethren and slightly altered its established patterns. E.G. Wood and C.R. Chase of All Saints, Plymouth, were to hold the mastership alternately until 1898. Not until 1924 would a London priest be elected Master again. In July 1888 chapter met for the first time outside London with a very successful meeting in Gloucester. Other meetings followed in Sheffield and Salisbury. Wood's priority was to emphasize SSC's potential to be a spiritual powerhouse. J.R. Sanderson addressed the Society on 'Special Devotions'[81] and had a powerful effect. Devotions to the Blessed Sacrament, Our Lady, days of the week and months of the year became common currency. Liturgical and theological papers continued to be read and published. However, three controversies in particular coloured these years. One was the trial of Edward King, Bishop of Lincoln, for relatively mild ritual offences. The second was the furore caused by the influence, again fairly mild, of critical scholarship seen most clearly in the publication of *Lux Mundi*.[82] The hurt and fury Liddon felt was echoed in the ranks of the SSC. Finally, the condemnation of Anglican Orders by Pope Leo XIII as 'absolutely null and utterly void' was another body-blow to Anglo-Catholics. Wood had been very close to T.A. Lacey, a fellow member of SSC, and to Lord

Halifax, the two most prominent Anglicans in Rome that year putting the Anglican case.[83]

In 1898 G.C. Ommaney of St Matthew's, Sheffield, was elected Master, and it was he who had to guide SSC through the next round of anti-ritual cases. There was some truth in the joke told about Mandell Creighton, the Bishop of London. He had spent so long studying medieval popes (of whom he was critical) that he acted rather like one. Public meetings of priests called for defiance if the bishops tried to suppress things which had the long sanction of ecumenical canonical authority. Incense and candles were small, if passionate, causes.[84] Reservation of the Blessed Sacrament went to the very heart of things. The Archbishop of Canterbury's 'Lambeth Opinions' of 1900 and 1901 found against all three. Creighton, however, saw the futility of much of this when Fr Wainwright of London Docks was threatened with prosecution. 'He will not appear before the Arches Court and will pay no attention to its sentence. Doubtless he will be ejected by the police ultimately amidst universal sympathy, and no one [else] will be able to work his parish . . . Incense will come back, and reservation for the sick will become general.'[85] Ritual details enshrined fundamental belief. 'To Catholics, the English Church was but a part of the greater whole and consequently she owed obedience in faith, morals and customs to the infallibility of the Church Catholic. To surrender such obedience would be *ipso facto* to cease to be a Catholic.'[86] Eventually Balfour's government set up a commission in 1904 on the worship of the Church of England and the law. Its report in 1906 concluded that the situation was a hopeless one. Both the law and the strict letter of the Prayer Book were too narrow for either to work satisfactorily.

Meanwhile the less spectacular side of SSC's life went on. Regular addresses on priesthood and priestcraft were a feature of Wood's years as Master. 'The Roman Question' was discussed endlessly from historical, practical and dogmatic angles. There was a steady stream of brethren who became Roman Catholics, but the numbers were never large. The SSC's printed minutes treated such resignations very discreetly. Retreats, missions and liturgical questions continued. The coronation planned for 1902, the first within living memory for most people, generated a row involving the Church Association over the King promising to uphold and defend the 'Protestant Reformed Religion'. The SSC was equally horrified that the Eucharist would be celebrated in Westminster Abbey in the presence of people of different faiths from other parts of the Empire.

Ommaney served as Master again from 1904 to 1907, and F.F. Irving from All Saints, Clevedon, from 1908 to 1911. Irving's ship was a tight one. He was particularly fierce about nonattendance at synod and nonpayment of subscriptions. Otherwise they were relatively quiet years, despite the early skirmishing around liturgical reform. This finally led to the revised Prayer Book of 1927, rejected by parliament the following year to the delight of many, if not all, Anglo-Catholics. Given this background, it was fitting that the liturgical scholar A.M.Y. Baylay, vicar of Thurgaston, served as Master from 1911 to 1913.

Irving was re-elected in 1913. As ever, there were issues which caused the SSC great concern. One of these was the stand made by an SSC bishop, Frank Weston, Bishop of Zanzibar, against intercommunion between Anglicans and Free Churchmen at Kikuyu. Closer to home, the modernist essays entitled *Foundations*[87] caused as much alarm as *Lux Mundi* had caused a generation earlier and *Essays and Reviews* a generation before that. Ronald Knox, himself never a member of SSC but a friend of many who were, answered this in his book *Some Loose Stones*, and attempted to undermine the whole approach with his parody of Dryden, *Absolute and Abitofhell*.[88]

By this time, however, Europe was on the threshold of war and the brethren of the Society of the Holy Cross, true to their principal calling, had their prayers to say for their parishioners and for a world in need of their prayers as much as ever.

Notes

1 PHL: SSC papers, Ch 71/A9, Mackonochie, Master's Address, May 1880, p 1. The standard modern biography of Mackonochie is Michael Reynolds, *Martyr of Ritualism: Father Mackonochie of St. Alban's, Holborn* (London: Faber & Faber, 1965).

2 J. Embry, *The Catholic Movement and the Society of the Holy Cross* (London: Faith Press, 1931), p. 22. Embry's book works carefully through the printed records of the Society now deposited in the Library of Pusey House. Although very scarce in booksellers' catalogues, it is available through the Project Canterbury website (justus.anglican.org/resources/pc/ssc/embry). Embry's purple prose can jar the modern ear. One can only assume that, writing in 1931, he had the Victorian style of Dr Liddon and Dean Church at the back of his mind. Care must also be taken with what might be called Embry's 'Whig view' of the history of the Society. With hindsight, Embry can give the impression that triumph was assured whatever the temporary setbacks. In fact, the possibility that the Society would cease to exist was a real one. Certainly Embry's book was written on his knees but it remains indispensable reading. His book may best be seen as one of a batch which accompanied the centenary celebrations in 1933 of Keble's Assize Sermon and, therefore, told a story of inevitable success. These celebrations proved something of a high-water mark for triumphant Anglo-Catholicism. S.L. Ollard, *A Short History of the Oxford Movement* (London: Mowbray, 1933) is perhaps the best-remembered example of the genre.

3 In recent years many important studies of the Oxford Movement have been written which have altered significantly traditional views of the Catholic Revival. Three books may be singled out. Peter B. Nockles, *The Oxford Movement in Context: Anglican High Churchmanship 1760–1857* (Cambridge University Press, 1994) demonstrates the vitality and range of the pre-Tractarian high church tradition in sharp contrast to the older Anglo-Catholic picture of a moribund eighteenth and early nineteenth-century Anglicanism. S.A. Skinner, *Tractarians and the 'Condition of England': The Social and Political Thought of*

the *Oxford Movement* (Oxford: Oxford University Press, 2004) examines in detail the importance of the Tractarians' social teaching, demonstrated clearly in their novels and journalism. The principle of social engagement, long attributed to the 'slum parishes', is dated to the beginnings of the Oxford Movement. Similarly, Nigel Yates, *Anglican Ritualism in Victorian Britain 1830–1910* (Oxford: Oxford University Press, 1999) argues against the received wisdom of a division between early Oxford theologians, uninterested in ritual questions, and a later generation of ritualists found in parishes and 'advanced' churches. Yates's use of the SSC papers is the most exhaustive study yet made of this rich archive. He shows that not all members of the Society were advanced ritualists, and not all advanced ritualists were members of the Society.

4 Numbers are difficult to give with total confidence and consistency until the printing of the roll became an annual custom from 1880. Before that date the roll was printed irregularly (1861, 1865 and 1866 were the first three occasions). Here we rely on the numbers quoted in the Master's Address at the May synods. These, however, can confuse. It is sometimes unclear who is and is not included in the total. There are at least six categories of names in the minutes: those being invited to consider joining; those proposed and seconded for election; those elected to the Lower Order; those admitted to the Lower Order; those elected to the Higher Order; and those admitted to the Higher Order. In some cases these distinct stages were compressed or ignored, particularly in the early years of the Society's existence. The relatively small number of ordinands, for example, constitutes a grey area. Furthermore, Mackonochie often quoted a different figure as 'last year's roll' when looking back. We use here the figures quoted at synod rather than those given twelve months later.

5 PHL: SSC papers, Ch 71/A55. This manuscript has the only surviving copy roll of May 1865, much annotated, pasted into its pages. The entries for the years 1855–65 clearly were compiled retrospectively. This explains the absence of the names of those who are known from the minute-books to have been elected and

MACKONOCHIE AND CONTROVERSIES

admitted but who left the Society before 1865. For example, only three of the first six members from February 1855 are listed. Similarly, the names of Dr Pusey, who joined and then left, and Oxenham, who left when he became a Roman Catholic in 1857, are not included. Dr Pusey was the fourteenth member to be admitted whose name in chronological order should come between those of T.W. Mossman and Bryan King. Yates claims that 'The allegation that Dr Pusey was one of the early members cannot be substantiated and his name is not on the extant role of members' (Yates, *Anglican Ritualism in Victorian Britain*, p. 73). However, this does not take into account the retrospective nature of the pre-1865 entries. See Chapter 4 of this volume for the details of Dr Pusey's membership.

6 Yates, *Anglican Ritualism in Victorian Britain*, pp. 76ff.

7 In the cases where the ages are known for certain this rule of thumb seems to hold true.

8 See Embry, *The Catholic Movement and the Society of the Holy Cross*, pp. 9ff.

9 Benson, founder of the Society of St John the Evangelist, was also living the religious life but is included here with the parish clergy as parish priest of Cowley.

10 See Owen Chadwick, *The Founding of Cuddesdon* (Oxford: Oxford University Press, 1854).

11 Yates, *Anglican Ritualism in Victorian Britain*, pp. 74ff. Of the large sample of 462 clergy ordained between 1841 and 1874 he analyses, 108 had been at one of four colleges: 32 at Exeter College, Oxford (Mackonochie's college); 30 at Trinity College, Cambridge; 25 at St John's College, Cambridge; and 21 at Christ Church, Oxford.

12 PHL: SSC papers, Ch 71/A8, Mackonochie, Master's Address, May 1867, p. 4.

13 This is a proposal first mentioned in the proceedings of the May 1871 synod. It recurred throughout the 1870s. It is unclear whether it was actually established.

14 PHL: SSC papers Ch 71/A1, p. 96. Bennett had first been proposed in 1856. It is unclear why he was not elected and admitted sooner.

15 In later years the boundaries were to be redrawn to give a better balance between provinces.

16 It is surprising that there was not more overlap in membership between the new religious orders for men and the SSC. However, living under two formal Rules of Life, as Fr Benson found, was always likely to generate tensions. At the same time, many of the founders of religious orders, as opposed to their members, joined the Society or had strong links with it. There is considerable overlap between the index of names in Peter Anson, *The Call of the Cloister*, (London: SPCK, 1955) and the roll of the SSC. A.B. Goulden, for example, was a long-standing and prominent member of the Society who founded the Community of Reparation to Jesus in the Blessed Sacrament to work as missionary sisters in his parish of St Alphege, Southwark.

17 The rolls and Masters' Addresses for 1894–7 inclusive are not among the SSC papers at Pusey House. Frustratingly, the reason for the substantial growth in membership during these years remains something of a mystery.

18 There were, in fact, a few SSC Freemasons who admitted as much in a startling debate on the subject in September 1875.

19 For a sociological and psychological treatment of the Oxford Movement which is sometimes controversial but always provocative see John Shelton Reed, *Glorious Battle: The Cultural Politics of Victorian Anglo-Catholicism* (Nashville, TN: Vanderbilt University Press, 1996).

20 PHL: SSC papers, Ch 71/A8, Mackonochie, Master's Address, May 1866, p. 6.

21 Ibid., *Acta* of June chapter, 1877 p. 6.

22 Ibid., Mackonochie, Master's Address, May 1868, p. 8. For all that Mackonochie insisted that reunion was an essential part of the aims of the Society he was surprisingly critical of Rome, especially after the definitions of Vatican I. He reserved some of his harshest words for brethren of SSC who became Roman Catholics. In 1868 Francis Wyndham, one of Lowder's fellow missioners in Wapping, and the secretary of SSC, went to visit a sick aunt in Kensington and never returned. Two of his fellow assistant priests joined him, one of whom, George Akers, withdrew the £4,000

he had planned to donate towards erecting a new parish. Mack-onochie praised Wyndham's hard work for the Society, but the final paragraph would have given him little comfort:

> We could bear the hatred of the world, and even the cow-ardice of our leaders, if only the line itself were firm. But alas! we know not when or where treachery may lie hid. The Priest who gives us Communion to-day may to-morrow tell us that for months he had been convinced that it was all a sham. If the very elements of the army be thus disorganised, who shall order the battle?

See L.E. Ellsworth, *Charles Lowder and the Ritualist Movement* (London: Darton, Longman & Todd, 1982), pp. 86ff.
23 PHL: SSC papers, Ch 71/A8, Mackonochie, Master's Address, May 1868, p. 6.
24 Mackonochie was firmly in favour of disestablishment. 'Church and State are a clog around the neck of each ... such a union always has had and always will have, God's curse upon it', pro-ceedings of May 1871 synod, p. 14. See below.
25 PHL: SSC papers, Ch 71/A8, Mackonochie, Master's Address, May 1870, pp. 7ff.
26 Ibid., p. 8.
27 Ibid., p. 4.
28 See J. Wickham Legg, *English Church Life from the Restoration to the Tractarian Movement: Considered in some of its Neglected or Forgotten Features* (London: Longmans, Green, 1914), pp. 252–80.
29 Cited by Desmond Morse-Boycott, *They Shine Like Stars* (London: Skeffington, 1947), p. 197. Confession has not entirely lost its capacity to excite strong opposition. The first website that the words 'The Priest in Absolution' offer the internet surfer via the Google search engine (in January 2005) is www.ianpaisley.org, which quotes a fiercely anti-confession tract by L. Atherton. The Anglo-Catholic father-confessor's vade mecum, *The Priest in Absolution*, was so exposed in the House of Lords that the then Archbishop of Canterbury denounced the book as 'a disgrace to the community'.

30 The long and detailed story of *The Priest in Absolution* affair is told in detail in Embry, *The Catholic Movement and the Society of the Holy Cross*, pp. 106–27, concisely in Ellsworth, *Charles Lowder and the Ritualist Movement*, pp. 138ff. and in a colourfully antagonistic way in William Walsh, *The Secret History of the Oxford Movement* (London: Swan Sonnenschein, 1897), pp. 93ff.

31 PHL: SSC papers, Ch 71/A8, Mackonochie, Master's Address, May 1866, p. 5.

32 Pusey's translation of the Abbé Gaume's manual was not published until 1878.

33 PHL: SSC papers, Ch 71/A8, Mackonochie, Master's Address, May 1867, p. 3.

34 Ibid., May 1866, p. 4.

35 Ibid., analysis of proceedings of May synod 1870, p. 1.

36 E.B. Pusey (trans), *Advice for those who Exercise the Ministry of Reconciliation through Confession and Absolution, being the Abbé Gaume's Manual for Confessors . . . adapted to the use of the English Church* (Oxford: Parker, 1878).

37 Francis George Belton, *A Manual for Confessors* (London: W. Knott, 1916).

38 Mackonochie was to face further prosecutions in 1875 and 1882.

39 PHL: SSC papers, Ch 71/A8, analysis of proceedings of May synod 1871, p. 4.

40 Ibid., p. 9.

41 Quoted by Ellsworth in *Charles Lowder and the Ritualist Movement*, p. 119.

42 PHL: SSC papers, Ch 71/A8, analysis of proceedings of May synod 1873, p. 9.

43 Ibid., *Acta* of July chapter 1873, p. 2.

44 Ibid., p. 2.

45 Ibid., p. 1.

46 See H.P. Liddon, *The Life of E.B. Pusey*, Vol. 4, (London: Longman, Green, 1898), pp. 261–70 for this account. See also Ellsworth, *Charles Lowder and the Ritualist Movement*, pp. 117ff.

47 PHL: SSC papers, Ch 71/A8, *Acta* of January chapter 1874, p. 1.

48 See, for example, John Betjeman's description of the importance for his faith of 'the things/That hearty middle-stumpers most

despise/As "all the inessentials of the Faith" ', in *Summoned by Bells* (London: John Murray, 1960).

49 PHL: SSC papers, Ch 71/A8, Mackonochie, Master's Address, May synod 1874, p. 7.

50 It is a safe assumption that many of Mackonochie's SSC would have enjoyed singing the later verse in the Walsingham Pilgrim Hymn, 'And this realm which had once been Our Lady's own Dower/Had its Church now enslaved by the secular power'. They might even have added the irreverent student chorus, 'Still is, still is, still is, still is'.

51 PHL: SSC papers, Ch71/A8, proceedings of May synod, 1876, p. 8.

52 Ibid., p. 16.

53 Ibid., *Acta* of chapter, June 1875, p. 4.

54 Ibid., proceedings of September synod, 1874.

55 Ellsworth, *Charles Lowder and the Ritualist Movement*, p. 137.

56 PHL: SSC papers, Ch 71/A8, Jackson to Bagshawe, 15 June 1877.

57 Ibid., Bagshawe to Jackson, 15 June 1877.

58 Ibid., Mackonochie, *Acta* of special chapter, July 1877, p. 3.

59 Ibid., proceedings of synod, September 1877, p. 4.

60 A second, linked proposal, dealt with the way in which the Society's finances would be wound up.

61 Ibid., p. 10.

62 Ibid., p. 12.

63 Ibid., *Acta* of chapter, October 1877, p. 3.

64 Bagshawe's health did not improve and he died in August 1879. By this date he had resigned not only as Master but from the Society. The August chapter sent its sympathy to his mother and, unusually, resolved that his name should be added to the list of departed brethren printed with the roll. In future years it was printed on that page in a box by itself.

65 Ibid., proceedings of synod, May 1878, p. 1.

66 Ibid., Bagshawe, Master's Address, May 1878, p. 7.

67 Ibid., Carter, Master's Address, May 1879, pp. 7ff.

68 Reed, Glorious Battle, p. 86.

69 Ibid., p. 86.

70 Ibid., p. 88.
71 This represents fewer than one priest in 40. In the late 1980s when membership was at its numerical height, the SSC could claim roughly one Anglican priest in ten.
72 Ibid., p. 88.
73 Embry, *The Catholic Movement and the Society of the Holy Cross*, p. 95.
74 PHL: SSC papers, Ch 71/Z1, a substantial bound volume of tracts produced during this period.
75 The most interesting collection of papers relating to the history of the OCR is found in the Ollard papers at Pusey House. See H.R.T. Brandreth, *The Oecumenical Ideals of the Oxford Movement* (London: SPCK, 1947), pp. 69ff. and H.R.T. Brandreth, *Dr Lee of Lambeth* (London: SPCK, 1951), pp. 118–45.
76 PHL: SSC papers, Ch 71/A8, *Acta* of chapter, January 1881, p. 7.
77 Ibid., proceedings of synod, September 1881, pp. 10ff.
78 Ibid., Mackonochie, Master's Address, May synod, 1882, p. 5.
79 Ibid., Nihill, Master's Address, May synod, 1885, p. 16. Embry, perhaps embarrassed by this, skates over this whole incident in a few confused paragraphs. See Embry, *The Catholic Movement and the Society of the Holy Cross*, pp. 161ff.
80 PHL: SSC papers, Ch 71/A11, Wood, *Acta* of chapter, January 1888, p. 5.
81 See Embry, *The Catholic Movement and the Society of the Holy Cross*, pp. 204ff.
82 *Lux Mundi: A Series of Studies in the Religion of the Incarnation* (London: John Murray, 1889) was a volume of essays edited by Charles Gore (1853–1932), founder of the Community of the Resurrection. Gore and his fellow contributors saw divine revelation as progressive and accepted the findings of biblical criticism so far as the Old Testament was concerned.
83 See Christopher Hill and Edward Yarnold (eds), *Anglican Orders: The Documents in the Debate*, (Norwich: Canterbury Press, 1997).
84 When the Archbishop of Canterbury pronounced against them, some priests gave them up, others ignored him and a third group, in defiance, used his condemnation as an opportunity to introduce them into their parishes.

Charles Lowder, Founder of the Society of the Holy Cross
(St Peter's, London Docks)

Dr Edward Bouverie Pusey
The bust of Dr Pusey by George Richmond
(The Principal & Chapter, Pusey House, Oxford)

Alexander Heriot Mackonochie
(The Hall Collection: The Principal & Chapter, Pusey House, Oxford)

Alexander Heriot Mackonochie with his clergy. On the right is Fr Wainwright
whose SSC Cross is visible.
(The Hall Collection: The Principal & Chapter, Pusey House, Oxford)

Alfred Poole, one of the original six members of the Society.
(The Hall Collection: The Principal & Chapter, Pusey House, Oxford)

Father David Houlding, Master of the Society, welcomes Dr Rowan Williams,
Archbishop of Canterbury, to the 150th Anniversary Theological
Conference, April 2005
(Stephen Parkinson)

The Rt Revd Keith Newton, Bishop of Richborough, preaching to the
International Synod of the Society, St Alban's Holborn, April 2005
(Stephen Parkinson)

International Synod, St Alban's Holborn, April 2005
(Stephen Parkinson)

Society Pilgrimage to the Shrine of Our Lady of Walsingham, April 2005
(Stephen Parkinson)

85 Cited by Embry, *The Catholic Movement and the Society of the Holy Cross*, p. 336.

86 Ibid., p. 336.

87 B.H. Streeter (ed.), *Foundations: a Statement of Christian Belief in Terms of Modern Thought, by Seven Oxford Men* (London: Macmillan, 1912). Streeter *et al.* accepted the findings of different criticism so far as the New Testament was concerned. Their empirical approach upset the traditionalists.

88 R.A. Knox, *Some Loose Stones* (London: Longman, Green, 1913); *Absolute and Abitofhell* (London: Society of SS Peter and Paul, 1912).

7

The winds of change: 1914–45

Luke Miller

'I recall, as others will, the solemn requiem in this church in 1878 on the death of Pius IX', said Fr Irving, Master of the Society, at the synod held in late August 1914, at St Peter's, London Docks, after the death of St Pius X. 'In some ways we seemed nearer to the Holy See then than we do now.'[1] There was a sense of the old order passing. The First World War was but days old; the world stood on the brink of immense changes. It was a time of 'unsettlement' in society and in the Church. Already, at the main synod of the year in May 1914, Fr Ommaney had suggested three great sources of 'unsettlement'. Schismatics were under certain circumstances to be allowed Holy Communion in Anglican churches; there was 'tolerance of priests denying the great facts of true religion', and the bishops were not driving away erroneous doctrines. These might seem at first to be small concerns in the face of the cataclysm of world events, but the Society was nothing if not focused on its mission to foster and uphold Catholic faith and discipline, practice and order in the Church of England.

For the Society these years of war and the changes it brought were difficult. Men brought up to the idea of revealed truth and inflexible principle were faced with a world which challenged truth and demanded new responses to new situations. There was an air of constant crisis in their meetings and discussions. As pastors in society they faced the need to respond to the circumstances of war and a difficult peace; as priests of the Church of England, they were faced with the proposed revision of the Prayer Book, and the response to both modernism and questioning biblical criticism; as priests of the universal Catholic Church they were required to consider their ecclesiology in the light of the Lambeth Conferences, and the newborn ecumenical movement.

Meanwhile the Society generated its own internal debates. Membership remained small (between 100–200 members), and it was secret. From the records which survive it would appear that three or four figures seem to have dominated the life of the Society at this time. There was a serious attempt to close membership to married men; the statutes were revised, and finances overhauled.

The Catholic movement had been a great success; but the very success of the movement and the concomitant broadening of opinion and variety of commitment among those calling themselves 'Catholic' in the Church of England led the brethren of the SSC to question some aspects of 'Anglo-Catholicism' itself.

The pattern of the Society's year is revealed in the printed copies of *Acta* which survive. There was through most of the period a main synod in May. This opened with a Mass for the 70 or so who attended, followed by a devotional address and the Master's Address to synod. The Master would resign, and elections would be held. Always in these years these elections were contested, usually with three or four candidates, but every Master elected served a full three-year term of office unless he had made clear previously at the short chapter held in March to plan the May synod that he did not wish to stand. Following the election of other officers there was a break for lunch and the business of the synod began with the reading and debating of papers on a specific subject for the rest of the day and the bulk of the day following. At the end of the second day there was a time for brethren to bring specific questions to inform their pastoral practice before synod closed. In July, August and November and or December there were shorter one-day meetings at which papers were read and business conducted. At either the November or December synod there was a much more substantial paper.

The paucity of surviving records for this period makes it difficult to gauge the life of the Society outside these main gatherings. Local chapters and synods were held in a variety of places around the country. Apart from the main gatherings in May and November these were attended by only small numbers of priests, on average as few as ten or eleven were present.[2]

In 1931 the Revd J. Embry published *The Catholic Movement and the SSC*.[3] The bulk of the book deals with the period before the First World War, though the penultimate chapter takes the story up to 1928. As a source for our period it is as remarkable for its omissions as for its contents. Fr Embry provides short biographies of brethren in the notes of the year of their deaths and lists of the Masters and officers of the Society. His is a work of record. Nevertheless, his style is engaging: discussing the proposed 1928 funeral service, Embry is pleased to see provision made for cremations, for the old book 'belonged to an age when cremation was considered a greater Christian act when practised on a living body than a dead one'.

Chapters and synods began always with a devotional address, whose content was carefully minuted. These addresses were often of very good quality. It is important in all the discussion of politics internal and external to the Society that the heart of every meeting was devotional. The brethren came together to pray with one another and to learn from one another how better to pray. They would discuss the devotional addresses and consider carefully their content and application. The whole of the May synod in 1925, at the height of the Prayer Book controversy, was given over to 'Devotion', the subjects of papers including: The History of Devotion; The Theology of Devotion; Original Sin and the Immaculate Conception; Our Lady's Share in Redemption; Practical Devotion; The Rosary.

None of these papers dwelt on the Passion of Our Lord. Despite its name, it is not clear that the Society of the Holy Cross fostered any particular devotion. As Master Fr Alban

Baverstock proposed the revision of the statutes on the basis that the Society promoted 'Priestly ideals' and *fraterna caritas*.[4] Three years later, however, he spoke of his 'deep devotion to the Holy Cross',[5] but this seems to be the exception in the records. While there is in the papers and devotions a constant concern for Catholicism, there is nothing particular about a devotion to the Holy Cross. In so far as there was a focus it was on the priesthood and its exercise: 'The priest is not to be a man of the world, but a man of God, God's man'.[6]

The brethren were hard-working parish priests meeting at a time when the Anglo-Catholic parish was understood to be the most effective missionary organization possessed by the Church of England.[7] In February 1914, in the context of a discussion of the best forms of altar bread to use (there being a debate whether the high starch content of wafers meant that they could properly be used for 'bread'), Fr Francis Belton explained that 'In my church there are about 6,000 Communions per annum'.[8] At this time SSC clergy refused Holy Communion to anyone not both fasting and shriven, and monthly rather than weekly (and still less daily) Communion was the norm (though hearing Mass, of course, was at least a weekly obligation on Sundays). Assuming that members of the congregation made a monthly act of Holy Communion, 6,000 Communions a year works out at 500 communicant members of Fr Belton's parish.

The discussion about altar bread is an example of the way the meetings of the Society gave the brethren a chance to discuss their work and its methods. Between the wars there was a number of papers and discussions on the holy oils and their use. Numerous discussions were held about the introduction in their parishes of the Midnight Mass of Christmas. There was concern that the Mass should begin after midnight, worry that communicants should be fasting for at least six hours, and that priests, already often saying two Christmas Masses, might end up saying three. The Master, Fr Irving, felt in the end that the whole business was a corrupt Roman Catholic practice better avoided.[9] Brethren asked questions about the translations of the creeds and brought pastoral questions to chapter for advice. The committee set up in earlier days to give specific guidance in issues arising from the confessional was, however, by this time defunct.

Synod was also sometimes given over to these practical questions. In May 1930, during the Lambeth Conference which moved the question of the Church of South India forward another notch, the Society gave extensive study time to work among children, with papers on Child Psychology; the Child's confession; the Child at Communion; the Child at Benediction; and a paper on the catechism. In 1942 the nascent Education Bill (to become the 1944 Education Act) was discussed. At the other end of life the same synod of May 1942 discussed cremation and the ministry to those who brought their dead not to church but to the municipal crematorium.

The 31 years from 1914 to 1945 were filled with events to which the Society had to respond, and in some of which it participated. Directly the First World War was over, the Lambeth Conference of 1920 brought to a head a number of ecclesiological issues that had already been exercising the brethren before and during the conflict. The 1920s were dominated by the struggles over the revised Prayer Book, but this was also the time of the Anglo-Catholic Congresses and the Life and Liberty movement, which led to the establishment of the General Assembly and parochial church councils. Modernism had been an issue before, but through the late 1920s and 1930s there were questions for the Society over the study of Scripture and the 'heresy' of Bishop Barnes of Birmingham.[10] Ecclesiological issues again came to the fore with the scheme for union with the Church of South India. During the Second World War there was an attempt to deal with what was called 'Church reform', the restructuring of the Church to deal with new circumstances.

Bishop Frank Weston of Zanzibar, a member of the Society, had caused a crisis in the Anglican Church in 1914. The Bishops of Uganda and Mombasa had gathered a meeting of Christian missionaries of all denominations (except Roman Catholic) in Kikuyu, East Africa, in June 1913.[11] Weston, however, was not invited. The meeting sought to develop a scheme which would allow African converts to ignore denominational differences if they moved between districts. It was a vision of a pan-Protestant church, but it was based on fudging doctrine and lowering the standard of ecclesial discipline to a bare minimum. At the end of the meeting Holy Communion was celebrated by the Anglican bishops and all the delegates except those from the Society of Friends were communicated. Bishop Weston protested to the Archbishop of Canterbury in the strongest terms. He sent an open letter to the Bishop of St Alban's, and when he came home in February 1914 there was a national ferment in ecclesiastical circles. Archbishop Randall Davidson was forced to intervene and the scheme was dropped.[12]

At home Weston's brethren in the Society were as shocked as he had been and offered him their support when he attended the February 1914 synod on his arrival. The dispute is largely forgotten now. The following year there was another conference at Kikuyu at which Weston was present, and the movement fizzled out as it became apparent that such a watered-down form of Christianity was not anyway attractive in the mission-field. But Kikuyu was the opening salvo in an ecclesiological battle which was to rage through the Lambeth Conferences of 1920 and 1930 and on to the South India debates of the 1940s.

Moreover, the Bishop of Zanzibar in his response to the Kikuyu Conference demonstrated the view that principle is far more important than pragmatism; an attitude that was to characterize the Society and its members in the other debates which lay ahead. In a pamphlet produced at the Archbishop of Canterbury's request for the committee of the Lambeth Conference in June 1914 Weston wrote:

> Easier were it to receive in brotherly love all who seek fellowship with us, honouring their principles as we honour their lives and labours. But He Who came to send a sword upon the earth will not have it so. Rather must we drink of His cup, and true to principle however unpopular and seemingly destined to bring

failure in its train, we must be content to become the scorn of men and the outcasts of the people.

For, whatever else may be said about reunion and the methods of attaining it, one thing is above all else true: without principle we shall accomplish nothing. And since the movement that produced the Kikuyu Conference is evidently at fault in the matter of principles, it is necessary to move backwards and return to prayer and study. Such a move backward is no loss: so to move along a wrong road is no gain.[13]

The ecclesiological debate was by no means over. When the Lambeth Conference finally met after the war in 1920 Archbishop Cosmo Gordon Lang brought forward his call to reunion. There was much debate behind the scenes, but the eventual support offered by the Bishop of Zanzibar to the resolution saved the 'Appeal to all Christian People'.[14]

That support was not total, however, and the Society as a whole was not as convinced as Weston. In July 1920 Frank Weston spoke to synod on the 'Appeal'. The Master, Fr Irving, responded. He felt that the 'Appeal' made use of an inadequate definition of the Church, and as a result merely looked to 'a big Pan-Protestant Federation or Fusion of Sects agreeing to differ'.[15] This in fact had been Weston's criticism of the Kikuyu proposals. Again and again the Society articulated the clear understanding that the Church of England could and should not be understood as a 'self going concern'[16] but merely as a part of the Catholic Church with no right or ability to make doctrine or change discipline.

Frank Weston is perhaps best remembered for the great speech he gave at the Anglo-Catholic Congress of 1923.[17] He was chairman of the Congress, and his work for it was much more profound and much greater than simply giving a well-turned peroration at its conclusion. The famous passage is from the end, when he told the 16,000 delegates:

> When you come out from before your tabernacles, you must walk with Christ, mystically present in you, through the streets of this country and find the same Christ in the peoples of your cities and

your villages. You cannot claim to worship Jesus in the tabernacle if you do not pity Jesus in the slum.

But this was not the whole speech. He spoke of Jesus as having leaped 'from the Father's throne across the gulf which separates Creator from Creation' and called his hearers to try to sympathize with others different from themselves: 'if God leaped a gulf for you, you can leap gulfs for God'. Then he spoke to his brethren in the priesthood when he said that 'Priesthood implies a strictness and a sternness in the following of Christ that is sometimes sadly to seek.' He asked the young for their vocations: 'What would you sacrifice to the naked Christ?' and of parents he asked, 'Can you give Jesus some of the joy that He has given to you? Dedicate your children'.

At the time and subsequently Anglo-Catholics have been delighted with this call to commitment and zeal. Weston's friend and biographer understands him as having been in full support of the Congress at least from his accepting the chair in May 1923. In the *Acta* of the Society of the Holy Cross, however, a different picture emerges. The Society and its members were ambivalent to say the least. Already in May 1920 the Master, Fr Irving, had spoken about his experience at the first Anglo-Catholic Congress 'offering high tribute to the executive, and in which he spoke enthusiastically... but ventured on some friendly criticism'.[18] Weston would have been aware of this ambivalence. At the SSC's May synod in 1923 (before Weston landed from Zanzibar) a resolution had been passed asking the Congress organizers not to begin the Congress with a service in St Paul's Cathedral (the Bishop of London was the Patron of the Congress) unless it was a Mass with incense. At the synod in October 1923 this rather petulant criticism was followed after the event by a full-scale discussion of the Anglo-Catholic Congresses as a whole. The fundamental criticism was that they were 'big gatherings with little or no spiritual result. The method of Congresses is not useful to evangelize the nation ... surely it is just about impressing the Bishops?'[19]

There were criticisms also of the Congress's failure to

examine its publications, some of which were believed by Canon Wood, who made a speech explaining what he saw as the Congress's failures, to contain theological error. Wood felt that the Congress was not clear in its ecclesiology, having sent addresses to various Primates (including one at Weston's instigation to the Holy Father at Rome) but not via the Metropolitan of the province where it had met. There was clearly a feeling that the Congress was more than a little about show and not enough about sacrifice and action. Wood was shocked that 'the priest who was first and foremost in the movement should have subsequently married a widow'. This was at the time a breach of the discipline expected of a Catholic priest in the Church of England, and was totemic for the synod of the view that the Congress was outward pomp and no inward reality.

As a result of these concerns and reservations the SSC synod passed *nem.con.*, a resolution which 'Regrets the use of the term "Anglo-Catholic" in connection with the recent Congress Movement'.

There was similar disgust amongst the brethren at the one concrete result of the Congress: a proposal for a pilgrimage to the Holy Land. Fr Taglis 'could appreciate the privilege of seeing the Holy Places and he could appreciate the cultus of the relics of the saints, but what is there in prayer in the Holy Land that cannot be obtained before the Tabernacle?'

Writing a decade or so later, Fr Embry gives the Anglo-Catholic Congress just one paragraph in his book, noting that 'as individuals' priests of the SSC 'have taken part in the Anglo catholic Congress, and some of them are on its Committee'.[20] The euphoria and the excitement, however, passed him by. There was no mention of the Anglo-Catholic priests' conventions of the 1930s in *Acta* or in Fr Embry's book. The SSC was at the least disengaged from the movement, and at times downright disapproving.

Perhaps we might also wonder whether the Bishop of Zanzibar did not share some of his brothers' concern. His great speech was a call to arms and a paean against complacency and outward form. He did not speak only of adoration, but also of suffering:

> Ideally we move in an atmosphere of self-sacrificing obedience. Ideally as I set out to go to the Altar of God, I step out in definite obedience to offer the sacrifice of Christ's obedience. I ask you, in the ordinary English parish church, how much obedience is there?... there is a sort of air of softness – yet He calls you. What does it matter if you get a headache when you are representing Calvary before the Father? Do you want to feel especially well and buoyant as you come from the contemplation of Christ on Calvary? Brethren, you know you don't![21]

Here is the spirituality of the Cross, and it was that, not a call to social action, which lay at the heart of Weston's speech and of his ministry. It was at the heart of his speech because it was the heart of his ministry. This is what the SSC nurtured in him and approved.

Frank Weston is not a figure widely remembered today, but for his great speech, while his work is sadly largely forgotten outside Africa. Alfred Hope Patten, however, was another member of the Society whose work at Walsingham is appreciated and remembered and whose Pilgrim Hymn is known with affection, despite its infelicities of rhyme and metre. He was in tune with the attitude of the Society both in his own time and the generation before when he wrote in that hymn, 'Her church was enslaved to the Secular Power'.

This is not to say that the brethren necessarily thought that disestablishment was the best way to achieve freedom for the English Church. The complexity of the position is illuminated by the Society's opposition to those who, in the interwar years sought to assert some ecclesiastical control over the Church's liturgy by proposing a revision of the 1662 Book of Common Prayer and over the Church's government through the establishment of the General Assembly.

The 1662 Book of Common Prayer was believed by the SSC to be inadequate. The structure of the liturgy had faults; the provision in the Kalendar for saints' days and festivals was poor, and the eucharistic canon lacked sacrificial terminology.[22] For all its faults, however, the 1662 Prayer Book had the benefit of having being imposed by that same 'Secular Power' of which Fr Hope Patten's hymn spoke in such frustrated terms. In synod in June 1924 the point was made that the 'Book of Common Prayer is acceptable because, though not good enough, it has been forced on us by the Civil Power. The Revised Book would be the Church's Book'.

Once the Church of England herself had decided on her own book, there could be no excuse or explanation of its failings; it was essential therefore that a Catholic Church adopt a Catholic book – or she would finally have proven herself to be not Catholic. Today the inadequacies of the Common Worship book may perhaps be accepted because the Book of Common Prayer remains normative for doctrine and worship; in 1928 no retention of the 1662 Prayer Book was contemplated. Prayer Book revision was to the fathers of the SSC a matter of the first importance; reflecting not merely an interest in liturgy but a statement of the very nature of the Church of England herself. Their position within that church was in jeopardy. No wonder they discussed the issue in such detail and watched with concern as events took their course, attempting to intervene when they could.[23]

Although there are well-known cases of use of the Latin rite, and though use of the Gelasian canon (silently and in addition to the Prayer Book canon) was widespread, and though the ritual forms of the liturgy were elaborate, these were priests who used the 1662 Book of Common Prayer in their parishes. It will be remembered that despite all the additions the English Missal prints the Mass in the 1662 form. Loyalty to the Prayer Book was a living reality for these priests. There was much debate for instance as to whether Mass at the beginning of synod should be said in Latin, but this was not a discussion of use of the Roman rite, but of the rubric in the 1662 Prayer Book stipulating that the liturgy be celebrated 'in a language understood of the people', and the case advanced made much of the Latin (Book of Common Prayer) Mass said in the University Church at Oxford at the beginning of full term.[24]

This loyalty to the Prayer Book of 1662 is seen in the response of the brethren to the Revised Prayer Book as it finally emerged in 1927. Their criticisms had been considered as the debates had rumbled on over the preceding decade, and by the time of the final deposition they were implacably opposed.

In some respects the new book met their requirements. The liturgy was rearranged, and the Kalendar was revised, though as Fr Embry pointed out, the ancient feast of the Assumption was omitted, while 'Some of her late medieval titles were included'.[25] Other omissions were regretted: 'It seems that the moldering pen which had erased the great name of St Thomas of Canterbury from the English calendar was still held stiffly in the dead hand of King Henry VIII'.[26]

More seriously, however, the new book presaged alterations which brethren felt the English Church had no right to make on her own to the liturgy of the West. As early as May 1915 the Master, who was a fine liturgical scholar, was worried that 'the master touch of disaster' had come in the provision making the Athanasian Creed optional: 'In other words, it might be omitted from public use altogether'. He was right of course, it has been; and this concern is not one of an ultramontane who is interested only in the Roman rite.[27]

In 1927, just before the book was brought to Convocation, the synod of the SSC adduced four serious criticisms. The new Prayer Book showed Nestorian tendencies;[28] the structure of the liturgy was still flawed; reservation of the Blessed Sacrament for adoration was ruled out; and the confirmation service seemed to allow an open altar – exactly what Bishop Weston had protested with such force twelve years before. A resolution was passed. The new Prayer Book was condemned as 'Heretical in tendency, subversive of catholic constitutional principles and mischievous in the highest degree, [the SSC] advises priests without hesitation or qualification to refuse acceptance of it'.[29]

The resolution appeared in the *Daily Telegraph* and caused a stir. In its preface the resolution had stated that it was passed 'by the Society of the Holy Cross in synod, representing nearly two hundred priests'. There were in fact about 60 brothers present and voting. The local chapter of St Wilfred wrote to the next synod to disassociate itself from the resolution, while in Liverpool the local chapter passed a further resolution in support of what had been said. Many more moderate Catholics supported the new book, but others agreed with the SSC. The resolution was clearly influential in highlighting Catholic opposition to the new Prayer Book.[30] The learned, well-informed discussion at synod, and the strong expression of the resultant opposition, did much to sway opinion in parliament and more widely in the Church of England against the book.

The SSC was not, however, unaffected by the winds of change. Voices in the debate had said that if the new book were to be agreed it could not be forced on priests. Fr Embry spoke in that same synod of May 1927 to ask: 'Shall we be bound if the Deposited Book is given communal sanction? The real fact is that no present English Book binds us now, save that we may be held to have individually assented to it.' Loyalty to the Book of Common Prayer was beginning to wear thin.

This was not true only of the fathers of the SSC. After the 1928 Prayer Book was rejected, some bishops gave permission for it to be used any way. In London, where SSC was strongest, Bishop Winington-Ingram told the diocesan conference that if the parochial church council agreed the new canon could be brought into use.[31]

Parochial church councils were new. Before the First World War the diocesan quota had been introduced, and synod had noted the development with disapproval. As the laity were asked to pay for their churches in a new way, so there was a move to involve them more in the management of the parish. This was coupled with a desire, only strengthened by the experience of seeing the 1928 Prayer Book thrown out by parliament, to achieve for the Church more freedom in the conduct of her internal affairs.

The PCC was the first, and perhaps most helpful, fruit of the Life and Liberty movement, most of whose other legacies have, as the brethren of the Society feared they would at the time, had a deleterious effect on the church they aimed to support.

For of the desire for self-government came not merely the PCC, but also the 'National Assembly', later the 'Church Assembly', from which has developed the structure of synods at General, Diocesan and Deanery level we know today.

The problem for Catholics has always been to understand, restrict and define the competence of such bodies so that they have no authority over teaching and doctrine. That in turn requires agreement of what is an issue of doctrine or teaching and what is an administrative matter. The development of the General Synod into a doctrine-making (and unmaking) body was anticipated by the SSC as early as the passing of the Enabling Act establishing the National Assembly and PCCs in 1920. In that year Fr Irving, Master of the Society, told the May synod that 'The Enabling Act and National Assembly represent the practical overthrow of the methods of government in Christ's Kingdom'.[32]

For Fr Irving, and for the Society, the Church was not a secular institution requiring a means of government, but a supernatural body whose Lord directs and guides her through Scripture and the Holy Spirit. This guidance is mediated through sacramental grace, especially in the gift of episcope or authority vested in the bishops through the sacrament of Holy Order.

The value of the PCC, at first rejected as contrary to this vision, came to be seen, at least by some in the Society. Collaborating with, but chaired by the parish priest, the PCC came to be appreciated. Fr Kirtland told the second day of synod in that same May of 1920 that he was working well with his PCC, though he reserved to himself all matters of doctrine and ceremonial. It was – and is when it functions well – a model of support for and cooperation with the grace of episcope locally exercised by the parish priest. This is not to say though that there was not some reserve about the PCC. In July 1942 synod heard criticisms of PCCs which it was felt were exerting too much influence over areas of parish life which should be reserved to the parish priest.[33] National Assembly, and latterly Church Assembly failed to establish the same pattern with the bishops, and from them has developed the parliamentary model we see today in General Synod.

Above all the SSC resisted in these years any tendency or action which established or expressed the idea that 'The Church of England is a self-going concern'[34] as opposed to being an obedient part of the Western Holy Catholic Church. As Bishop Weston would have emphasized, the Catholic faith is not just about theory – it is as much about practice. Weston, as we have seen, set a demanding standard for himself and for others. Standing in the shadow of the Cross, how could he accept second best as an adequate response to the enormity of Christ's love for us? In their teaching and practice the brothers of the Society of the Holy Cross were rigorous in their demand for obedience to the disciplines of the Western Church, often more rigorous than others in the Catholic movement in the Church of England.

In November 1915 one of the brethren raised for discussion a pastoral issue that had arisen. A woman, not normally a member of his congregation, had approached him before the 9 a.m. Mass to ask to make her communion. Her own parish priest, a member of the Confraternity of the Blessed Sacrament, had given her permission on account of her weak constitution to have a cup of tea at 6 a.m. and told her this should not bar her from Communion at 9 a.m. The SSC priest had contradicted her own parish priest and refused her Communion: he asked the brethren what their view was.

The discussion was wide-ranging. A rumour that French soldiers at the front had been in certain circumstances dispensed from the eucharistic fast was discussed and found in fact not to be true. By and large brethren agreed that to communicate someone, even a soldier in danger of death, who was not fasting for at least eight hours was wrong. There was one voice which gave a more moderate view: 'If the sustenance makes it *possible* for the person to get up and go to the altar, does it not seem much more fitting they should do so than remain in bed only to get up after reception [of sick communion]?'[35] The CBS Priest who had allowed his communicant a cup of tea would surely have said yes!

The matter of the marriage of the clergy was another in which the Society was divided in its view. All agreed that for a priest to marry a widow was contrary to Catholic discipline.[36] There was also a feeling that, following the Orthodox discipline, while a married man might be ordained, one who was ordained should not contract a marriage. This was not however enshrined in the Rule, which did stipulate that priests marrying a second time in contravention of the injunction in 1 Timothy 3 should be asked to resign.

For some years Fr Ommaney had been attempting to move the Society definitely in the direction of celibacy. He was elected Master in May 1916 and at once sought to put his programme into action. At the November 1916 synod he publicly deprecated clergy marrying a second time and after ordination. He announced that he had asked a Brother to leave the Society who had contracted a second marriage, something he did again with three brothers before the May 1917 synod. At this latter synod he sought to extend the roll which was maintained of celibate priests, and to encourage the younger men to make a vow of celibacy.

In May 1918 Ommaney returned to his theme. The SSC has often, he said, been called 'a society of celibate priests who often get married'. A priest, he continued, who has to concern himself with wife and family cannot be fully dedicated. A proposal was brought to synod that no priest could marry after joining the Society and remain a member, and this was carried.

In September of that year Ommaney tried to take the Society further. A motion was proposed by Canon Lay to make the SSC a society of celibates. In the debate that followed, Canon Wood pointed out that six of the first members of the Society had been married men; Fr Wainwright, Lowder's successor at London Docks, spoke against the motion. It was lost by 25 votes to 23. In May 1919 Ommaney's three-year term of office came to an end. He spoke to synod as he relinquished his office, looking forward to the celibacy of the Society.

This though was not the end of the matter. Ommaney was succeeded by Fr Irving, who let the matter lie. Then in 1922 Fr

Alban Baverstock was elected Master. He sought to revise the Rule. Mainly he wished for less frequent chapters, which would then, he hoped, be better attended by clergy who had many meetings to go to, and he wished for these to be more focused on the Society's 'primary purpose, the cultivation of sacerdotal holiness'.[37] Baverstock also sought to put the Society's finances on a sounder footing, and to invert the principle whereby everything at chapter and synod was treated as a secret unless explicitly made public so that everything could be considered public unless specifically said to be confidential.

Fr Ommaney, however, seized the opportunity offered by the revision to reopen the celibacy question. Baverstock had voted for his proposals, and could hardly object when Ommaney brought them forward again as amendments to the new Rule in May 1922. The proposal was that married men should 'die out' from the Society, though Baverstock thought that if the statutes were changed most married men would seek to leave immediately. The Master called for a referendum of the whole Society (rather than simply a vote of those present in synod) so that an 'undeniable majority' should be obtained for any change. The results of the three questions put to the Society were announced in September 1922. The status quo, 'That there should be no restrictions except that brethren who marry a second time should be asked to leave, and a separate celibate roll would be maintained', received 44 votes. Twenty-four brethren voted for a system which would in addition to the current rules have forbidden anyone, being already a brother, to contract a first marriage.[38] The proposal not to admit any more married priests received nine votes; not to admit married priests unless they had married before ordination attracted seven votes, while eighteen brethren voted to make the Society immediately celibate. Those were the days before single transferable voting. The Master proposed to synod that the present rules be maintained, and this was passed *nem. con.*

None of this is narrated by Fr Embry. The protagonists were, as he wrote, still alive, and the wounds may have been sore. It seems clear that the 200 or so members of the SSC ran the risk of seeing it become a very small and extreme group on the edge of the Catholic movement. It would have been the Society as a whole which would have 'died out', not simply the married men from its ranks. Baverstock, who had some sympathy with Ommaney, must take much of the credit that it did not. He managed, by splitting the question into many options, and calling for a plebiscite, to make it very unlikely that Ommaney's position would be accepted. The matter was dropped and not raised again. SSC moved forward.

A sign of the transition to a stance which while no less principled than of old was yet open to new thought is the way the tone of debates about modern theology and biblical criticism shifted between 1914 and 1945.

At the beginning of the period the modernist debate was filling the air and synod was discussing with horror *Foundations*, a series of essays edited by B.H. Streeter. The Master, Fr Irving, said that the crucial essay in the collection was that by the Revd William Temple, Chaplain to the Archbishop of Canterbury (and later, of course, himself Archbishop) which though good in part, contained 'stark naked heresy' when dealing with the divinity of Christ: 'The identity predicated of God in Christ consists only in a oneness of Will and purpose'.[39]

'Modernism' is applied by theologians to a specific theological school; for the brethren of the SSC the term applied – for all their learning and ability to deal with abstract ideas – to a wide range of new attitudes and ideas which they felt attacked or undermined the Catholic faith. In May 1929 Fr Kingdon was Master and Fr Baverstock addressed synod, criticizing Bishop Gore's biblical commentary published for the English Church Union as 'modernist'.[40] Baverstock asserted himself to be opposed to the Tübingen School of critical biblical studies, and called on the Society to witness against 'Anglo-Germanic' Christianity, which must be in opposition to Anglo-Catholic Christianity.[41] A motion was passed condemning the commentary for asserting that the Bible 'contains some parts we must believe and others we need not'. There were, however, other voices more willing to use critical scholarship. Fr C.E.

Douglas appears to have been more interested and open to the new methods than many of his brothers. Douglas responded to the debate at the next synod[42] with a paper dealing with these issues. It seems the brethren were either embarrassed or ill-equipped to deal with the argumentation. The minute reports: 'A very short and desultory discussion followed'.

A decade later Fr Embry gave a paper setting out the classic patristic and scholastic interpretations of Scripture: 'Literal; allegorical; tropological; anagogical'. He summed up his position in a splendid peroration: 'These things David sang, Isaiah preached, Zechariah heralded forth, Moses recorded, Justin Martyr taught'.[43] Fr Douglas, however, told the same meeting that, 'Anything in the results of Criticism is helpful which helps us to understand the writings of the New Testament'.[44]

Pope Leo XIII had encouraged a new approach to biblical studies in the Roman Catholic Church in the first years of the twentieth century; Pope Pius XII had continued to encourage the Pontifical Biblical Institute, and by 1939 the winds in Western Catholicism were blowing in the direction which would lead to the subsequent publication of the Jerome Biblical Commentary in the wake of the Second Vatican council. This was the beginning of the great flowering of modern Roman Catholic biblical scholarship. Within the Church of England's Catholic movement Bishop Gore had led the way, but despite the best efforts of Fr Douglas, many in SSC thought that he was dangerously ahead of the Western Church.

Despite this, the brethren did not turn away from the study of Scripture and retire into an Addulamite enclave. In 1938 and 1939 there were major debates on Scripture, that in 1939 following a paper on 'The witness of Scripture to the Doctrine of the Church'. The Society had chosen to turn outwards and engage with the 'Modern' world; unbending in principles, but prepared to listen, study and reapply the truth of Catholic doctrine to new situations.

There were plenty of new situations to face. Some were old ones in new forms. The question of the union of the Church of South India, a Presbyterian body which had no apostolic succession or ordained ministry, with the Anglican Church raised again similar questions as had been raised at Kikuyu. The question was raised in 1930, as the Lambeth Conference gave the scheme qualified approval (though it was not enacted until 1948). The SSC synod gave the matter long discussion, and debated the issue again in February 1944 as the Second World War hung in the balance. In October 1943 Fr Baverstock had spoken of the 'Present crisis' over the South India question, in a paper entitled, 'Jurisdiction, Schism and Heresy on Holy Order – Its Satanic Origins', and in May 1945 as the world celebrated VE day the Society again concerned itself with the scheme.

Inevitably the war itself called for consideration. In May 1940 the synod debated papers on 'The Christian Ethic of War'; 'The Moral Justification of this War'; and 'The Christian Basis of a New Peace'. During the war there was in the Church of England, as there was in the nation, a debate about the shape and nature of the institutions which should be established after the war. Beveridge was working on the report on social insurance that would lay the foundations of the welfare state, and plans were afoot for the nationalization of key industries and services. There was a concern that the mistake of the 1920s should not be repeated when the Homes fit for Heroes which were promised turned out to be homes in which only heroes could live. There was much talk in the last years of the war of 'Church Reform'. What shape should the postwar parish take? How should it be ordered and what roles should it share?

In May 1942 the SSC considered 'Catholics and Church Reform',[45] discussing parishes, churches and schools. How should finances be ordered and parishes administered? There was concern for the mode of appointing bishops, and a paper was given by a brother who was working full time in a crematorium. He explained the work and the way he interacted with the parochial clergy. Far the biggest concern was the 1944 Education Act, which brought church schools within the ambit of the local education authorities. In September there was a consideration of the balance between Church and State. There was in all of this opportunity to rebuild in new ways, but also a fear that big government (to use today's term for it) was coming to interfere in matters which were no concern of the 'secular power'.

There was a cloud the size of a man's hand on the horizon. The brothers of the SSC had been, along with the Catholic movement as a whole in the forefront of encouraging and nurturing the ministry of women in their parishes. Many had nuns working alongside them. Most would have had in post someone, often called a 'mission woman' to aid parochial visiting, especially of women and children. All had Sunday school teachers and catechists who were women. In May 1917[46] the SSC concerned itself with the 'Position of Women in the Church'. The positions taken were remarkably advanced. 'Three Proposals might be thought dangerous.' The first was that women be allowed to vote in church assemblies. Fr Ommaney said that suffrage should be allowed, for women had voted in vestry meetings and had been elected as churchwardens for centuries. Secondly, there could be no real danger in women teaching in the parish, and Ommaney even felt, (despite 1 Corinthians 14.34) that some preaching was legitimate. The third 'dangerous proposal' was that women might be admitted to Holy Orders. Ommaney was sanguine: 'This move can hardly be called dangerous. I cannot take it seriously. The conclusive answer is, "We have no such custom, neither have the churches of God"' (1 Corinthians 11.16).[47] He continued to say that women were not admitted to the apostolate, and not even those like abbesses or queens regnant who are invested with some of the vesture proper to Holy Order, and who have authority in the Church are admitted to Holy Order. The same view was expressed at the end of our period, when Fr C.E. Douglas said that women could be allowed to rule the Church, and to preach, but not to minister the sacraments.[48]

In May 1945, as Fr Kirtland began his second year as Master, the Church and the Society looked to the world in the wake of the Second World War. There was much to do, and despite much continuity there was also a clear break with the past. The world of Bishop Frank Weston was long gone, and new thinking and new attitudes were beginning to grow in the Society and in the universal Church. Already, just before the outbreak of war[49] the Society had discussed the liturgical movement. Soon the changes in attitudes and methods would be expressed in radical reshaping of the church buildings in which these priests spent such significant – in all senses of the word – parts of their time and ministry. The Second World War was much more destructive of church life and property especially in the urban areas where most SSC priests served, than the First World War had been. Historians have emphasized the changes wrought by the impact of that earlier conflict; the discontinuity, effected by the Second World War was, however, in some ways far greater.

In 1941 the theme of the synod was 'The Priest in Current Conditions'. Synod had been booked to meet in St Alban's, Holborn. The destruction of the church by German bombing was a powerful symbol of the passing of the old ways. The rebuilding would nevertheless be glorious, and glorious precisely because it retained and maintained so much of what had been there before:

One day a new St Alban's will rise in which the splendid work carried on to the very last day (one might truthfully say the very last minute) in the old one will be perpetuated, and a fresh and not less holy and fragrant shrine will stand where now the ashes of the old one are lying.[50]

Notes

1 PHL: Ch 71/A23, *Acta* August 1914.
2 There is in the archive at Pusey House a manuscript minute-book from the Chapter of St Thomas Aquinas in Cambridge for the years of the First World War; and there are lists of chapters in other parts of the country; but no record of these meetings has survived in the principal Society archive. The dedication to St Thomas Aquinas is significant. Pope Leo XIII had revitalized

Roman Catholic theology in the last quarter of the nineteenth century by encouraging Thomist studies. The dedication expressed both intellectual credibility and loyalty to the Western Church.

3 J. Embry, *The Catholic Movement and the Society of the Holy Cross* (London: Faith Press, 1931).

4 July 1921.

5 PHL: SSC papers, *Acta* June 1924, on his retirement as Master.

6 Ibid., March 1938, Brother deJorge.

7 See for example Roger Lloyd, *The Church of England in the Twentieth Century*, Vol. 1 (London: Longman, 1946), Ch. 7, especially p. 139, quoting Friedrich Heiler: 'the renaissance of evangelical Christianity is to be sought ... in the revival of the Catholic spirit ... Anglo-Catholicism is one of the most hopeful and fruitful movements in the Western Church of the present day'.

8 PHL: SSC papers, *Acta* February 1914.

9 Ibid., July 1914.

10 Bishop Barnes was ultra-liberal in his approach to biblical criticism. To his opponents he reached the edge of acceptable Christian belief and sometimes fell beyond it. He was also highly intolerant of Catholic ceremonial and ritual, and several Anglo-Catholic churches in his diocese incurred his displeasure and were under his episcopal ban.

11 See H. Maynard-Smith, *Frank, Bishop of Zanzibar* (London: SPCK, 1926), esp. Ch. 8; also Embry, *The Catholic Movement and the Society of the Holy Cross*, pp 373–5.

12 The Archbishop made a statement which while overtly criticizing the Bishop of Zanzibar in fact justified him in every point. The SSC synod in June 1915 voted to 'disassociate' the brethren from the Archbishop's statement and to support the Bishop of Zanzibar.

13 Maynard-Smith, *Frank, Bishop of Zanzibar*, p. 159.

14 J.G. Lockhart, *Cosmo Gordon Lang* (London: Hodder & Stoughton, 1949), Ch. 23, especially pp. 270ff.

15 PHL: SSC papers, *Acta* May 1920.

16 Ibid., May 1928, Fr Baverstock, in the context of Prayer Book

revision: 'My quibble in it all has been that the C of E has seen herself as a self-going concern'.

17 For all the following see Maynard-Smith, *Frank, Bishop of Zanzibar*, Ch. 16.

18 PHL: SSC papers, *Acta* May 1920.

19 Ibid., October 1923.

20 Embry, *The Catholic Movement and the Society of the Holy Cross*, p. 386.

21 Maynard-Smith, *Frank, Bishop of Zanzibar*, p. 302.

22 PHL: SSC papers, *Acta* July 1924: 'What Catholics really want from a Revised Liturgy'.

23 The opposition to the revision was led in Convocation by the Revd Dr Darwell Stone, the Principal of Pusey House. Although not a member of the Society, he employed the same arguments. He was chairman of the Federation of Catholic Priests.

24 PHL: SSC papers, *Acta* November 1914.

25 What would Embry have said of the 'General Synod all Purpose Mary Day', now commended by Common Worship for 15 August?

26 Embry, *The Catholic Movement and the Society of the Holy Cross*, p. 384.

27 PHL: SSC papers, *Acta* May 1915.

28 I.e. dividing the two natures of Christ so as to assert two persons; sadly *Acta* does not pin down the precise point at which this is the case, though there was some concern over the prayers proposed for the baptism service.

29 PHL: SSC papers, *Acta* May 1927.

30 See S.C. Carpenter, *Winnington Ingram* (Oxford: Oxford University Press, 1949), Ch. 10.

31 Ibid., p. 209.

32 PHL: SSC papers, *Acta* May 1920.

33 Ibid., July 1942.

34 Ibid., May 1928, Fr A.H. Baverstock, Master.

35 Ibid., November 1915.

36 Ibid., October 1923. Cf. the shock expressed by Canon Wood at the marriage of the 'Priest who was a leading light of the Anglo-Catholic Congress'.

37 Ibid., May 1922.

38 At what point the resolution of May 1918 (above) was rescinded is not revealed in the records I have seen.

39 Ibid., August 1913; B.H. Streeter (ed.), *Foundations: A Statement of Christian Belief in Terms of Modern Thought, by Seven Oxford Men* (London: Macmillan, 1912). (See Ch. 6, n. 87, this volume.) For Temple's defence of his position see F.A. Iremonger, *William Temple* (Oxford: Oxford University Press, 1948), Ch. 9.

40 Charles Gore, Henry Leighton Goudge, Alfred Guillaume, *A New Commentary on Holy Scripture: Including the Apocrypha* (London: SPCK, 1929).

41 PHL: SSC papers, *Acta* May 1929.

42 Ibid., July 1929.

43 Ibid., September 1938.

44 Ibid., September 1938.

45 Ibid., May 1942.

46 Ibid., May 1917.

47 Ibid., May 1917.

48 Ibid., February 1944.

49 Ibid., May 1939.

50 Ibid., May 1941.

8

Postwar and pre-crisis: 1945–92[1]

Owen Higgs

The Society had survived the war years and now entered a changed world. Its early meetings, however, took up familiar themes: the conversion of England, the interpretation of Holy Scripture, authority in the Church of England, the sacrifice of the Mass, rules for marriage and nullity, the hopes and fears of the reunion of Christians, the music of the Mass, the Lambeth Conference of 1948. This last was criticized for its 'confusion of thought' on several issues arising from its 'equivocal use of terms which belong to the Catholic vocabulary, but which are used in a novel sense' and also for 'the uncertainty of [its] doctrinal basis'.[2] That point of view shaped the Society's response to many issues in the coming decades. The discussions at chapter were a characteristic mix of the practicalities of priesthood and its spiritual underpinning, the legal and the liturgical, the political and the problematic. All these concerns were to occupy the brethren as the postwar world developed, but there were dark clouds gathering and the role and position of the Society was not necessarily secure. Fr Kirtland continued as Master until 1947, when he was replaced by Fr Whatton who served until the election of Fr Simmons.

In the 42 years between 1950 and the 1992 vote on the ordination of women measure the SSC grew almost tenfold from at least 114 members, largely resident in the United Kingdom, to about 1,150 in 1992,[3] spread across the Anglican Communion. At the start of this period the Society's continued existence was in doubt, and so, in a different way, it was at the end. As a society of priests concerned for the Catholicity of the Church of England, and especially of her clergy, the SSC was particularly concerned about those threats to the Catholic faith and order of the Church of England which struck at the priesthood. These were the foundation of the Church of South India, the proposals for unity with the Methodist Church, the covenant proposed between the Church of England and the Nonconformist churches and the ordination of women. Although the Society did not take a lead on these issues, its members did. Fr Simmons in his second term as Master began the opposition to the Methodist unity proposals at a time when other Catholic societies were divided on the issue. This was the major reason for the growth of the Society; it stood for the traditional faith and order of the English Church. However, the Society is not a campaigning organization. Indeed, there were problems in the 1970s and 1980s with brethren who thought that it was. Its concern, rather, was to spread the Catholic faith and to encourage the spiritual life of the priesthood. So, during this period brethren were also concerned about the introduction of reforms in the wake of the Second Vatican Council, and the care of and mission to their parishes, which were often at the heart of racial or industrial unrest. Slowly and repetitively the statutes of the Society were revised from their original Latin with a great emphasis on ceremony, to the modern English statutes designed for a religious institute which would promote the traditional faith and order of the English priesthood and Church.

The year 1950 was a landmark for the SSC: in that the Bampton Lectures at Oxford were, for the first and, to date, last time, given by a brother of the Society, Fr Tom Parker. There were also changes in the SSC's personnel. Fr Alban Baverstock, a former Master and noted spiritual writer died, and Fr Alfred Simmons replaced Fr Geoffrey Whatton to become Master for the first time (at this point the mastership was for one year at a time, typically held for a *triennium*).

As for much of this decade, attendance at the May synod was poor, 23, with thirteen dispensations granted, in total, barely a quarter of the membership. Indeed, until the Society grew again, meetings were quiet and secretive. Yet, the Society did provide a network of clergy who understood each other, and confessors to clergy who were otherwise isolated. In his address to the synod, the new Master spoke about the successes the Catholic movement had enjoyed, despite persecution by the authorities: improvements in Sunday worship, the parish Communion movement and the reservation of the Sacrament. As he put it, the sacrifice of the Mass should be at the heart of the Society. This devotional stress was balanced by a concern about the wellbeing of the Society: how it could be more effective; how its Statute Book might be revised. These were to be major themes of Fr Simmons' first term as Master. They were propagated through *Acta* in some detail, necessarily so when so few brethren attended meetings.[4] In this year two articles approached these issues.

The first was a piece by Fr Seaborn, the secretary, on the nature of the Society. He argued that the SSC's main object was to gather and support such Anglican clergy as accepted the Catholic faith and its discipline, who wished to live according to the best models of priestly life, in an association of mutual benefit and support. To do this the Society had a Rule, containing voluntary and obligatory parts. Some of the Rule was now generally accepted as best practice in the Church of England and this meant it could benefit current members of the Society while not putting off new members. It should be remembered that at this time membership of the Society was by invitation and *Acta* were very discreet in their reference to individuals.

Fr Seaborn continued, saying that in its early days the role of the Society had been twofold: to defend the faith and practice of the Church, and to lead missionary work at home and abroad. Much of that work had been taken on over time by other societies formed for a specific purpose, for example the Society of St John the Evangelist, formed for missionary work, so that the SSC now concentrated on building up the way of life of its members, who in turn would benefit the Church by their more holy life.[5]

He continued with the issues of celibacy and the hope that the Church of England would be united to the Holy See: two issues which he saw as linked. He believed that the celibate life was of value to the Church of England, and, with echoes of past SSC debates on the issue, argued that in future members who married might have to leave the Society. This suggestion seems to have been squashed by the Master in the following months.

The life of prayer, Fr Seaborn continued, for SSC members never should be just Morning and Evening Prayer; rather, he believed, the Latin Office or the Book of Common Prayer supplemented by the Common Hours should be used by brethren.

He concluded by emphasizing the importance of the Master in ordering the Society, and in September of 1950 Fr Simmons also took up this theme and set out the beginnings of a vision for renewal. He began by noting that the Society had lost its fervour to such an extent that one of his predecessors now thought it should be dissolved. The Society had been in decline during and after the Second World War, both in attendance at chapter and overall numbers. Work was being done and done better than by other organizations of the Catholic movement. To remedy this situation, he proposed: (1) that more local chapters be set up so that attendance at chapter was easier; (2) that the policy of not advertising continue, but more personal contacts be made; (3) that, as had originally been the case, ordinands might be allowed to join; and (4) that the Statutes and organization of the Society be revised. By the end of the year some action had begun to be taken when the secretary appealed for help in revising the roll, which suggests that the organization of the Society was in bad order. At the same time, the records suggest a continued split amongst members when the papal Bull on the Assumption was promulged: papalists in

148

the Society accepted the Bull on the Pope's authority; while others argued on scholarly grounds that Catholics should pass over it in silence. This sort of debate seems to have been typical amongst the brethren, although as the Society grew there appears to have been a tailing off of the depth of learning aspired to by Fr Lowder and typical of the *Acta* of the 1950s and 1960s.

In the following year some further progress was made towards the Master's vision of bringing the Society back to life. The May synod approved the admission of ordination candidates to the Society and the Master continued to press for regional chapters, not least because of the cost of rail imposed by the 'socialist railways' – one of the few references to politics in the *Acta* of the 1950s.[6] He emphasized that the Society was not a group of London clergy: local chapters now existed in Cumberland (Our Lady of the Fells); York (St Wilfrid) and Northampton (St Edmund, King and Martyr).[7] At the same time he looked beyond the Society and in the pamphlet *A New Deal for the Catholic Movement*, he suggested that the weakness of Catholics was not due only to the hostility of the hierarchy but to the failures of Catholics, especially the clergy, in their personal lives. Where once the movement had been noted for personal holiness, loyalty to the Church of England, especially in its historic formularies, and a zeal for souls, so that it became the leaven in the lump, now the clergy routinely disparaged the Church of England, were indifferent to their parishioners and were flippant in outlook. The Society, he said, had a role to change this. It was a Society whose only programme was to foster the priestly life. No other Anglican society did this. SSC members should be loyal to the Church of England and zealous in the Catholic cause as a means to combat spiritual introversion. Loyalty to the Church of England should not be belittled and priests of the Society should be equipped for the Church of England and not for Catholic ghettos, and they should show charity to one another.[8]

After this burst of activity, 1952 was a quiet year for the Society though a significant innovation was a synod in the north, at the proposal of the St Wilfrid chapter. This began as a one-off but became an annual event, and the forerunner of later provincial synods.[9] Most of the talks given centred on the liturgy and the devotional life of the priest. A requiem was celebrated for the late king, George VI. The Society's bank account could not be used for a while, as the treasurer had died in post and until his will was proved, funds could not be accessed.[10]

There were also hints of changes to come with a discussion of the new Holy Week rites in the Apostolic Constitution *Maxima Redemptionis Nostrae* and a discussion of Saturday evening masses and the relaxation of fasting, introduced in the constitution *Christus Dominus*. Both these changes, and experiments with westward-facing Masses and offertory processions were discussed by brethren and generally commended as the way forward. The changes were to provoke trouble. By 1956 one order of Sisters had withdrawn from all parishes which had introduced the new rites and, in the beginning, there was resistance, especially from the northern clergy, to Saturday evening services, since these were seen as a mark of Protestantism: the changes in rites meant that the landmarks of Anglo-Catholic devotion had been removed, the full impact of which was to be felt after Vatican II. *Maxima Redemptionis Nostrae* was discussed by the Master three years later, posing the question whether to follow the Book of Common Prayer or the Roman use. He argued, that to begin with, the Sarum use could not be employed to supplement the old rites. The old rites were just that: they had no authority, and deliberately to choose them over the modern rite would be an exercise of private judgement. However, following the SSC's custom, a brother should use his own judgement in bringing his people to a better understanding of the rites, or to put it in later terminology, full faith was an aspiration, not a requirement.

Christus Dominus was discussed in detail at the May synod of 1953 by Fr Whatton, who replaced Fr Simmons as Master in that year. He argued that the Church of Rome could make changes to its regulations because, unlike the Church of

England, it considered itself to be *the* Church, rather than a national or local church. In the absence of an ecumenical council, it was proper for Anglicans to follow the Pope's lead: the Anglicans at the Malines Conferences had recognized that the Pope had a certain responsibility for the whole Church (a view later endorsed by ARCIC, though not by many Anglicans in the 1950s). Contrary to those who said that the Church of England should remain where it was at the time of the breach with Rome in the sixteenth century, he argued that too much had changed in our religious life to make that a practical option, citing the controversies over aumbries and the loss of religious communities. Rather, to move forward was to show loyalty to the founders of the Catholic movement, and if Rome made a change it was difficult for Anglicans not to follow. Indeed, there was a need to live the true life of the Church in the Church of England. The 1928 Anglican position had been that fasting was commendable, but it was a matter left to the individual conscience. This did not reflect the true mind of the Church, which must always be the mind of God and not necessarily that of an episcopal clique. So change had to come and it was up to good priests and the Confraternity of the Blessed Sacrament to provide instruction and teaching. The same went for evening Masses which it was difficult to criticize since the Romans had authorized them for the eve of the Coronation, with scant regard for ecumenical concerns. These Masses were, after all, originally an initiative by Pope Pius X to return to the Early Church's devotion to Our Lord.

The rapid grasp of the implications of the Apostolic Constitution was echoed by a talk at the same synod by Fr Carter on the liturgical movement. He noted the widening use of Communion services in the Church of England following the Parish and People movement which had started from Queen's College, Birmingham, in 1950. This was a movement supported by those of diverse churchmanship and was acceptable in many parishes because it did not provide overtly Catholic teaching.[11]

In Europe liturgical change had begun earlier, at first with a traditionalist and romantic strain amongst the Benedictines, followed by a Dominican pastoral concern to lead the common man to Christ in his mysteries; hence the use of evening services, the time when people were able to come to Church. The work of the Church in France was particularly apposite to England, since both countries were deChristianized.[12] Other notable features of these changes were the emphasis on the Bible as the message to non-Christians and as the source of dogmatics, and the experiments in worship made in parishes with changes in the rigid timetables and reforms to baptismal rites. However, Fr Carter went on to note that the other Apostolic Constitution of 1952, *Mediator Dei*, censured the neglect of private and extra-liturgical prayer, the urge to innovate for innovation's sake and the mania for primitive usages without Catholic understanding which too often accompanied liturgical change.

He further argued that the Parish and People movement could not be ignored because it posed such fundamental questions as how to be the Church, how to build up an ordered congregation in a disordered society, how worship could be ordered to give a sense of mystery, how the people could be instructed in what is relevant.[13] These questions had to be answered, and in Fr Carter's view the Church of England either followed the French model or became a period piece. In many respects Vatican II as implemented decisively impelled Catholic Anglicans towards the French model. Later on that year the Master raised, as a more domestic matter, the idea of setting up a home for retired clergy and a centre for Ignatian retreats which was the germ for the foundation of the Holy Cross Trust.

The following year, 1954, was again quiet, despite it being the centenary of the Society. The treasurer spent £10 on celebrations. The Master, Fr Whatton, abolished the order of probationers and noted that he had no funds because the previous Master had spent them all on travel. He also stopped the annual readmission of the Master to his post on the grounds that the practice reflected little more than the founding brothers' love of elaborate procedure. Preparations were made for the centenary of the Society. It was to be a Mass followed by a dinner, not advertised and with only priests of the Society present. (So quiet an affair was it, that there is no reference in the following year's *Acta* as to when or where it took place.) The year ended with the death of Fr Wreford, who had belonged to the Society since 1906 and who, as a boy, had known Lowder, Stanton and Suckling. He had loved to talk of the great priests of old and was devoted to the Sacred Heart, the Blessed Sacrament, Christ the King and Our Lady of the Cross. He opposed liturgical change, preferring to make up the Book of Common Prayer with the Missal. His funeral was attended by some 2,500 people.

In 1955 a number of simmering disagreements within the Society finally came to the boil. In August the Master proposed in the London chapter that the Society be divided into two coequal provinces: 'to give greater weight to the Northern brethren of the Society in view of their greater seeming fidelity to the spirit which inspired our forebears'. He pressed this idea again in the September synod with the suggestion that the Master should be head of the northern province and that more chapters be founded in the north. Tension between London and the rest of the Society had been exacerbated by the claims to greater Catholicity by southern clergy who had introduced the new Roman fasting rules.[14] The Master's idea was rejected by the council who preferred, at a time of national rail-strikes, to urge a greater involvement in the Society by the northern brethren. A number of schemes to improve the life of the Society, such as days of recollection and the revision of the Office, had had little effect, and with so much of the Society's work done by other societies and standards of clerical life much improved, the Master clearly felt unhappy about the state of the Society.

The controversy over the Church of South India seems further to have lowered morale. Under this scheme churches in South India came together and new clergy were episcopally ordained, although existing nonepiscopally ordained clergy were not. The scheme was eventually recognized by the Convocations in 1958. In some ways it foreshadowed the later practice of the Church of England pushing forward ecclesial experiments in the name of Protestant mission and goodwill which often implied that the example and teaching of Jesus had no ecclesiological implications or was merely human and contingent. The Church of South India was discussed by chapters during the year and at the September synod the Master argued that it was not a resigning matter. He noted that the Church of Rome had recognized the priesthood of some heretical churches. But do as the non-Jurors was the way to extinction. Rather, the best thing was to follow the path of the Tractarians and continue to Catholicize the Church of England, where much progress had been made. Nevertheless, the Church of South India was an important issue because there was the danger that it would become the thin end of the wedge in easing the Catholic priesthood out of the Church of England, and that necessarily struck at the roots of the Society.

The second major fault-line in the Society which was exposed that year was what it believed about authority. The issue appears to have arisen because of the Church of South India. Though it was argued that the SSC as a spiritual organization should leave campaigning on this issue to the more political Federation of Catholic Priests, there was uncertainty about the stance of the Church Union and it was decided that a clear statement of Catholic principles needed to be made. So it was that Canon Rich presented a paper to the September synod which brethren were asked to sign. His first five of six propositions were agreed. Canon Rich argued that the Catholic faith is wholly God-given. It may be developed or explained. It was to be received not primarily as a set of historical truths but as a gift to the Church and handed on by the Church. John Henry Newman had recognized this. Dr Pusey had feared its consequences and had blocked any development in doctrine. This static view of faith handed the initiative to Gore and the *Lux Mundi* group.[15] Canon Rich argued that Anglicans needed to recover that understanding of faith as a whole and a given.

On this basis he asked the brethren to assent to the following propositions:

1. The Catholic faith is a divine gift.
2. There is a genuine need that it be truly understood as a connected whole and that it comes underpinned by the teaching authority of the Church, which itself is under-pinned by God.
3. The Church is helped by the Spirit to give an unfailing witness to the Deposit of Faith.
4. The historical facts which have given rise to the Christian revelation are not bare facts but come interpreted and passed down by the Church. Therefore the fullest under-standing of the faith comes not by research into historical facts but as the present experience of the Divine Society.[16]
5. Therefore the Church is the final test of belief and not historical evidence and critical reason.
6. The Papacy is the duly appointed, visible centre of unity. It is hoped that Anglican and Roman theologians might overcome their mutual fears and at the same time preserve Anglican spirituality.

The first five propositions were printed and sent to members to be signed. Thirty brethren agreed to the six points; one member left the Society.

In October a letter on this issue was sent to the Church Union asking whether Canon Rich's principles were in line with the Church Union's charter and whether the membership was divided over its own charter. The Church Union replied that it believed Catholics were divided over the Church of South India. As a consequence, the Master and another representative of the Society were invited to join the Catholic Council (previously the Catholic Advisory Council),[17] a body of about a hundred members. The threat to the priesthood which the Church of South India posed had drawn the Society into political struggle. In many ways the action which the Society took over the Church of South India was a dry-run for what happened with the Methodist proposals; though in the

1960s, the contacts which the Master had made with the Church of Rome opened up an ecumenical dimension and the possibility of some form of Anglican Uniate Church. In turn, that was to be the great hope of Fr Colven at the time of the Ordination of Women debate. In the 1950s, the Society's role in pulling together the different Catholic groups had begun, and it did so, as it did in the later controversies, because it was a society of priests which sought to defend the integrity of the Anglican priesthood as a part of God's way to save his people.

The problem of the Church in South India rumbled on into 1956. Archbishop Fisher wrote to the Catholic Council to say that ministries in the Church of South India were 'unequal' and receiving communion in the Church was a matter of conscience. This does not seem to have reassured the brethren, and rightly so, since others took the Church of South India as a signal that the Church of England's ministry was negotiable; hence later frustration when the scheme for Methodist unity failed.

In the May synod of that year, Brother Thomas was made Master, and later in the year the Fraternity of Christ the Eternal Priest was publicized. This had originally been a fellowship for Catholic ordinands in the armed forces which was now opened up to all ordinands and affiliated to the Society, the latest in a long line of guilds and lesser orders for those in training. At this time it provided a number of future members of the Society. Br Thomas encouraged retreats, and especially a Society retreat to Walsingham, though this proved unsatisfactory.

Brother Thomas's mastership came to a sudden end in 1957, when he was appointed head of Bishop Gray Theological College in Zoonebloom, South Africa, where the following year he helped found a local SSC chapter in South Africa. He was replaced by Fr Allso as acting Master. In his brief time as Master Brother Thomas emphasized prayer as the only way to build the Kingdom of God, as opposed to Church assemblies packed with state appointees who merely expressed their own opinions and whose chief aim was to avoid extremes.

In 1958 the Master, Fr Allso now elected, moved to

strengthen the Society through local chapters and this led to the re-founding of the St Dyfrig chapter in Wales and that of St Benedict in Lancashire. chapters continued to focus on spiritual issues while at the same time offering insights into the state of the Church. In this year the problems of divorce and the remarriage of divorcees were discussed, with the suggestion that a nullity procedure would be both faithful to Scripture and ecumenically proper.[18] The lack of impact of Catholic Anglicans in the universities was discussed, over against the presence of the Christian Unions and the Student Christian movement; although it was noted that this latter had become increasingly distanced from mainstream Christianity, demanding a pan-Protestant alliance to which the Pope would be forced to submit: a curious understanding of ecumenism.

Fr Whatton introduced the Society to Pope Pius XII's *Instructio de Musica et Sacra Liturgica*, noting how it emphasized that the laity had a part to play in public worship, taking up one of the themes of the Protestant Reformation and offering a foretaste of some of the reforms of Vatican II, which had been held up in the Church of Rome because of the need to defend a proper understanding of the Mass.

At the time, however, the most serious domestic event in the Society's life was the removal of Frs Hum and Blagdon-Gamlen from the roll by the Master. The dispute seems to have begun when Fr Blagdon-Gamlen opposed the election of Fr A.B. Andrews on the grounds he had written an heretical letter to *The Dome*, a newspaper run by one of the brethren. The London chapter supported Fr Allso, the Acting Master, in his decision that there was no heresy. On his own authority, Fr Allso then removed Frs Blagdon-Gamlen and Hum from the roll, though they were given the chance to rejoin, not, it seems, because of the original controversy but because of the damage to their reputations which removal from the roll might cause.[19] Fr Allso was re-elected Master that year, 1959, though, unusually for this time, he was opposed and attempts were made to formalize the nominations for the mastership.[20] Discussion in the Society continued on the usual topics, though the Master noted it was sad that attendance at synods was down on what it had been 20 years previously. Despite obvious distrust it was agreed to approach other Catholic societies to make a submission to the Liturgical Commission which would produce the experimental Series 1 rite.[21]

The hint of ecumenical activity in 1959, when there is a tantalizing reference in the Society's papers to a reply from the Vatican to a letter 'sent some time ago', became a major theme of the Society's work in the early 1960s. By 1962 the Society had its own ecumenical committee. Ten brethren and the Master visited Rome that year for a private audience with Pope John XXIII. In the October synod of 1972, the Master claimed that as a direct result of the meeting with Pope John his Holiness had introduced the clause 'Blessed be His Most Precious Blood' into the Divine Praises. The Pope spoke of his admiration for the principles of the Society, and in later years it became the hope of Fr Simmons that if and when Pope John was canonized he might be made patron of the Society. The party also had an audience with Cardinal Bea and saw Mgr Willebrands at the Secretariat for Unity. At the same time Bishop Holland, coadjutor of the Portsmouth diocese, had set in motion discussions between the new Roman Catholic Committee for Unity in England and the Society. The Society had insisted that any unity scheme should accept the validity of Anglican orders and sacraments – a frequently repeated position of the Society, hardly surprisingly since it went to the heart of is *raison d'être*, though Bishop Holland had difficulty understanding how it was possible to accept the authority of the Holy See while at the same time rejecting *Apostolica Curae*.[22]

Discussions about uniate status had also taken place with Fr Cleane OP at Blackfriars, Oxford. Fr Cleane had wanted to know if SSC clergy would be able to bring their parishes with them out of the Church of England; would the people come if their buildings stayed behind; would uniate Anglicans be prepared to celebrate in Mass centres while worshipping in their accustomed fashion (any uniate status would be directly under the Holy See through an Apostolic delegate, and so separate from the English hierarchy)? No indication of the Master's response to these questions is given in *Acta*, his emphasis being that it was important that SSC clergy should move as a body with their parishes, while recognizing the importance of individual conscience. If approval from Canterbury was forthcoming, it was hoped that joint meetings between the Society and Rome might continue.

The ecumenical enthusiasm continued at the September synod. The Master reported that the idea of a conference between the Society and representatives of the Church of Rome had been supported by Roman Catholics in the UK, though this could only take place once the Vatican Council had sat because they would need to know in which direction the Church was moving before they could act. While respecting the consciences of individual members of the Society, he emphasized that it was the Society's unity which had impressed Rome. Canon Rees was able to tell members that the Holy Father had told him he was much impressed by the priestliness of the SSC clergy he had met and the synod was addressed by the Revd Dr Buckley, a Roman Catholic, on the next council, which would be a council of unity. He mentioned, in passing, that ecumenical dialogue in the UK was difficult for historical and ethnic reasons.

The year 1962 ended on a more domestic note, with complaints sent to the Archbishop of Canterbury and Brigadier Watkins of the Lord Chancellor's office about the Brigadier's public comments that it was a sad state of affairs that patrons had to look at men who were almost Roman Catholics when making appointments. The correspondence petered out after the Brigadier said he was opposed only to unsuitable Anglo-Catholics and maintained that there was no question that his remarks implied a bias against Anglo-Catholic clergy.[23] In 1962 the London chapter bemoaned the public utterances of Dr Alec Vidler[24] as undermining the Christian faith and there were continuing rows between the London chapter and the rest of the Society which reflected, to some extent, a continuous tension between the provinces and the capital.

At the start of 1963 the roll stood at 150, and for the first time there is reference to the report about unity with the Methodists. In January members of the Society had attended a unity service in Westminster Cathedral, for which they were condemned as disloyal to the Church of England by the *Church Times*. *The Sunday Times* had also referred to the SSC's work for unity with Rome and had written of the Society as if this were its chief aim. The May synod concentrated on matters of Church unity. Fr Whatton gave a paper on the Catholicity of the Church of England, noting how bishops such as John Robinson of Woolwich were not representative of Anglican teaching and how Rome was not too hard-and-fast in its definition of church boundaries. He argued that it was essential to recognize that the Church of England claimed only to be a part of the Church and not the whole Church, hence it should not act as if autonomous. Fr Hum noted how uniate status overcame the problems of difficulties such as sacramental order, though it would require disestablishment and pose financial problems.

In this year the report *Conversations between the Church of England and the Methodist Church* was published. This built on the 'Interim Report' of 1958, drawn up by a committee of theologians from the two churches and which had received support from the Lambeth Conference, as well as from the Methodist Assembly. The 1963 *Conversations* advocated the unification of the two churches, and the proposals were sent to the dioceses and to the Methodist Conference. Problems with the proposals were examined in a talk give by a Methodist, Mr Dawson. He noted that the episcopal function in Methodism was to be found in its Conference rather than in individuals, and that Methodism taught that bishops were not necessary to Catholic faith and witness. Any service of reconciliation for them could not be an ordination. Likewise, their ecumenical agenda was that they should not compromise their relations with the Free Churches. At a local level, he said, there was ignorance of the Church of England and fear that it would simply swallow up Methodism which would lose its distinctive culture of temperance and no gambling. In discussion it was noted that there were dangers in external unity without internal unity, made worse by the different language used by the two sides. Further, a service of reconciliation where the intention on either side was different would be defective in intention.

The proposals for unity with the Methodists now became a central concern of the Society. After the synod the Society was represented at a meeting of the Catholic societies about the proposals, and members began to keep a close eye on what the Church Union was doing. From now until 1968 the Society was the main Anglican opposition to the unity proposals, and its members suffered accordingly. The September synod further discussed the problem. The Revd Clucas Moore spoke on the divisions within Methodism and the difficulties which opponents to the proposals would have in simply going to Rome. A catechism for Methodists and Anglicans was drawn up on the proposals, while at the same time it became increasingly clear that the Church Union's public stance was at best indecisive. However, at the start of 1964 the chairman of the Church Union had written to the Master saying the Anglican–Methodist Report was not acceptable; although in March of that year it was noted that though the SSC, Catholic League and Annunciation Group were working well together it was still necessary to bring the other Catholic societies on board.[25] At the same time, the Master was in contact with Methodists who opposed the report and in the spring sent a list of problems with the report to all Methodist ministers at the request of the *Voice of Methodism*. Later on in the year, public meetings were organized by the Catholic societies at St Matthew's, Westminster, to inform and persuade about the report.

Relations with the Church of Rome continued to develop over the year. The Master had attended a reception given by the papal delegate at Westminster Cathedral at the start of the year. Archbishop Cardinale spoke at the May synod, where he suggested that the validity of Anglican orders should not prove a great problem, nor should married clergy since that was a matter of discipline. The Church of Rome was concerned for outreach to the whole of the Church of England and the work of the SSC might be part of God's providence to achieve this. He did not think much of uniate status, but envisaged centres of further education for converting Anglican clergy, the 'Evening Beda'. Later in the year, the Master reported on confidential discussions with the Archbishop, when Cardinale had said the Pope would be prepared to make concessions on married clergy. He advised the Society to work with the Benedictines and Dominicans rather than the parish clergy, and to ensure all correspondence was copied to Canterbury. This proved to be the kiss of death to these discussions. He thought reconciliation with the Holy See might be possible in three to four years, although he emphasized the importance of acclimatizing the laity to any changes. The Master later reported that the issue of orders might be dealt with by recognizing the sincerity of Anglican orders and that the Society might be able to keep some form of its identity when it had been reconciled. The events post 1992 showed that this was not a practical option.

In terms of the Society's structure during the year, numbers on the roll grew to 181, and plans for a newspaper, trust-fund and Friends' Society were begun. By the end of 1964 the number of Friends ran to 712 of whom 400 were laity. A new Chapter of Our Lady was proposed for the south-west, and the Chapter of the Holy Martyrs for Birmingham. The reform of the Society was planned, with a new deputy-Master for the northern province and a new and simplified set of statutes in English. Admission to the Society was still in Latin, though dispensations had begun to be granted to those who did not have Latin.

The Birmingham chapter was inaugurated in the January of 1965, and in his address the Master argued for the importance of the Society in providing a space where clergy could speak freely and maintain a Catholic discipline. The SSC hoped for reconciliation with Rome, while at the same time it needed to maintain discipline in the face of such threats as the proposed Methodist unity.

The *Catholic Standard* was now being published under the

editorship of Fr Mitchell. Frs Arrowsmith and Preist ('Cosmas and Damian' as they signed their editorials) were to become editors in 1973. It was a successor to *The Dome* and *Crux*, which though produced by Society clergy were not answerable to the Society in the way that the *Catholic Standard* was. This journal contained a mixture of devotional articles, pictures of 'high dos', correspondence and teaching about issues of the day. From the start it had chronic problems of selling enough copies, typically 2,000 against a break-even of 4,000, and finance (typically clergy not paying their dues).

The controversy over the Anglican Methodist Report continued. In this year the Methodist Conference approved the unity proposals in principle and the Convocations accepted them so as to allow further consideration over matters which had come to light. At the same time, the high hopes of reconciliation with Rome were dealt a severe blow by Lambeth Palace. Following Archbishop Cardinale's suggestion, correspondence had been copied to the Archbishop of Canterbury who insisted that all such negotiations be handled by his Unity Committee. The Master was summoned to Lambeth for a meeting, about which he was vowed to secrecy. It is apparent, however, that he said to Dr Ramsey that he did not intend to leave the Church of England and that in part the discussions with the Church of Rome were forward-planning against Anglican unity with Methodism.

In this highly charged atmosphere Fr Simmons was re-elected as Master to serve for five years because of the dangerous state of the Church of England. There was anger amongst the brethren that the Bishop of Southwark had been invited to preach at Walsingham.[26] His later appointment as a guardian of the Shrine in 1971, at a time when there were no SSC guardians, led the Society take a more active role in the life of the Shrine.

At the same time the Vatican Council was beginning to undermine many of the outward signs for which Anglo-Catholics had fought. At the October synod, the Master listed the replacement of stone altars by wooden tables, the abolition of private masses, concelebrations which took place after an *agape* breakfast and dissent about birth-control. Cardinal Heenan had talked in the Council about the Beatles. Earlier in the year Fr Howard had highlighted how all recent change in the Church of England had been generated by Protestant liberalism, including Dr Ramsey in his criticism. From now on the agenda for change would increasingly be set by Rome. The Society was not master of its own destiny and in the following year there was concelebration for the first time at the national synod.

The Society continued to grow. In 1966 its numbers rose above 200 and a new chapter of St Edmund, King and Martyr, was inaugurated at All Saints, Kettering, and later one in Hove. Relations with the Church Union improved after a letter from the chairman, Fr Coleman, which explained it was the Church Union's policy not to oppose the work of the Church of England but to work within its structures for the advancement of the Catholic faith. Even in the 1980s the Master had to encourage brethren to vote and take part in General Synod elections.[27] As a result of this correspondence it was agreed that the Society should write articles for the *Church Observer*.

The Master's main business in the year was again with the Methodist unity proposals.[28] Though he remained in contact with Archbishop Cardinale, a proposed visit to Rome was cancelled owing to opposition from Lambeth Palace. Cardinale had suggested that it would be easier for Rome to deal with a Church outside of the Church of England, which in the light of the Methodist proposals was a possibility.

It is significant that during the year, Prebendary Timms of the Anglican–Methodist Commission approached the Master requesting help in the matter of 'Dissident Catholics'.[29] He wanted to know what judgements of conscience opponents to the proposals would make, how those judgements could be resolved; and if the proposals were pushed through, what opponents might do and how they could be helped. In his reply, the Master, writing as one of the leading Catholics in the Church of England, began with the lack of doctrinal agreement. Plain issues were fudged by formulas which were designed to mean different things to different people. Above all, there was a lack of agreement over sacraments.[30] A Methodist minister needed to know that he was not a priest, and that any reconciliation service would require his ordination. That was simply not possible before there had been a growth in order and discipline; to do otherwise was to put the cart before the horse. The growth in discipline would require fixed forms of practice in such matters as the disposal of the sacrament and an end to lay celebration. Furthermore, because ecumenical schemes involved the whole of Christendom, any unity scheme should be considered sound by the great churches of East and West, as Methodists were insisting that the scheme should be acceptable to the Protestant churches. More practically, clergy who opposed the scheme should have the moral and legal right to remain in the cures to which they had been lawfully admitted and they should receive a fair share of appointments and of the temporalities in the Church.

In the following year the Master reported back on this exchange. He said that the bishops had respected the Catholic position and there was some recognition that what was being proposed was contrary to the reply to *Apostolica Curae*, not that this seems to have held the bishops back. He had been pressed on whether there was a move for a continuing Anglican Church. He felt not, though the scheme as it stood would put Catholics outside of the Church of England. He further reported that the Bishop of London believed that if a large number of clergy across the country opposed the scheme, it would fail.

In the same year, 1967, there were Church of England reports proposing a General Synod to replace the Church Assembly and, in *Partners in Ministry*, a reorientation of the ministry with the work of the parish priest being modelled less on that of a pastor and more on that of a facilitator. It was noted that the Synod proposals would mean laity, who were largely outside canon law and would not necessarily have much theological education, would help make Church law – authority was being removed from those to whom it had been given by Christ.

165

The end of the year saw the inauguration of the Bristol chapter and the roll at 241. Next year the roll continued its rise, to 266 and then 309 at the end of 1969. The London chapter was formally inaugurated in 1968 and the Leeds and Wakefield branch celebrated its centenary. Finally, after much delay, the Holy Cross Trust, with the intention to raise funds for a priests' retirement house or centre for study, was authorized by the brethren in 1969. That same year the St Wilfrid's chapter by its own resolution put the Master and the then officers in place 'until such time as the Society may wish to review the situation again'. This time was when the Master died. The reaction of other chapters to this *coup* is not formally recorded, though there was clearly a great deal of bitterness and the revision of the statutes in the 1970s was partly designed to make the Society return to its more democratic origins. The Master was to tighten his already firm grip on the Society in this year when the Master's council was dissolved because so many local vicars lived out of London and could not attend. Instead, an executive committee was set up, comprising the Master, the secretary, treasurer and the two deputy-Masters. These, in the style of the Council, acted collegially. Further structural changes included the elevation of one meeting a year of the Bristol Chapter of St Jude, covering the West Country and Wales, to synod status which became permanent in 1970. Ordinand members of the Society were to be called 'Probationers', and rules for their conduct were drawn up. A new Rule for the Society as a whole was drawn up, available to all members from 1970.[31] Fr Simmon's 1970 revision of the Rule is a little longer than the 1964 Rule it replaced. It maintained the emphasis of the Society as forming a special bond of union between Catholic priests and working to extend Catholic faith and discipline. On his own say as Master, Fr Simmons gave instruction for a Society cincture.

During 1968 and 1969 the main issue facing the Society was the final moves towards the Anglican–Methodist agreement, which was blocked in the Church Assembly of 1969. The Master recorded the Society's thanks to Graham Leonard, then

Bishop of Willesden, for his leadership. He noted that the Society's role had been to stand alone against the proposals until others finally took up the political fight. In the following year, at the May synod, the Society was to be addressed by Dr Geoffrey Fisher, the former Archbishop of Canterbury, who warned that the bishops were determined to bring back Methodist schemes until they succeeded: as has proved to be the case. At the same time, the Society's hopes for reconciliation with Rome were dented by a 'disastrous' meeting with Cardinal Heenan at which he told representatives of the Society that there was no point in a uniate rite and that Anglican orders were simply invalid. The Master believed that any hope for unity would have to lie with the new generation of Roman bishops.[32] One of these, Derek Warlock, was to suggest in the following year that the Society was a parallel to the Oratory since it had no vows but a customary Rule. This idea was to be developed in the revision of the statutes, initially in the revision of 1970-1 and the later revision during Fr Shields' term of office.[33] More positively that year the possibility of SSC missions was raised after a successful mission to Holy Redeemer, Clerkenwell, returning to one of the Society's original aims. At the end of the year the roll stood at 357.

The sense of continual change or revolution in the Church and the pressure to change was addressed by the Master in the 'In and Out' Club,[34] at the April synod of 1971. The Society was to send comments to Anglican Roman Catholic International Commission (ARCIC)[35] to support the reports on authority, the Church and the Eucharist, and continued to oppose, ultimately unsuccessfully, the new open Communion policy.[36] At the same time the Society was addressing social changes in what became known as the 'Permissive Society'.[37] The Master produced a statement on morality directed to the Anglican clergy, critical, *inter alia*, of sexual deviation and promiscuity. This provoked resentment, since it was adopted without prior consultation. He continued his address with a discussion of the impact of the Second Vatican Council. After fighting for vestments, reservation of the Sacrament, confession, and largely succeeding in having these tolerated and often accepted, the new Roman minimalism seemed to threaten all which had been achieved. His own view was to accept change as part of life. He believed that Catholics in the Church of England could also be proud of their own heritage, its music, restraint and vernacular liturgy, and not simply assume everything in Rome was better, as the experience of converts often suggested otherwise.

It is difficult to assess how quickly and where the changes of the Vatican Council were brought in to SSC parishes. Anecdotal evidence suggests that in the first instance the Council had an impact because of the move to the vernacular liturgy. Whereas previously the Roman rite had been in Latin and esoteric amongst Anglicans, the liturgy in English was clearly seen to be superior to Series 3[38] and was much easier to introduce into parishes than the Latin rite. At a time when Prayer Book Catholicism was on its last legs, however long-lasting some of those legs proved to be, Anglo-papalism had been given a powerful means of propaganda. The introduction of the new liturgical styles seems to have depended very much on the character and opportunities of individual clergy, while at the same time the tide flowed in favour of change as the modern style was the only liturgy taught in seminaries. For many of the younger clergy the choice was either to follow the new, authoritative way or be left in the past; and if the new ritual pricked the bubble of pompous Anglicanism, so much the godlier.[39] By the mid 1970s, parishes such as St Paul's, Tottenham, and St Mary's, Somers Town, were noted for their reordering and wholehearted adoption of the new rites of the Council, and were quoted as such in *Acta*. Equally, there were parishes where the laity refused any change from the English Missal. One, taken at random from amongst many, being the leading Catholic parish of All Saints, North St, York (parish of Fr Alban Howard, later deputy-Master), which only accepted the Roman rite in the 1990s. And in the early 1970s disagreement over the reforms of Vatican II was seen to be one of the reasons why the London chapter was in disarray.[40]

An important development in 1971 was the presence of Fr Carter, secretary of the Church Union, at the June synod asking that Catholic societies work together, and the ready agreement that the Church Union take the lead in resisting the suggestion of the ordination of women to the priesthood. A new Catholic Societies Working Party began to meet that year.

Liturgical reform was on the agenda and Series 3 was discussed at the northern synod, meeting in Dean Court Hotel in York. The Master typically felt no need to admit members to the Society in Church. It was noted that the new, 'definitive' rite (the 'Rite of King Canute') had been drawn up without any Catholic involvement, which it was felt was almost an invitation for Catholics to ignore it. The reference to International Commission on English in the Liturgy texts was criticized because, as later with *Common Worship*, the texts were rarely left alone. Again, as was to happen later, prayers of offering acceptable to Nonconformists were considered impossible in the Church of England, and in a non-partisan spirit a rite was offered which suited evangelicals and broad churchmen, but not Catholics who were, therefore, by definition, partisan.

In 1972 the proposals for unity with Methodists were defeated in General Synod. The Society numbered 380 by the end of the year and its rapid growth in previous years led the Master to emphasize that it was not a campaigning body: that was the work of such organizations as the Church Union and League of Anglican Loyalists.

The importance of General Synod as a body generating change became apparent for the Society in the 1973 synod, when proposals for the ordination of women began to be discussed. If SSC commentators at the time are to be believed, this occurred as much by organizational error as from any groundswell of opinion, though it is difficult to believe that pressure for this innovation would not have built up. The Catholic societies set up a working party to deal with such matters as the authority of Scripture, the theological implications of the differences between the sexes and the significance of male analogies for God. Professors Mascall and Macquarrie were invited to write papers. Branches of the Society began to draw up resolutions critical of the proposals in the following year although, from the start, notions of priesthood varied greatly amongst Anglicans.

Professor Macquarrie was also behind a conference at Oxford that September which looked to do for Catholics what the Keele Conferences had done for evangelicals. In the event, it was the less academic Loughborough Conferences which led to Catholic Renewal. This more outward-looking Catholicism is mirrored in the evidence of what local branches of the Society were discussing at this time, not only liturgy and the spiritual life but also evangelism and pastoral method, how to encourage and maintain a sense of the numinous in worship. There is a dearth of information of social and political engagement at a time of significant social and industrial unrest.[41]

In 1974 there were attempts to organize the Catholic vote for the elections to future General Synods. Too often Catholics had stood against each other and SSC, the Federation of Catholic Priests and the Church Union now set out to work together.[42] At the same time there were attempts made to ensure regular attendance at branch meetings and that these meetings were fruitful. The view was often expressed that many who had joined the Society at the height of the campaign against the Methodist proposals did not really understand or share its aims. Equally, the Master at the October synod warned local officers of the Society to avoid scandal, which may suggest why some newcomers fell away from the Society. There was correspondence between the Master and the London chapter about resolutions on moral matters at the May synod which had, again, been put with scant consultation. It is clear that members felt the Master had acted in too autocratic a style and, on the basis of a memorandum drawn up by Fr Shields, the London chapter set up a committee to propose a revision of the statutes. One intention at this point was to make clear the limits on the Master's powers. More positively, the revision of the statutes in the 1970s represented the Society moving from governance by the Master in synod to governance by the Master in council; a necessary change as the Society grew. The proposed revision became the basis of the revised Rule, of Fr Shield's term of office, a term of office which began with the statement that the new Master was not an autocrat. Fr Simmons in the following year addressed the London chapter more in sorrow than in anger and noted that parts of the Society in the rest of the world had accepted his resolutions without demur. He believed it was his duty to articulate the Catholic faith on behalf of the Society and he hoped that the brethren would unite behind him. At the end of the 1974 synod the roll was 462.

The next three years were quiet ones for the Society. The year 1975 was designated a Holy Year, and as part of the Master's design to encourage the brethren to deepen their commitment to the Society and priestly life, he arranged for Dom Godfrey Stokes OSB to write a commentary on the Society's Rule. There continued discussions about the problems for the Society of clergy who had joined as part of the opposition to the Methodist unity proposals but who were not Catholic-minded. Papers were put up about the ordination of women and though there was disquiet about this, the papers suggest that it was felt this would go the same way as the unity proposals. These themes continued in 1976. In the June synod that year the Master noted that he had raised with the Welsh synod the possibility of fresh elections of the Society's officers, and they had demurred. In Birmingham the response had been the same. He does not seem to have taken the view of the London chapter. He proposed that Fr Hinton, now retired, should step down. He mentioned the names of other officers who might go as well. For himself, he 'enjoyed' being Master and would not step down until he saw someone good enough to take his place. In the event no such candidate stepped forward, death intervening. The following year, 1977, the Master went so far as to say in his final synod that the ordination of women to the priesthood was a matter of custom, not faith, though one which required the agreement of the whole

Church. He also noted, that having once favoured a continuing church as the mechanism to hold the brethren together against the Methodist proposals, he now felt this would simply be schismatic. At the same time some of the enthusiasm for unity with Rome, at least amongst some of the more elderly brethren, slackened as the effects of Vatican II became clearer.

The previous year, Dr David Hope, Principal of St Stephen's House, had addressed the brethren on the crisis in ministry. Shortage of funds, a decline in the number of ordinands, the status of auxiliary ministry, uncertainty over matters of faith and prayer, a crisis in the Catholic interpretation of the priesthood; all these things called for a renewal of ideals and spirituality. SSC brethren by that time were working on the renewal of the Society and the seeds of Catholic Renewal had been sown. The sudden death of the Master, Fr Simmons, in 1977 gave an opportunity for change.

Fr Shields had been a comparatively new member of the Society, his business background leading to his appointment as treasurer a few years after joining. When senior members of the Society declined the opportunity to become Master he stood, and though Fr Alban Howard was prevailed to stand as well, Fr Shields was elected comfortably.[43] At the synod of his installation there were proposed alterations to the statutes setting out which posts of the Society must be elective and giving more ample time for nominations to be made; the mastership was to be for four years at a time, and for no more than eight years consecutively. These proposals were agreed by the different synods within a year. At the same time, to cope with the growth of the Society, the four provinces in Britain were recreated, plus a new province in the Pacific, to make a total of seven in all.[44] These were in place with vicars provincial by 1979, so that the Master's council was now the executive, plus the vicars provincial. Smaller chapters were encouraged to help members to come together more often.

Fr Shields' early addresses showed a determined attempt to restore the Society to its early fervour, to end its reputation for 'gin, lace and backbiting', and to work as a religious congregation. Not all members of the Society understood it to be anything so formal as a congregation, but the new statutes which were eventually approved, modelled the Society on those lines. From the start the Master raised the possibility of the restoration of a Society cross[45] as the outward sign of a congregation which now, like congregations in the Church of Rome, was returning *ad fontes*, to the vision of Fr Lowder and the other founders of the Society. As described by Fr Shields over the next eight years, this was a Society of priests founded on the principles of St Vincent de Paul:

1) to defend and strengthen the spiritual life of the clergy
2) to defend the faith of the Church
3) to carry out and aid mission work
4) to meet in prayer and confidence.

In particular the brethren should be bound together in charity and not take part in ecclesiastical one-upmanship. It was again re-emphasized that the Society was not a campaigning society. There continued to be a slow series of resignations of members who had joined it as such during the height of the Methodist unity proposals. As a confidential, rather than a secret society, members were now encouraged to talk openly about its work. All this was to take tangible form in the new Rule.

Beyond the internal debates about the Society there were the continued threats to Catholic order and practice from the ordination of women.[46] To counter these, brethren were encouraged to become more involved in the Church of England's synodical structures,[47] to provide reasoned, prayerful opposition[48] under the guidance of the Catholic group; an appeal that was made repeatedly before synod elections. At the same time there was hope that ARCIC would provide a way to unity with Rome.

In this year the *Catholic Standard* ceased publication. Its circulation had rarely been above 3,000, and moves, in particular that of Fr Preist to Beverley Minster, and illness amongst its editors were the final straws that forced its closure.

The Loughborough Conference held in 1978 was widely

believed to have been a success. About 80 brethren from a roll of 510 went to the conference, and the Society was visible for the first time through the lapel cross.[49] Some believed that there was a new spirit abroad amongst Catholic Anglicans. The Catholic societies were cooperating better than they had for some time. They were in a unique position to bring the insights of Vatican II to the Church of England and following the decree *Perfectæ Caritatis* and the instruction *Renovationis Causam* there was a sense that the Society as an 'other institute' should reopen and renew its common life set against the background of serious absenteeism from the Society's meetings. Debate continued whether the Society was a brotherhood or no more than a group of likeminded priests. Catholic Renewal itself was a much broader movement than SSC or even Catholic Anglicanism. The conferences were addressed by such leading lights as Richard Holloway, Colin Buchanan, who as Bishop of Woolwich was to work so hard to water down the most Catholic of the Alternative Service Book's eucharistic prayers (though he had also worked against the Methodist unity proposals), and Ken Leech, the leading Christian socialist. New ideas and new liturgy were experimented with. The ordination of women did not seem an issue to provoke serious division. In years to come, renewal pilgrims in their thousands from the Catholic north went to Lindisfarne or Walsingham; parishes from out of the Catholic mainstream would attend large open-air Eucharists where, on one such occasion they watched Bishop Goodrich of Tonbridge administer Benediction, and then, like a good Cranmerian, consume the Host.

Nevertheless, there were continued threats to Catholic faith and order in the Church of England. During 1978 and after, the Catholic societies worked closely against the ordination of women, but there was also concern over that year's Lichfield Report on the remarriage of divorcees and the publication of *The Myth of God Incarnate*.[50] The publication of the ARCIC elucidations on Eucharistic doctrine and ministry and ordination did little to lift the sense of gloom reported in some chapters. In 1979 Robert Runcie was translated to the see of Canterbury.

For once, there was an Archbishop with a good knowledge of the aims and purpose of the Society, though there were the usual mutterings that he was not a 'proper Catholic'.[51] During that year the Society supported opposition to the Incumbents' (Vacation of Benefices) Measure, which was one of a series of measures proposed over the following years to bring discipline to the parochial system through the centralization of power. The Society opposed the measure on the grounds it made bad law, that there was no definition of pastoral breakdown and no right of appeal, and clergy could be blacklisted without being told. It was in this year that the Abbot of Nashdom called a meeting of the Catholic societies, which finally happened in 1980 under the secretaryship of Fr Peter Geldard, then General Secretary of the Church Union. This was the first of a series of meetings designed especially to work against the covenanting proposals.

The year 1980 was the 125th anniversary of the Society. It was marked by a Mass at the Chapel in St Barnabas, Soho, where the Society had begun. Following the moves to make the Society more of a congregation, there was an opportunity for the renewal of the Society promise. At the same time, the revision of the statutes was finally completed, although it was not until 1983 that new statutes were issued to all brethren, some of whom had never had a copy of any statutes. (It was thus hardly surprising that some brethren did not know what the Society was about.) The new statutes allowed for divergences in what was becoming more and more a global society. This had been the case throughout the period, but the Society had grown abroad most rapidly in the 1970s. New structures to deal with this only came into place gradually, and it is only in 1983 that there are minutes for the Master's council.

As part of the renewal of the Society, the post of episcopal visitor was created. The hope was that the visitor might represent the Society's views in the centres of power and act as guardian of its statutes.[52] Alongside this continued work of renewal, the decision was taken to focus more on mission. It was also decided that the Holy Cross trust was unlikely to raise sufficient funds to buy a house to be a centre for the Society, and it was turned into a grant-making body.

In the same year, the Alternative Service Book was passed through General Synod. It was the most Catholic service book in the Church of England in modern times, although the improved rites were often ignored by those who had the opportunity to use the full Roman rite, despite the exhortations of the Master. As usual, progress on one front was counterbalanced by what were seen as threats to the Catholic integrity of the Church of England. In this case it was the proposed covenant with the United Reformed Church, Methodist Church and Moravians, by which the Free Churches would become episcopal – though that episcopacy would be ambiguous. Although it was felt that the Protestant churches would be making concessions, the overall effect would be to make the Church of England firmly Protestant; lay celebration would continue and doubtless spread into the Church of England, and the URC would continue to communicate the unbaptized. In short, the proposals struck at the foundations of the Society and the ecclesiastical foundations of the Church of England. Partly through the work of the Church Union, the covenant was defeated the following year.

In 1981 the revision of the statutes was finally completed and agreed. Fr Shields was re-elected Master without any other candidate being put forward. In the following year Dr Graham Leonard, Bishop of London, became the first episcopal visitor of the Society, having previously advised on the role of the episcopal visitor when the new statutes were drawn up. He immediately said that the most serious problem which faced the Anglican Communion was not theology but personal discipline, especially in the priesthood. The Society had an important task to set standards of priestly integrity for others to copy. During the year the possibility of parish missions by SSC clergy was raised. This project had been previously considered, but was now to lead to the 1987 Barkingside mission and Mission Direct. In addition, many 'Fan the Flame' missioners were SSC clergy. Three deputy-Masters, Frs Hum, Tute and Howard, stepped down during the year, all three now retired and a single deputy-Master, Fr Mander, was appointed by the Master.

In 1982 the Pope visited Great Britain, but there was no official SSC involvement. Although the official communiqués raised hopes of unity in due time, the response of the Sacred Congregation for the Doctrine of the Faith to the ARCIC final report and the continued problems over the ordination of women in the Anglican Communion dampened any excessive hopes.

The following year, 1983, was the 150th anniversary of the Oxford Movement, the term sesquicentenary becoming commonplace among clergy and people. The second Loughborough Conference took place in this year. It was considered good for morale even if its content was limited. Issues raised, if not faced, at the conference included the common perception that Catholic Anglicans were 'no' sayers and that the nature of renewal was something to be sought rather than organized. The Catholic Renewal movement from this point was clearly running out of steam. Nevertheless it can be seen to have generated an important, if mixed, legacy, ranging from Affirming Catholicism to Fan the Flame and the Caister Conferences. Its charismatic offshoots seem to have had little popular success.

The 150th celebrations and conference need, however, to be put into context. The Bishop of London addressed the Society on the need for love for the brethren: a striking illustration of how even those friendly to the Society doubted its spiritual strength. The Master made a similar point, noting how the Society was founded as a Society for mutual edification, not as a political body; one whose leaders were not necessarily big names in the Church at large. At the same time proposals for the ordination of women to the diaconate were put forward in General Synod. This was to be highly significant for it was the admission of women into the House of Clergy which broke the Catholic block on the ordination of women to the priesthood. When in 1985 General Synod voted to prepare legislation on the ordination of women, only the House of Bishops gave a two-thirds majority in favour. At this time, however, the tactical implications of this were not recognized and they were related to the decline in Catholic numbers, the importance of which again seems not to have been recognized. Indeed, the diaconate seems to have been so little thought about that the theological implications of voting for women deacons were not recognized.

In this year new proposals from General Synod on the remarriage of divorcees were considered. Speaking to the Society, Fr Brian Brindley, then an influential chairman of the Synod Standing Committee, had noted that something had to be done to avoid a complete breakdown in what were now recognized to be increasingly unworkable laws. The favoured Catholic option of some form of nullity procedure had little support. In the event the proposals came to nothing, but remarriage after divorce was eventually piloted through synod by the bishops in 2004.

The *Acta* for 1984 give few indications of new concerns. However, at the synod for London and the south-east, concerns were raised as to how to help priests whose marriages were in difficulty. This, and the question of clergy partners, was to become a more pressing issue. The year 1984 was Fr Shields' last as Master. He left the office with the Society at a strength of 731 priests. During his time the Society had become much more open. Fr Shields had been proposed for membership without his knowledge, and it had taken some ingenuity to find out who his seconders were. All that was now of the past, but the growth of the Society meant that great strains were placed on the Master. In his farewell letter to his congregation at St Stephen's, Gloucester Road, Fr Colven, the succeeding Master, would apologize to his people for neglecting them at the expense of the Society and the wider Catholic movement.

Fr Colven replaced Fr Shields as Master, Fr Mander, the then deputy-Master having withdrawn when it became apparent that the London clergy would not support him. Fr Colven was then Administrator of the Walsingham Shrine and would become Vicar of St Stephen's, Gloucester Road, in 1987.

In his first *Acta* the new Master addressed some of the themes which would dominate his time as Master. He noted the difficulties of the Society becoming more international and how that was dealt with became a major concern of the Master's council. In the previous year it had been suggested that Australia and New Zealand form separate provinces and that happened in this year. He noted also that the *Faith in the City* report was being produced by a body which, typically, had no SSC representation on it, even though SSC clergy worked in some of the most deprived parishes in the country and had been involved in helping to bring the respective communities together after the Handsworth and Tottenham riots. Arguably, one of the reasons the Society was marginalized in the Church of England was that the people it often cared for were themselves the marginalized. He felt that it was important too that the Society should not just merely rest on its laurels but rather maintain its work.

However, the main concern the Master addressed in his first *Acta* was the ordination of women. The recent General Synod vote that there was no theological reason not to ordain women had depressed some Catholic clergy. There were now five years or so before legislation would be brought to synod. In the meantime, as well as mobilizing support, a key concern was relations with the Church of Rome. The Bishop of London, Dr Leonard, posed the question, 'Is there a Catholic future for the Church of England?' in September at a conference in Oxford. He had argued that, in the event of the ordination of women in England, clergy should not leave the Church of England as individuals, but in a temporary group of bishops, priests and people; not as a continuing church and not as a new body. If there were to be a parallel jurisdiction, that had to be an interim measure while the ecclesial situation worked itself out. The Master interpreted this, surely correctly, as the description of a uniate church. The minutes of the Master's council show that the council was much of one mind in its opposition to the ordination of women, though it had doubts about the brethren; at least one member in Southwark diocese belonged to the Movement for the Ordination of Women. In the event the Society would not directly oppose the ordination of women, this would be done by Cost of Conscience, which was formed as a specifically campaigning body. It was within this perspective that the Master wrote that there were different kinds of Catholic Anglicans, but he himself did not believe that the Church of England was an end in itself; indeed it was defective while not in communion with the Great Church.[53] Though recognizing the breadth of Catholic Anglicanism, it was his view that the Society was papalist in intention because it recognized this defect within the Church of England and that this represented a 'fuller vision' than other kinds of Catholic Anglicanism.[54] This, as the Master implicitly recognized, was to move the Society in a 'full faith' direction which was new.[55] Union with Rome through a uniate church would appear to have been the Master's, and perhaps the council's, goal. To this end, clergy were advised to present ARCIC to their parishes as a means to gain their acceptance of the Church of Rome.

The campaign against the ordination of women linked with the possibility of a uniate Anglican Church dominated Fr Colven's term of office. The internal organization of the Society as an international body, especially with the impact of the ordination of women to the priesthood in the different Anglican provinces, took up much of the Master's council's time. It may be a misleading impression of *Acta*, but except in response to political pressures, holiness of life was not a theme of the Master's Addresses.[56]

In 1986 the Master wrote reviewing current developments in the Church of England. *Faith in the City* had largely ignored the traditional Catholic's work in the poorest parishes. The proposals for locally ordained priests were a managerial response to the decline in clergy numbers rather than an idea developed from a belief that priesthood is given by God for the whole Church. However, the bishops' report *The Nature of Christian Belief* was generally to be welcomed. Even if it lacked clarity, it did not directly support Dr Jenkins' demythologization of Christian belief.

As for Society business, there was again the problem that priests had joined without really understanding what the Society was for and what its core beliefs were. The London chapter was working to have all its members sign up to the Bishop of London's petition on the ordination of women: a sign of the pressure to mobilize and to make sure the Society spoke with one voice. At the same time, the Master's council had to deal with a problem of women training for the diaconate who had demanded entry to a chapter meeting in Oxford. The council noted that attendance at meetings of the Society was by invitation only, and that because deacons were only admitted to meetings of the Society on the understanding that they would become priests, those in the permanent diaconate could not become members.

In 1987 the ARCIC statement on authority in the Church was accepted by the General Synod. The Master welcomed this, though he noted that since the Church of England was not the Universal Church, any such decision had limited standing. Arguably this emphasis on the fact that the Church of England does not claim to be the Universal Church, and the conclusions to be drawn from that, has been a major stumbling-block to the successful presentation of the Society's position on the ordination of women.

During the year, Fr Roy Fellows, SSC, replaced Fr Colven as Administrator at Walsingham, and Fr Ross Thompson, SSC, replaced Fr Geldard as General Secretary of the Church Union. There were continued discussions about the international dimension of the Society. The province of Central Africa was inaugurated. There were also suggestions that there be devolution of powers to the provinces. This was further discussed the following year when it became apparent that, with the exception of the New Zealand brethren (who by this time seem to have admitted women clergy), there was a desire to maintain a central organization. Plans for an International Synod in 1989 were begun that year.

In his address to the May synod of the Society the Master focused especially on the recent General Synod debate on human sexuality. He noted this was a problem area for Catholics and as such care should be given to avoid particular cause for scandal. Indeed, it had happened that brethren had lost the sense of their priestly calling to wholeness of life because of their sexuality, or had reneged on their calling to accept posts from the establishment. He reiterated a favourite theme that true priesthood involves pain and rejection to stand by Mary at the foot of the Cross.

Contacts with Roman Catholic dignitaries had continued. The Master had seen the apostolic Pro Nuncio, Mgr Barbarito, in 1987, and the general officers of the Society had visited Rome during 1988. In writing up the visit, Fr Davey noted that the position of the Vatican on the question of women's ordination was quite clear: as Pope Paul VI had said, the ordination of women would not be one obstacle among many but a threat to unity.[57] Mgr Barbarito had urged opposition to women's ordination through the Society's brethren because the bishops would be of little help in this. Fr Davey further noted that what was not clear from the Vatican was how those who opposed the ordination of women would be dealt with. Requests would be taken on merit, though, significantly in the light of the Master's comments, the moral problems of individual clergy would need to be regularized. Further, there was the impact any agreement would have on the Church of Rome in the United Kingdom, including its relations with the Church of England. Local bishops would not want independent-minded clergy who were used to ignoring their own bishops and who were, despite everything, not culturally Catholic and thought to be too concerned with ceremonial niceties and vesture, and it would be easier to receive married priests than married bishops. As often in the past, Fr Davey continued, one of the key questions for Rome to consider was how many clergy they would have to deal with, and as Cardinal Willibrands noted, was the ordination of women their only reason for leaving? Willibrands had further asked how the Church of England could seek unity with Rome when it was so disunited in itself. The Society's representatives had also had a very brief word with the Pope and were given to understand that he regarded organizations as the SSC as very important as part of his concern for similar world movements.[58] Later in the year the synods of the Society passed a motion from the oldest and largest synod of the Society, London, supporting ARCIC and urging that the bishops of the Church of England not place any obstacle to the unity of the Church.

In his July letter the Master noted how at the Lambeth Conference it was clear that the different provinces of the Anglican Communion were in effect autonomous local churches.[59] His main concern, though, was the spiritual and political weakness of Anglican Catholicism. As had been so often analysed in the past, unlike the evangelicals, Catholic Anglicans had not dug themselves in very effectively against the liberal establishment, and the evangelical emphasis on sexual morality would be problematic for Catholic Anglicans. The Society was not a campaigning society, though by its nature its members took a stand on some issues. Rather it was a spiritual society, and here it seemed to lack enthusiasm and fervour – something which appeared not only in sexual behaviour but also in personal spirituality, pastoral work and the use of money.[60]

The main event for the Society in 1989 was the International Synod which took place over four days in April. During the synod talks were given on the origins and ideals of the Society by Fr Cobb, on priesthood and Christ the high priest by Professor Macquarrie, intercommunion today by Dr Leonard, and whither ARCIC? by Canon Christopher Hill, the Archbishop's secretary for ecumenical affairs. Devotional addresses were given by Fr Sheehy, chaplain of New College, and there were discussions and reports on the work of the Society. There was worship at Fr Lowder's church of London Docks, at St Stephen's, Gloucester Road, and pilgrimages to Walsingham and finally Canterbury, where Dr Runcie celebrated and Bishop Clarence Pope of Fort Worth preached.

The conference was largely organized by Frs Geldard, Wilson and Bedford, and began with greetings from the

Archbishops of Westminster and Canterbury, presented in that order. Amongst the addresses, that of Canon Hill was perhaps the most significant. He noted the inconsistency of the Lambeth Conference voting to support ARCIC while at the same time maintaining provincial autonomy. He did not believe that the ordination of women would be accepted by Rome in the foreseeable future since Rome did not have the power to change the Church's tradition.[61] It was not a first-order issue and so not one which fell within ARCIC's remit, but it had a very important bearing on the Eucharist, which was a first-order issue. ARCIC was a forum to provide a framework for discussion, but he could not see Rome coming to an agreement with any part of the Anglican Communion, since the Reformation ecclesial settlement left it with no juridical embodiment: it was not possible to come into union with a body which had no locus of unity.

Christian unity was the focus also of the Master's Address, and a motion was passed which called for all Christians to work for unity under the primacy of the Bishop of Rome, and for Anglican bishops not to hinder unity by unilateral action. The Master's Address began with the assertion that a Catholicism separated from the See of Peter ran great risks. The Church of England was the Catholic Church of this land, but nationality was not the same as Catholicity, so it could not be a free or independent Church. The transitional nature of the Church of England had been held by Archbishop Fisher and reiterated by Dr Runcie at the Lambeth Conference. It was the nature of Catholicism that it is the Gospel of Jesus Christ. Catholicism is the proclamation not of a faith but the Faith. Nothing should obstruct that work of mission, certainly not negative, old-fashioned or misogynistic clergy. Likewise, the divisions of the Church were a great bar to mission and so ecumenism was vitally important, and especially unity with the Great Church. Thus the Society could not be a single-issue body: its concern was for the Gospel, not for opposing Methodist unity or the ordination of women, though its members had done so in the interests of Christ's mission. Now the Society faced a crux and he hoped that if its members left the Church of England, they did so retaining their pastoral identity.

That was a rallying call to a Society of 900 priests, one which in the light of future events might be taken as a signal that for some, at least, their time in the Church of England was over. Indeed, it was significant that the Master and Frs Bedford, Wilson, Geldard and Broadhurst visited the Fort Worth synod. Two hundred SSC clergy were attached to the synod and its representatives spoke at the international conference. The Ecumenical Catholic Mission, the umbrella group for the synod, was seen as providing a possible model for a response to the ordination of women in the Church of England.

At other times in the year it was agreed that divorced and remarried clergy should not be put up for membership of the Society, and that in general if a member did remarry, he should withdraw. Divorced and now single clergy could, however, join. There was also a plea from Fr Stephen Trott that Catholic clergy should involve themselves in the new continuing ministerial education. Fr Lindsay Urwin, Chichester diocesan missioner, gave a talk, later printed, on the need to re-evangelize the Church, emphasizing appropriate music, ceremonial, preaching and the participation of the laity. This was to become the 'Fan the Flame' missions.

In 1990 Dr George Carey was translated to the see of Canterbury and Dr Hope to that of London, and both were taken as signs that traditionalists would not continue to be marginalized. Dr Carey was welcomed for his clear orthodox teaching, though it was noted he supported the ordination of women and had little experience of Catholic Anglicans. Some fears were expressed by brethren that Dr Hope did not stand out enough in defence of Catholic truth, but he was to become the second episcopal visitor of the Society.[62] The year 1990 was also the beginning of the Decade of Evangelization, as the Church of Rome and the Society called it. Mgr Barbarito spoke to the London synod about the necessity of Christian evangelism, not just as proclamation but also as lifestyle. Evangelism required a concern for justice, peace, for human dignity and freedom, and evangelism was weakened by disunity – a theme of the great Protestant missionary societies and a motivation for the work of the pan-Protestant alliance, though they rarely recognized Barbarito's further point that a united mission of the churches could not work if it was based on a fudge.

It was decided that there was a role for the Society in mission, and the SSC's resources and the fund-raising in parishes would be best served by using the already existing structures of the Society and sending money directly to Catholic parishes through Mission Direct. The first year's donations were given to the Company of Mission Priests' parish of St Oswald, Hartlepool, and the diocese of Aipo Rongo, Papua New Guinea, whose bishop, Paul Richardson, was a member of the Society. Sadly, this was also the year when the New Zealand province was dissolved after it had admitted women clergy. By the following year under the deployment officer, Fr Turnbull, £12,000 had been raised, but the growth of the work was held back by the ordination of women debate.

The debates and manoeuvrings over the ordination of women continued to take up time and energy which brethren might have preferred to be spent on mission. The Master lamented this as well as the thinness of much of the Society's theology; as he put it: Does anyone understand Hauke?[63] However, he was confident that the legislation would be defeated, though as usual, he lamented the loss of good priests over the year and reminded the brethren of the need to vote in elections. During the year there were press reports about 'Open Catholicism', once known as 'Cuddesdon Catholicism', but which soon became 'Affirming Catholicism'. The belief that mainstream traditionalist Catholics would not join this party was misplaced; in recent years the issue of human sexuality, in particular homosexuality, has been a reason for a number of brethren to leave the Society. It was an issue addressed by Fr Colven in that year.

After consultations, which had begun at the start of Fr Colven's mastership as part of an exercise to divine the mind of the Society, guidelines on divorce were published for the

Society. Some provinces had already drawn up their own guidelines, including nullity procedures, some brethren had remarried after divorce and others had married divorcees. The basic principle was that the Society was obedient to Christ and the constant teaching of the Church. The founders of the Society had been clear that the teaching authority applies to morals. Priests who are characterized by the lifestyle of the Cross need to scrutinize their lifestyle to ensure it follows the teaching of the Church. From this it followed that since members of the Society, which was, after all, a voluntary organization, should be obedient to the Catholic tradition in ethics as well as dogma, so if there were marital breakdown and a brother remarry, that brother should leave the Society, though be treated with pastoral love.

The need for these guidelines brought out the need for a fuller discussion of human sexuality. The Master was mindful of the need to avoid a double-standard, since while remarriage after divorce automatically led to expulsion from the Society, prohibited sexual acts outside of marriage did not. At the same time, however, he emphasized that it was not possible to equate the moral problems of remarriage with those of homosexuality. Marriage was God's will for creation and was a commitment to love as Christ had commanded. A homosexual relationship, even a non-genital one, could not be the same. The Church had always distinguished between homosexual acts, as sinful, and homosexual orientation, which was not, and had taught that the real difficulties which homosexuals faced could be overcome by grace, and where there was human failing, the confessional provided the proper place to work out problems of sexuality.

In 1991 the membership of the Society stood at just over 1,100. In this year the Master and Frs Bedford, Wilson and Hawkins visited Dr Carey. The meeting proved unsatisfactory: the Master having wanted to talk about evangelism and the Gospel; Dr Carey nervously talking about the East End, the ordination of women and the possibility of alternative episcopal oversight. The SSC was not in fact campaigning on those issues

– they were the work of Cost of Conscience. A similar sense of crossed purposes occurred when, in the following year, the Archbishop addressed the London synod and much of the Society, at St Stephen's, Gloucester Road. He spoke about hearing the pain of clergy who opposed the innovation of women's ordination and of his desire to encourage that part of the clergy who took seriously the fact that the Church of England was not created at the Reformation. He spoke of the importance of the sacraments and of creation, of loyalty to credal forms and value of Catholic spirituality, but he believed that the New Testament did not give warrant for splits in the Church over ordination. In response to questions, he noted the Society was simply one pressure group amongst many. This was not appreciated. The synod was not in an emollient mood and some members directed harsh and insulting words at the Archbishop, who (it is said) was greatly angered by his reception; though Dr Geoffrey Rowell's address on Anglican inclusiveness was greeted with possibly even greater scepticism. The synod probably did the Society more harm than good.

The year 1992 was dominated by the November vote on the ordination of women. In preparation for the legislation being passed Fr Colven urged the need for members of the Society to stay together and move together. At the May synod he was voted by acclamation an extra term as Master in view of the situation. At that time the Society had 1,051 members. General Synod voted to legislate for the ordination of women to the priesthood on 11 November. A meeting had already been arranged for the Society for 9 December at St Alphege, Solihull, and 650 priests attended, in a mixture of shock, confusion, bluster and anger. For some the vote marked the end of their time in the Church of England; others were much more uncertain. A questionnaire soon afterwards suggested that the majority of the Society would stay in the Church of England, and of these, most would want alternative episcopal oversight. A few supported the new legislation.

In November, immediately after the vote, Fr Colven had had discussions with Mgr Barbarito, who had worked hard to make the Anglican establishment see how serious was the step they were taking. Fr Colven later reported to the Society that there was a good possibility of some corporate vehicle for it to be received into the Roman Church. At this stage the evidence suggests that Cardinal Hume had in mind his own personal prelature for the Society and its members' congregations, which would be given uniate status; however, the plan was given up after news of the discussions leaked to the press. Fr Colven did not bring to the wider Society's attention Barbarito's comment that individual conversions would be easier for Rome to deal with, as proved the case, or the extreme sensitivity any mass conversion would need to be treated with *vis-à-vis* the Church of England. Local hierarchies, who had frequent meetings with their Anglican counterparts, would especially not wish to take advantage of the situation. A process of discernment had begun.

Notes

1 The main source for this chapter is *Acta*, but there are some minutes from the Master's council and personal reminiscences that I have been able to draw upon. However, this must give a partial description of the Society, and often one seen through the eyes of the Master. There remains scope for a larger consideration which searches parish archives, synod papers, personal reminiscences and a comparison with other Catholic societies. This chapter is, by contrast, more of an institutional survey and a commentary by members of the Society on the changing Church of England. My especial thanks are due to the Rt Revd John Broadhurst who gave his time for an interview about some of the events described, to Revd Canon Michael Shields who also gave time for an interview, loaned some of his private papers and kindly read a first draft of this chapter; to all those brethren who so patiently answered my telephone requests for information; to the Principal and chapter of Pusey House for their hospitality. None of the above should take any blame for any errors in what follows.

2 PHL: SSC papers, *Acta* November 1948.

3 I have found no extant rolls of the Society at this time. The figure

of 114 is based on the number given to a brother joining at the May synod.

4 A distinguished member such as Fr Alfred Hope-Patten is only recorded as attending one chapter and that when it was held at Walsingham. He was, on that occasion, the only brother present. He said the High Mass, recited the Society Office and, as *Acta* for July 1946 laconically notes, 'There were necessarily no further proceedings'.

5 The brethren represented less than 1 per cent of the total Anglican clergy: they must have been a very powerful leaven to move that lump.

6 Fr Simmons in his latter years as Master would escape the tyranny of the nationalized railways by arriving at synods in a chauffeur-driven car, from which he would descend in scarlet mozetta.

7 His attempts to found more local chapters met indifference.

8 The continued calls by a succession of Masters, at least until the Methodist scheme, and then renewed over the question of the ordination of women, for loyalty to the Church of England, and at all times the repeated calls for holiness of life and brotherly charity, suggest there was always an element among the brethren who were not loyal to the Church which ordained them, and that there was much gin, lace and backbiting: a case of *semper ecclesia, semper reformanda*.

9 See below for 1960–1.

10 That it could happen shows how slight the Society's resources were; a similar situation was to arise in 1993 *et seq.* when no accounts were produced.

11 It is arguable that this has been the root cause of failure of Catholic Anglicanism: the inability to win mainstream Anglicanism to the basics of Catholic dogma, even though at the same time the outward signs of eucharistic worship (in itself more puritan after Vatican II) have become more acceptable (alongside services of the Word) to the mainstream. The argument, used to justify staying in the Church of England in the face of unity proposals and the ordination of women, both of which struck at the Catholic order of the Church of England, that the Church of England was inherently Catholic began to sound as hollow as the

POSTWAR AND PRE-CRISIS: 1945–92

acceptance of Catholic practice was in reality. Hence the later concerns of both Fr Simmons and Fr Colven to create short-lived continuing churches or prelatures to take the priests of the Society and their people out of the Church of England.

12 Note that this was being said before the 1960s, so often taken as the time of great change for the Church.

13 The parallels with today's (2004) synod concerns are striking.

14 The northern province was in 1969 to return the compliment when it made Fr Simmons Master for life by popular acclamation (and without reference to anyone else in the Society).

15 Canon Rich's position seems to have been that development in doctrine should be taken from the Church of Rome, raising the question, what is the point of the Church of England, other than God's providential vehicle for English Christians in the immediate aftermath of the Protestant Reformation?

16 In this respect the SSC might be considered a precursor of postmodernism.

17 From the late 1970s it became customary for the Master or his representative to be on the council of many of the Catholic societies.

18 In 2002 the General Synod finally rejected this in favour of remarriage at the discretion of the parish priest.

19 The full details of this controversy, finally resolved the following year when the St Wilfrid's chapter put pressure on the Master, are currently time-embargoed at the request of the late Fr Blagdon Gamlen, who subsequently headed the Society's roll.

20 It is not clear from the lack of evidence what happened to these proposals, but over the years the process of electing the Master was not always very transparent.

21 There are no records extant in the Society's archive for 1960–1. This is unfortunate because they might have thrown some light on the second election of Fr Simmons as Master. In this time the Society statutes were revised and considerably slimmed down and, as best as can be judged, Fr Simmon's old idea of a southern and a northern province was put in place.

22 In the following year in a memorandum to Bishop Butler the Master acknowledged that Anglican orders were the main stumbling block to unity; he believed Anglican clergy would

submit to retraining, but they would also be very concerned to bring their laity with them.

23 Nowadays this would be called spin.

24 Dr Vidler was a distinguished Anglican historian and theologian. In 1962 he edited *Soundings*, a volume of essays whose contributors included, among others, H.A. Williams. Vidler edited the journal *Theology* from 1939 to 1964.

25 This was to be a perennial problem. In 1970 the Master noted to the Society of Mary that councils of the Catholic societies had so often petered out.

26 Dr Stockwood was fairly orthodox at this time.

27 Relations with the Church Union improved at the time Fr Douglas Carter SSC became General Secretary, and were to become especially strong in the 1980s when Fr Geldard became General Secretary.

28 As part of his work in mobilizing opposition to this scheme, Fr Simmons was instrumental in setting up the League of Anglican Loyalists. Later Masters of the Society were *ex officio* theological advisers to the League.

29 We must presume the Anglican establishment thought its position so right that any opposition, even before decisions were made, was contrary to Anglican teaching.

30 In the following year this would be brought into sharp focus when the Accra diocese allowed communion regardless of church affiliation. The split was clearly whether communion was the goal of unity or its means.

31 But brethren often found these rules so brief that recourse had to be made to the 1952 manual.

32 But even Bishop Butler told the Society in 1971 that Rome would not negotiate with dissident groups, the Anglican clergy would probably need to be conditionally ordained and that Anglicans should hold on to what was good in their tradition.

33 Fr Simmons became wary of statute revision, perhaps fearing, justly, that it might be organized against his perpetual mastership.

34 The practice of admitting brethren to the Society in hotels was later to be severely curtailed.

35 Although it had no representation on it, which places its ecumenical activities in perspective, it may be there was a lack of
serious theological expertise in the Society.

36 The point at issue was one of the fundamental points at issue in
Methodist unity; was communion the means or the end of unity.

37 It was not yet seen how far the Church of England would be
persuaded to accept these as her own moral norms.

38 Another aspect of Anglican life which greatly concerned the
Society, and on which it had no direct impact.

39 Some chapter secretaries could be equally pompous when it came
to when to wear the cincture (especially in Rome).

40 Other reasons were listed as a lack of Christianity, unease at the
Master and the inaudibility of both the Master and the local vicar.

41 The political opinions of members of the Society seem to have
varied enormously: in the 1984 miners' strike one of the brethren
was injured by the police while on picket-duty, while another
was the only Tory councillor in Doncaster. As far as I can judge,
Society priests worked to keep communities together and were
generally most sympathetic to those in greatest hardship, dis-
tributing food to those in need without being too closely iden-
tified with one side or another in industrial disputes, so as to be
trusted by all.

42 Later evidence suggests that Fr Simmons' work to bring the
Catholic societies together was held back by personality clashes
and turf-wars. It was not until 1980 that the societies began to pull
together seriously.

43 One of the first changes introduced at this time was that officers
were to be voted in post for four years at a time (the previous
Master had, in effect, become Master for life).

44 The north of England and Scotland, the west of England and
Wales, the English Midlands, London and the south-east, the
Pacific, North America and South Africa.

45 The Second Vatican Council was ultimately to put an end to
much of the lace.

46 By the same token, he noted that the officer's scarlet cincture was
resented by those outside the Society as a claim to minor dignity,
while the ordinary cincture was perhaps worn most frequently by

those clergy who were least zealous in living the Society's Rule. Later there was to be a brief controversy when Fr Shields as Master sought to restrict the number of occasions when the Master wore a scarlet mozetta or *cappa magna*, and even in the 1980s there was a brief spat when the Bishop of Johannesburg objected to a deacon coming to his priestly ordination wearing the cincture.

47 The Master continually warned against misogyny.

48 As the Master noted, these might be wearisome and hard on the soul, but the Catholic faith would not grow without personal cost.

49 The possibility of positive reform in General Synod hardly seems to have been raised.

50 At the time of writing, in some dioceses it is still not uncommon for most clergy never to have heard of the Society.

51 The 1981 Doctrine Commission report, *Believing in the Church*, showed just how little agreement there was about Anglican teaching. *The Myth of God Incarnate* was a volume of essays edited by John Hick (London: SCM Press, 1978) which upset many traditionalists, both Catholic and evangelical.

52 In the event he was to promote his own cadre of Westcott and Cuddesdon men, reckoning later that none had proved disastrous. See Humphrey Carpenter, *Robert Runcie: The Reluctant Archbishop* (London: Hodder & Stoughton, 1996), p. 146. Bishops whom he promoted reckoned Runcie's cronyism was overstated.

53 The Society is unusual in that most congregations are required to have a Visitor by the hierarchy.

54 Fr Colven stated this point against Tractarian and Eastward-looking Catholics, unfairly, since there is a tradition outside Anglo-papalism of making this point, for example, Geoffrey Fisher said as much.

55 Which may be interpreted as meaning that in the graded levels of communion with the Holy See, the papalist Anglican was more advanced than other Catholic Anglicans. I have found no evidence that previous Masters held this view or presented it as Society policy. Previously the hope had always been to convert the Church of England from within, and Fr Colven did occasionally refer to that 'leaven in the lump' view. Increasingly,

remain one of those moments when we can all remember where we were and what we were doing when we first heard the news. I had listened on and off all morning to the debate on the radio and had heard the then Bishop of London, David Hope's powerful contribution opposing the move but later in the afternoon, with a number of friends, had settled down in my sitting-room in Gospel Oak to watch the debate live on television. It had been a long afternoon. We numbered about ten priests with one ordinand who was on placement with me at the time and who testifies to this day to the emotion with which we all received the news. For him it was a formative experience as he subsequently went to St Stephen's House and on to ordination, and finds himself now a member of the Society. Of the others who were there, five were to leave the Church of England subsequently and are now ordained in the Roman Catholic Church. We had listened to the debate. We saw our friends on television, John Broadhurst, Stuart Wilson and Peter Geldard, and the Master of the Society, Christopher Colven. Several of them had spoken and, inevitably, emotions were running so high that it was not a good debate. Many people on our side of the argument had not spoken particularly well that day, but Archdeacon David Silk had done his very best to signify to the Church of England the depth of division that a decision in favour would bring. Peter Geldard too, in his speech, had warned that the Church could never be the same again, and that division would go to the very heart of its life. For the last hour of the debate the speeches had become increasingly in favour of the innovation. What had happened to our side of the argument? The Bishop of Southwark, Roy Williamson, whose contribution had clearly been saved until the final throes of the afternoon, pulled every emotional string he could with his arguments about justice and integrity. There was no going back. The result was staring us in the face. It was only a few remaining speeches in favour that had to be given in order to fill the time that remained before the vote, yet still we did not believe that the Church of England could do this. It was not possible and we hoped against hope. So 5 o'clock came and we fell silent. The tears began to roll down our cheeks. No one could say anything. The television was immediately switched off and we sat motionless and speechless. Then, one by one, people left the vicarage, without even a word of goodbye. Within a quarter of an hour I found myself alone.

A few minutes later, one of my oldest friends rang from the USA. He too had heard the news. He simply said 'Welcome to the club!' It was not the most helpful remark at that moment. Everything was in turmoil. It was St Martin's Day. I remember going to St Martin's, Gospel Oak for their patronal festival. The clergy in the sacristy beforehand were hardly able to speak when the local Methodist minister exclaimed what great news it was and invited our reaction: we certainly gave it to him, the force of which I suspect shocked both him and us. Fr Simon Evans SSC tried to preach without commenting on the day's events but could not avoid referring to the fact that the Church of England had, at a stroke, lost its Catholic credentials. It was a bizarre evening. None of us wanted to be there. The next evening, I remember saying Mass at All Hallows for our regular Thursday evening celebration. I could hardly get through the eucharistic prayer. It seemed to me that everything I believed about the priesthood had been destroyed. Everything I believed I stood for had been removed. It felt desperate.

I suspect that this experience was true for very many. It was not so much a question of whether a woman could or could not be ordained to the priesthood, as we might have discussed from time to time, but rather how could the Church of England make this decision; what authority did this General Synod have; how could a number of votes sway our particular part of the Church to depart from the received tradition of the Church Universal? It was a crisis of authority. It was in every sense as if death had occurred. Fr David Paul SSC, who had been with us that fateful afternoon and who subsequently was one of the many who left the Church of England, later described the experience as a bereavement. We were all in a state of shock, incredulous at what had happened, and we went through many of the feelings that bereavement brings. We were bewildered and disillusioned. We were upset and broken. We were afraid and lost. And we were angry.

Over the next few years these emotions were to surface again and again in the life of the Catholic movement. Many priests were angry and, perhaps regrettably, our behaviour showed it. Bishops who tried to sympathize with our sense of loss did not always meet with a polite response. The light had been put out and I suspect many clergy were so totally disillusioned that the darkness seemed to overwhelm them. Things somehow had to be kept going on the surface but many priests neglected their own devotions. They ceased to pray. They neglected to go to confession. The daily office was forgotten. It is easy for us, when we look back, to forget how deep the hurt went and how immense was the damage.

So it was that on 12 November 1992 the leadership of the Society of the Holy Cross met with others from the Catholic group in General Synod in Faith House, Westminster. Something had to be done immediately which would draw in all who found themselves unable to accept what had happened. It was recognized immediately that no one organization could meet the need of the hour. The Society inevitably only covered the clergy; the laity too needed to be brought on board. The Church Union in 1992 did not have the political clout that was required to meet the crisis. A new organization was needed to embrace clergy and laity in the widest possible sense. Forward in Faith was born. The Society immediately gave £10,000 from the Holy Cross Trust in order to set it up. Stuart Wilson became its first secretary and Christopher Bedford a member of its executive. Christopher Colven himself, though it had been very much part of his vision, took something of a back seat. Anthony Prescott from the Additional Curates' Society and Geoffrey Kirk from Cost of Conscience were brought in to help. The choice for chairman lay between David Silk and John Broadhurst. David Silk had borne the heat of the day in the Synod debate by leading the opposition from the platform. John Broadhurst had been leader of the Catholic group in General Synod. John Broadhurst was chosen. From the outset the Society has worked alongside Forward in Faith in its political struggle to secure an honoured place for everyone who found themselves in the position of being unable to identify with the Synod's decision.

Christopher Colven, throughout the latter part of the 1980s, had been an influential figure and had done much to coordinate the opposition and to rally clergy and people. He was both Master of the Society and Master of the College of Guardians at Walsingham. In so many ways he was the recognized leader of the Catholic movement at the time. In 1989 he had called an international synod of the Society, which took place in Church House, Westminster. There he had spoken of the need to embrace a complete Catholicism and had encouraged us 'to look to the rock from which we were hewn'. They are both themes which I have reiterated in recent years. He was deliberately making the attempt to mould both priests and people to be ready to make a move. He was looking earnestly to the Church of Rome so that Anglican Catholics might find a way to embrace Peter as a focus for unity and enabler of full communion. His was a vision of some great realignment of Catholicism in this country. Yet the vision was not clear and it was hard to see, even before 1992, how things would pan out. Rome had already been questioning the status of the ARCIC agreements and casting doubts on the Church of England's sincerity to pursue the ecumenical vision which they contained. That Rome would not fully endorse ARCIC's work led many to change their mind at the eleventh hour and vote in favour of women's ordination. The Church of England seemed to speak with forked tongue: it was saying one thing and doing another. Although Rome courteously responded to the vote to ordain women to the priesthood by saying it did not present insurmountable barriers, it clearly did see such a departure from Catholic order as being a grave obstacle to continuing the ecumenical discussion at the level it had reached. For Anglican Catholics who had had an understanding of corporate reunion and who shared the Master of the Society's vision for some Catholic realignment, the withdrawal on the one hand by the

Church of Rome of approval for the ARCIC documents and the actions of the Church of England on the other left this vision in pieces, and there was a real confusion as to the way forward. Christopher Colven approached the Archbishop of Westminster. Could he come to our rescue? All that he had worked for over the ten-year period leading up to 1992 seemed to be threatened. What were we to do?

For some, the answer was very clear. Their minds had been made up long before the vote had taken place. They were only waiting for the right moment and the right circumstances to leave the Church of England and seek reconciliation with the Holy See. But for a few, there was from the outset a determination to stay in the Church of England and to resist the innovation. For most of us, however, there was a real sense of uncertainty as we recognized, on the one hand, our loyalty to the church in which we had been baptized, formed and ordained, but at the same time questioned our own integrity if we were to remain in the new dispensation. I did not know what to do. I admired Fr Colven and the leadership of the Society, and was deeply influenced by them. I felt compelled to look into 'the Roman option', as it became known. Looking back, something told me that I would never catch the train, but I was certainly on the platform with all the other passengers, and was excited by the prospect of the journey ahead. So it was that Cardinal Hume did come to our rescue. He invited us to Archbishop's House in Westminster in order to receive us and assure us of a warm welcome. He did not want any instant decisions and wanted to provide plenty of space in order for us to make up our minds. There were perhaps 200 priests who went to meet him that evening. The Catholic Church was overwhelmingly sympathetic and friendly to us. It was very alluring. Many possibilities were in the air. The Cardinal himself had yet to go to Rome to discuss it with the Holy Father and, for that matter, with his own bishops in England. It was clear from the outset that there was going to be a massive breakdown in the life of Catholic Anglicanism as we then knew it. At the same time, the newly formed umbrella grouping of

Forward in Faith was going about its work. Not by accident had it taken its name of Forward in Faith. It was definitely about moving forward, and it was definitely concerned about embracing a positive agenda which would indeed rekindle our faith. It was quite clear initially that the agenda of entering into a fuller and deeper communion with the Church of Rome was what moving forward meant. Finding a way across the divide, not just on an individual basis but for us all, was what Forward in Faith envisaged, as well as pursuing a short-term political agenda to maintain the pressure on the Church of England to provide what Catholics within it needed to retain their integrity. In the next few years things were to change very greatly regarding the aims and objectives of Forward in Faith, but I do believe that, as it was set up, it was never envisaged that the organization would develop in the way that it has. There was a goal and it was to be reached as soon as possible with as many as possible on board.

The Cardinal clearly loved us. His heart went out to embrace us in our predicament, but he was equally firm in pointing out that Catholicism was a set menu, table d'hôte, and not à la carte. We could not pick and choose, and the discipline of the Catholic Church was to be accepted as much as the doctrine. Nor was it appropriate that we should be allowed to embrace Roman Catholicism simply because of one issue. He understood only too well that the ordination of women was the presenting issue which had caused us to go knocking at this door. He wanted us to bring with us our English traditions and culture, our traditions in music and of high standards in the performance of the liturgy, but he emphasized how crucial it was to embrace a full Catholic way of life. Without being judgemental at all, he did not want us to convert on our own terms but rather to come with enthusiasm and commitment to all that the Church of Rome might ask of us. So he wanted to provide a space and time for reflection and he predicted, rightly as it turned out, that a great many of us would not take the road in the end. He did not want to see the Catholic movement in the Church of England completely depleted. He believed that it was in the interests of the Gospel for there to be a strong Church of England and for the Church of England to have a strong Catholic movement within it.

Looking back, what he succeeded in doing for us was to receive with open arms those who were already convinced, and to help those who had yet to make up their minds, one way or the other, about what to do to make their decision. He affirmed our right to stay in the Church of England and to witness to Catholic truth and order in whatever way we could.

The way was still to be found as more and more priests left, or retired earlier than they might otherwise have done, so that those who remained became more exposed and, often, isolated. Forward in Faith set about its work and began to fight for a political solution within the synodical structures. A hasty set of provisions was cobbled together by the House of Bishops, which would form an Act of Synod in the February 1993 session of General Synod, and which would provide for extended episcopal care from bishops for parishes who saw the fullness of their communion with the diocesan bishop impaired. Again, I believe that all this was envisaged very much as a temporary measure to see us through what everyone recognized on both sides of the debate would be a turbulent period. Maybe 'flying bishops' would be needed for five years or so. Certainly they would not be needed for longer than the ten-year period during which provision would be made available to assist those priests who could no longer in conscience minister in the Church of England. By 2004, the opposition would have dwindled sufficiently to be of little significance in the Church and would certainly not warrant any such episcopal ministry. All the evidence suggests that however firmly the then Arch-bishop of York expounded a fair understanding of the meaning of reception in the matter of Holy Order so far as the admission of women to it was concerned, none the less it was generally felt it would only be a matter of time before all opposition dwindled and became of no consequence in the life of the Church of England.

The Archbishop of York was fair. He came to address a large

synod of the Society at St John the Divine, Kennington, and assured us of our honoured place in the Church of England, both in principle as well as in practice. As a sign of his commitment to that, despite not having any theological objection to the innovation, he would refrain from ordaining women to the priesthood. He kept his word, and even to this day, as occasion has given rise, he has come to the defence of traditionalists within the Church, clearly recognizing increasingly that our position is one of theological conviction and integrity. The Catholic movement of the Church of England and priests of the Society of the Holy Cross owe much gratitude to the support of John Habgood.

I went to the first ordinations in Westminster Cathedral when a dozen or so of my close friends were being ordained. It was a difficult occasion and I was greatly torn by it. I felt guilty that I was not with them, and yet I was angry with them for leaving. I felt strangely alone, lost in the Church of England, but nor had I found my way into the Church of Rome. The ordination, as well as being inspiring, and an occasion with which I could identify on so many levels, also convinced me that this path at that time was not for me. There was indeed too much to salvage in the Church of England, too much was at stake. A real gap had opened up and a great chasm was emerging. It needed to be filled.

By 1995 the hole in the Catholic presence in the life of the Church generally was all too obvious. It needed mending and bridges needed to be built. Forward in Faith by this stage had established itself; it had held its first annual national assembly in 1994. Outside the General Synod, it was clearly the largest democratically elected ecclesiastical meeting of its kind, and it represented a wide spectrum of the Catholic life that remained in the Church of England. This wish to remain for the foreseeable future had clearly taken preference to that of leaving the Church of England to its own devices. In 1995 Forward in Faith became a membership organization, and it adopted a strong political stance in order to face the situation and be representative of such a wide constituency. Yet it too struggled to draw people into a clear unity of purpose. It was an organization in its infancy, and just as the circumstances which had brought it to birth were painful, so too it was now suffering from growing pains. After much debate and amendment a statement on communion and a code of practice had been adopted. This was perceived by some as being far too hardline and, in practice, increasing the feeling of division in the Church of England. It was essential, however, for Forward in Faith's members to set some boundaries within which the Catholic life could flourish and the highest possible degree of communion could be maintained. Bishop Jack Nicholls of Sheffield was to appeal some years later, when he preached at the National Pilgrimage at Walsingham, for the walls not to go too high and to remember that they did not reach heaven. It was a timely reminder maybe, but at the same time it must be remembered that we have had to pay a very high price to maintain a Catholic integrity, without which those who would claim the term 'Catholic' for themselves, though they may have accepted women priests, could not have continued in the way they have. Too many bishops have tried to affirm Catholicism from both sides of the divide and have failed to understand the consequences of their actions when they have departed from the practice of the Universal Church. Both enthusiasts and critics alike have been in danger of forgetting how permissive the code of practice on communion is, as Geoffrey Kirk has so often been at pains to point out. There is no hardline policy here, but simply a way of living together in the highest possible degree of communion with conscience respected on both sides. Inevitably, there will always be individual circumstances where the exception proves the rule.

Despite its restrictions the communion statement has proved itself to be of enormous value in providing a way forward in living with the Church of England as it is and giving recognition on both sides to the theological integrity of those who remain opposed. Even at Walsingham, where some flexibility remains regarding concelebration, the Guardians laid down very early on that no bishop who ordained women to the priesthood would either preside or concelebrate on Shrine occasions. This too helped the Shrine to recover from the 1992 vote and enables it to flourish today, retaining its integrity while being open to all.

Somehow we weathered those winter months. The Society's records show that meetings of chapters of clergy were more frequent than ever and attendance was high. Everyone was looking to the Master for his lead. Wisely, Christopher Colven took time before he called a national synod. In April 1993, there was to be a meeting at St Alphege, Solihull. Priests travelled from all over the country to Birmingham; coaches even set out from London to go north! Quite probably this was the largest meeting the Society has ever held, either before or since. The huge church was packed to capacity, with every seat taken. I remember sitting next to Fr Martin Warner SSC, whom I met for the first time that day. We began with a celebration of the Eucharist which was low-key as it was a low mass. Nothing was sung, and only Fr Colven celebrated. Depressing as it was on one level, I remember being overwhelmed by a deep sense of God's presence and fervent prayer for the guidance of his Spirit. After the Mass and throughout the afternoon, the various options were laid before us. The clergy were not going to be appeased. Rome was the answer. Michael Shields tried hard to give integrity to the position of those who wished to remain, yet he stood apart from the rest of the leadership. He appealed to the Anglican pastoral tradition. What was to happen to the people we had been sent to serve; people for whom at one level the choices were far easier, but who were also by this stage beginning to make their voices heard? They were going to remain in the Church of England and wanted their priests to do the same. This was clearly the cry that lay people would take up at the national assemblies of Forward in Faith as time went by. It became clear that a real gulf lay between those who would go to Rome, and hopefully take as many people with them as would follow, and those who for the sake of their people would remain where they were, and fight the cause from within. There was no clear resolution at the synod but the options were clarified for us.

Then came the next bombshell. Father Colven resigned as
Master. It was half-way through his third term which he had
accepted at the request of the brethren in order to meet the
'special circumstances' that existed in the Church. Christopher
Bedford, at that point secretary of the Society, was proposed as
Master and appointed by acclaim at the synod held at St Stephen's, Gloucester Road, in June 1994. Many now were
confused about what to do. Christopher Colven was clear
about his own agenda and felt that he could not carry the
Society with him. Having led us for twelve years he felt it
necessary to pass on the cross to the more feisty Christopher
Bedford. It was inevitable that the Society would divide and be
split. Fr Bedford set about the task of giving priority to the
Roman option in order to see many priests safely across the
Tiber. In different circumstances he would have been an
inspired leader. He had all the determination and courage
needed to speak out and to unite such a group of priests, yet his
mastership was dogged by opposition. Wherever possible the
Roman rite was to be used for the celebration of Mass and the
Holy Father's name to be included in the canon. He would not
concelebrate on any Society occasion as other priests could not
necessarily be relied upon to share his vision of full communion
with the Holy See. Admission to the Society was now closed
and aspirants abolished: Christopher Colven had ceased to
admit deacons in 1987. It was clear that the Society was pulling
up the drawbridge in order to be ready for the great move.
However, moving day never came and a reaction, beginning in
the northern province, set in. The signs of the split in the
Society were no longer covert and sides were taken. Painful
though it might have been at the time, it clearly helped many to
decide, however reluctantly, where they belonged. Fr Bedford
knew this and decided to be proactive. He called an international council meeting at the Tower Thistle Hotel in London
in the spring of 1996. Deputy-Masters and provincial vicars
from around the world met together to decide the way
forward.

By that time, I had become the newly elected local vicar for the London chapter. Howard Levett, Vicar of St Alban's, Holborn, at a chapter meeting at St Mary's, Somers Town, had called the leadership's bluff and forced us to address the issue of whether we could continue as we were. Within the chapter, we had a series of meetings to discuss the options. Amongst the various speakers who addressed us, Graham Leonard came, having just been conditionally ordained, and encouraged us not to take fright. I wrote a paper with Fr Richard Arnold addressed to the London clergy about the imperative of remaining in the Church of England and building up the Catholic movement again. It was the only one given to discussing what I called the Anglican option. We held forth for nearly an hour at Holy Trinity, Hoxton, where the meeting took place. It was a painful meeting. I had disillusioned my friend Stuart Wilson, the parish priest at Hoxton, who had up to that point thought that I had been a Roman option man. We realized that the parting of the ways was inevitable. The London chapter itself would have to divide. Roger Reader was elected as local vicar for the 'Romans' and I was elected local vicar for the 'Anglicans'.

On the basis of what the London chapter of Christ the King had already done, so too the Society would have to divide. At the Tower Thistle Hotel it was agreed that the Society would split into provinces, each one being autonomous and responsible for its own affairs and governed by its own elected Master. The provincial Masters would elect an overall Master of the Society. America and Australia had already gained considerable autonomy with their deputy-Masters as it was becoming impossible to run everything from England. At the same time, Wales, which had only recently become a separate province with a provincial vicar, now voted to separate completely from England. The Church in Wales had not as yet voted to ordain women, and their political agenda was inevitably slightly different. Despite there being only two chapters in Wales, they too would become an autonomous province with an elected Master. Most significantly of all, there would be an international Roman province. David Paul was elected Master for the

Roman province, funds in the UK were divided accordingly but the Holy Cross trust should remain with access for all UK brethren. The Trust had paid for the international conference and was subsequently used to assist many priests who were experiencing hardship as they moved from one communion to another. The job of drawing up new statutes was given to Michael Shields. In the summer of 1996 at the London synod – the principal synod of the Society – the new statutes were finally adopted, although it should be noted that the northern provincial synod, as it then was, voted against them. At the London synod, I argued strongly that the statutes should be adopted. Even though I was not happy with the arrangements, I could see no other way of taking the Society forward at that time. Elections would take place in the autumn. When the provincial Masters were in place, they would elect the first Master-General. The new provinces would come into existence on Founders' Day, 1997.

Owing to the circumstances which had developed within the London chapter, I had already decided to make a bid for the mastership in order to bring about a sense of unity that I felt the Society desperately needed. Here again a sense of bereavement was at work. I knew that in order to foster this unity there had to be a greater distance between us and the Roman province. Indeed, I was dubious from the outset whether the Roman province could survive. Many of my friends were now in it, and relationships became estranged and difficult. In the end, it was their decision to withdraw from the Society. No longer did the spirituality that the Society promoted seem appropriate to their situation. They did not face a political struggle, nor was there any need for a Catholic tradition within the Catholic Church. They had found for themselves the fullness of Catholicism for which they had been longing. As time moved on, the discipline of the Society faded. No longer did they need to meet in synod, and no longer did they find themselves saying the Society prayer. The Roman province had served its purpose in seeing them safely home, but it had already outlived that purpose. I had written to Cardinal Hume, shortly after becoming Master, expressing my doubts about whether the presence of the Roman province within the Society was helpful to our ecumenical endeavour. I know the Cardinal showed that letter to others but, to this day, I do not know what influence he brought to bear upon the demise of the province.

With the ending of the Roman province, the Society began to rekindle its confidence and set about an agenda to unite the brethren once more. Shortly afterwards, the Holy Cross Trust was wound up and given to the English province, where it was felt the money belonged. Hardship payments were stopped.

In 1997 admissions were reopened. At the first national synod of the English province, over 40 priests were admitted to membership. The Pusey Guild was set up for ordinands, in order for them to become aspirants to the Society. Mission Direct was resurrected. The numbers on the roll in 1996 had fallen to just over 400. By 2000 that figure had risen to 700. The Welsh province too grew substantially, bringing the total number of brethren in the United Kingdom to 750. By the time of the Society's 150th anniversary in 2005, the roll worldwide stood at 1,100.

The Forward in Faith national assemblies have been significant events each year. Gradually they have helped to mould the constituency and bring it together with a vision for a Catholic future. Forward in Faith had established itself as a truly democratic organization, speaking for an extremely large body of people. At the same time it has not been without its controversial moments, and not everyone has found themselves in agreement with the stand it has taken. In the past few years we have seen close cooperation between clergy and laity. In case of any future development in Holy Order, ideas for a free province with a model for alternative episcopal jurisdiction at its heart have been much debated and agreed. To the extent that there is no credible alternative on the table it has now become the backbone of our future agenda. The Society is working, in the closest cooperation with Forward in Faith, for 'a new dawn for our Catholic movement'.

Yet there have been other events and initiatives over these

past years that have done much to revive confidence and to give fresh impetus and determination to Anglo-Catholics in the Church of England. In so many ways the clergy of the Society have helped to regenerate Catholic life by giving themselves wholeheartedly to the various initiatives, none of which should be underestimated for their significance. Bishop Eric Kemp, recognizing the spiritual poverty of our depression, called a meeting of the Catholic bishops to discuss what they might do in order to give the lead and help revitalize the confidence of the movement. The need first of all was for prayer and a re-awakening of a truly Catholic spirituality. A conference for the clergy was planned and Bishop Lindsay Urwin was given the task of delivering it. Thus in 1996 nearly 200 clergy gathered at the Haven holiday camp at Caister-on-Sea for the first Caister Retreat Conference. It was a real turning-point. Priests found themselves again. Their vocation was re-called and a commitment to mission was reborn.

It must be remembered, however, that the Society at this time was almost dead. It had lost its way. Although I knew what was happening in London I recognized the need to follow through nationally the vision that Lindsay Urwin had placed before us. Another Caister Conference was planned for the following year. It was to include the laity: the very best decision that Bishop Lindsay could have made. This time the Society was on board and subsequently has been a co-sponsor each year with the Confraternity of the Blessed Sacrament, as we have watched these conferences grow and contribute towards the renewal of the Catholic movement as a whole. Each year a synod for the clergy has been held at Caister with significant contributions from Bishop John Hind, Fr John Gribben CR and Fr Andrew Sloane, among others, and, as Master, I have been asked to address the whole conference in successive years. These have been happy days and we have rejoiced once again in our Catholic heritage.

The Shrine of Our Lady of Walsingham has become for many a focal point of renewal and rediscovery of confidence. As we have watched the Shrine develop its amenities, so more and more have gone there. Inasmuch as Fr Hope Patten was himself a member of the Society and looked for the support of the then leadership of the Society in order to fulfil and sustain his vision, so too over this past decade we have been able to support Walsingham in its outreach to so many who go to 'England's Nazareth' on pilgrimage. A number of priest-Guardians, including the former Master, who had become Roman Catholics remained for some years as Guardians. This inevitably led to tension, both within the College and beyond. It was part of the vision left over from the 1980s which had not been realized. As we look forward twelve years on to what now lies ahead of us, it is not difficult for us to understand the disillusionment that Christopher Colven and his close friends felt. Walsingham remained as it had always been, very much part of the Catholic life of the Church of England and priests of the Society were there to support it. The Society was pleased to support the millennium initiative as the image of Our Lady of Walsingham was taken round to various cathedrals in England and Wales to celebrate the 2000th birthday of her Son.

Yet the Shrine remains a symbol of reconciliation for our broken Church, and this vision for unity must still lie at the heart of the Shrine's witness. What may not have been achieved before may still have significance in the future in helping us bring about a great Catholic realignment for the Church in this land. Certainly, in whatever the future holds, Walsingham has a significant part to play and continues to hold a place dear in our hearts. The priests of the Society as they pioneered an enhanced devotion to Our Lady in the Church of England continue to think of Walsingham as home, and we continue to be at one with its work and witness.

The provincial episcopal visitors, the 'Flying Bishops', have each held festivals for their episcopal areas. Part of our story has been the great gatherings over these past few years in York Minster, Liverpool Cathedral, Bristol Cathedral and St Albans Abbey. Many thousands of laity have joined their priests in these celebrations and helped to raise the profile and identity of Catholicism within the Church of England. Each of the provincial visitors, along with John Broadhurst, the Bishop of Fulham, who acts as episcopal visitor in the capital under the 'London Plan', as members of SSC, have been given a pectoral cross resembling the Master's Mackonochie cross at their consecration, as have the Bishops of Whitby, Burnley and Pontefract and, most recently, Blackburn, where Nicholas Reade became the first diocesan bishop appointed from among the ranks of the Society since 1992.

At the same time the provincial episcopal visitors have celebrated the Chrism Mass each year in a number of locations within their areas. These too have become key events in the yearly calendar and have drawn priests both from the Society and far beyond. The Bishop of Fulham, celebrating each year on the Tuesday in Holy Week in the Church of Christ the King, Gordon Square, regularly attracts 120 priests together with over 200 laity for his Chrism Mass. The five regional synods of the Society held each year around the country are always well attended and have been key points in reinvigorating the clergy's commitment to the Society with its commitment to priestly formation and discipline. Since 1997 there have been over 30 of these occasions with two significant national synods in 1997 and 2001.

When we reached the time for the elections for the General Synod in the summer of 1995 nothing had been organized. The Catholic group had been depleted and was demoralized. In London, the diocese which had always returned a pre-dominance of Catholics to the Synod, there was not a single Catholic candidate planning to stand in the election. The same was true all over the country. The chasm was opening up. We had to move quickly and find people prepared to offer them-selves for election. I recognized the hole in London that had been left. The Edmonton area of the diocese alone had suffered a loss of over 20 priests who had either become Roman Catholics or had taken early retirement. Bishop Brian Masters began working to persuade people to stand. Throughout the crisis he had held his ground, using the image that the captain was the last to leave the ship. In reality, looking back, he never in fact came to terms with what the Church of England had done. He lost that sharpness and vitality for which he was renowned during the 1980s. No one had a sharper political mind than he, and I (along with others) was simply told to stand in the forthcoming election. I never dreamed at that time I would get anywhere near the Synod of the Church of England. The new Catholic group elected in 1995 was small and timid. It was not at all clear what our contribution was to be. Yet the newly elected leader of the group, Robin Ellis, the Archdeacon of Plymouth, saw us new members in gently and welcomed us with great affection and enthusiasm. The Catholic group, though struggling to find its way, was a real point of identity for many of us who had, somewhat surprisingly, found our way on to the Synod and it gave us the determination to work for a Catholic future. Andrew Burnham was to take over on Fr Ellis's retirement and, with his grasp of the issues, he gave the Catholic group an agenda to tackle. Catholics engaged thoroughly in the synodical processes once again; they stood for election to boards and councils and contributed to a wide range of debates. The Catholic flag had been hoisted once more and we began to discover we did have something to say to the Church of England after all. As our confidence returned, so the Church began to sit up and listen. Yet we were still not strong enough to win the votes we needed. Nothing more illustrated this than at the end of the 1995–2000 General Synod, during the first debate on the ordination of women as bishops, with the motion to set up a theological working-party, subsequently to be called the Rochester Commission, when we lost all three amendments that we proposed. These included one put by Geoffrey Kirk who spoke characteristically well and persuasively on the removal of a time-frame for the work of the commission, in the light of the Church's understanding of reception in this matter, and the ecumenical amendment which I put to request consultation with other churches in the course of the theological reflection. The group had agreed beforehand that were the ecumenical amendment to be lost, then we would have no choice but to vote against the whole motion. This we did, and to a man and woman the Catholic group voted solidly against the motion. We were proud of our achievement that day to act together decisively and in this way were able to put our mark on the debate, even though we lost the vote. In the days following, the Archbishop of Canterbury agreed that Forward in Faith should set up its own theological working-party to shadow that of the Bishop of Rochester and, in the fullness of time, that working-party published *Consecrated Women?*, edited by Jonathan Baker, the Principal of Pusey House, Oxford. That July Synod was a turning-point in our determination to stay together and to build up the Catholic group once more into a strong political voice which would be heard and respected in the next quinquennium. Once again the sight of many lapel crosses was to be seen in the chambers and corridors of Church House and around the campus at the University of York.

Following Andrew Burnham's consecration as Bishop of Ebbsfleet, at the opening of the new synod in November 2000 I found myself being elected as chairman of the Catholic group. It was to tie in well as I was elected at around the same time to serve for a second term as Master of the Society.

Tying up with all the growth and new life that was being regenerated throughout the Catholic movement, the millennium came to be the focus of thanksgiving for much that had been achieved, pointing us forward to all that lay ahead. A great celebration was planned for everyone for whom the term Catholic in its traditional sense was a point of identity in the Church of England. Forward in Faith's national secretary, Fr Geoffrey Kirk, dreamed of a celebration: Christ Our Future. It was to be the largest gathering of Anglo-Catholics in the history of the Church of England. The London Arena was booked three years in advance, and a programme of preparation in study and devotion was promulgated in many of the parishes. The Archbishop of York would be the principal celebrant, the Bishop of London would preach, and the Bishop of Chichester, who would be 85 years old in 2000, the other principal con-celebrant. Ten thousand people were needed to fill the Arena and it all happened as planned. Ten thousand people, including one thousand priest concelebrants, were there. All the Catholic societies had come together to support this event, masterminded by Forward in Faith and financially supported by the Confraternity of the Blessed Sacrament. The next day a stunning photograph appeared in *The Sunday Times*, showing rank upon rank of priests, and the following week the front page of the *Church Times* pictured the deacon, James Patrick, reading the Gospel with the hundreds of priests banked up in front of him. It was indeed a great vision of the Church, militant here on earth, but looking forward to being triumphant in heaven. The queues of traffic caused gridlock on the Isle of Dogs and the start of the Mass had to be delayed by three-quarters of an hour. The entrance procession alone lasted for 45 minutes. The Master of the Society was the Master of Ceremonies, the Superior of the Confraternity assisted the Archbishop of York and the Guardians of the Shrine escorted the image of Our Lady of Walsingham into the Arena to tumultuous applause. The Mass took over three hours, but it was the sign to everyone who had ears to hear and eyes to see that the Catholic movement in the Church of England was back on track and that nothing could deflect us from the task in hand. From then on, our faith was immeasurably more confident and our hope much more secure. Our love binds us together for all the future.

Inevitably this has been a very subjective account, as I recall my own experience and inevitably too, as I recall how we picked ourselves up and regained our confidence, this very much reflects my own understanding of what happened to us in the years following the momentous vote in General Synod on that bleak day back in November 1992. Many readers will be able to identify with these feelings and will have their own particular memories. We all have our own stories to tell of how we moved through this period. The records of the Society covering these years are, tragically, incomplete, so it is not easy to be objective. There are many aspects of the story that we cannot yet tell. I am sure much that took place during the months and years that followed has yet to be recorded, and only history will be able to make a true judgement of what took place in the last decade of the twentieth century in the history of the Church of England.

Index